Contents

Preface

On the brink of the new millennium the language profession is brimming with challenges and opportunities. The development of national standards and performance assessments provides us with a direction and vision for the future of language instruction in our country. With this vision, however, comes the challenge of connecting new curriculum, instructional strategies, and performance assessments to the classroom—a classroom filled with diverse learners. The changing face of demographics in America and an increasing globalization of the economy are finally beginning to change the way parents, students, and administrators view the importance of learning languages. As we focus on our new learners, we must look at the new possibilities for them—advanced technologies, research on how languages are learned, and language learning for specific purposes in non-traditional settings, to name just a few. But above all, we must emphasize to our students that the learning process requires their active involvement! In sum, this volume presents ways that we can be informed by research about the learning process and work to make systematic changes in our delivery of instruction. Thus, the learners of tomorrow will be engaged in the process and see themselves as lifelong learners of language and culture, thereby continuing to change the face of America and how American citizens are viewed by the global community.

Such ideas led me to the theme of this volume. However, I am deeply indebted to the many colleagues who helped see these ideas to fruition. For their support and assistance, I would like to thank all the members of the Board of Directors of the Northeast Conference on the Teaching of Foreign Languages (NECTFL), with whom I served from 1994–99, as well as the dedicated staff of the NECTFL office, Rebecca Kline, Executive Director, Susan Cavenaugh, Exhibits Manager, and Susan Shaffer, Administrative Assistant. I would like to thank the authors of this volume for their informed research, superb thinking, and reflective instructional practice that provide the basis for this work.

Above all, I am grateful to Margaret Ann Kassen, Editor, who collaborated with me on every aspect of this volume and who really made it happen. I appreciate her insight, dedication, perseverance, and friendship throughout this endeavor.

This volume is dedicated to the memory of Glenn M. Knudsvig, Professor of Classics at the University of Michigan, who died tragically before he could complete the chapter he had undertaken for this volume. Glenn's excellent research and thinking are reflected in the chapter by John Muccigrosso and Deborah Pennell Ross, former students of his, who willingly and faithfully picked up where Glenn left off and provided this volume with a chapter based on his work.

Martha G. Abbott,
1999 Conference Chair

Introduction

T he 1999 Northeast Conference theme, *Language Learners of Tomorrow: Process and Promise*, offers language teachers the opportunity to reexamine the role of the learner and the teacher in the context of current pedagogical and sociopolitical concerns: recent research on language acquisition and learning, the demand for accountability in education, and expectations for the fast-approaching 21st century. Language educators of today and tomorrow face serious questions about the competencies learners will need given the increasing reality of cross-cultural communication, the rapid expansion of distance learning and virtual classrooms, and the growing use of English throughout the world. Many of these issues point to the need to develop learners who are more capable of and responsible for managing and directing their own learning in order to make the most of the various educational experiences they will encounter in their lives. This volume, which shares the name of the conference theme, furthers our professional dialog on learning by incorporating the student into the teaching-learning process as an active partner. Indeed, the voices of teachers and learners are tightly interwoven throughout the chapters you will read here.

Over the last 15 years, much has been said about the learner-centered classroom and the need for teachers to recognize and address the diversity that exists among learners, including such variables as motivation, anxiety, learning styles and strategies, age, gender, cognitive differences, etc. This discussion has often remained at a theoretical level, expressing visions for the future and recommending that students be actively involved in communication and learning. As an example, Magnan envisioned learner-centered classrooms where learners were "beg[inning] to direct the curriculum" (1990, p. 11) and proposed that "along with the instructional focus, control and responsibility too must shift to the learner" (1990, p. 13). Shifting control and responsibility to the learner is fundamental to what has come to be known as autonomous learning, "the ability to take charge of one's own learning" (Holec, cited in Nunan, 1996, p. 15). While some experts consider learner autonomy to be an ideal or a rarely attained goal for adult learners (Benson, 1996), Nunan (1996) sees learner- (and learning-) centeredness in the classroom as a means of working toward this end.

Further impetus for enhancing the role of the learner comes from the *Standards for Foreign Language Learning* (1996), which sets the course for language instruction into the 21st century. The learner is the key figure in each standard: "Students engage in conversations …" "Students demonstrate an understanding …," "Students use the language…." By codifying learner outcomes and providing us with the language needed to talk about what learners know and do with the language, the National Standards point us in the direction of increased teacher–student collaboration in order to attain these goals.

The purpose of the 1999 *Reports* is to demonstrate how such visions for language learning have been carried out—specfically, how they have been translated within instructional settings. The chapters in this volume present approaches teachers have developed to involve learners in their learning, to help students become more responsible for their education, and to guide them in acquiring skills for directing their own learning. The present volume not only includes the teacher's voice, describing these approaches and techniques, but also highlights the voices of learners, who demonstrate their ability to reflect on their own learning processes and the instructional process itself. These learner voices, ranging from elementary to secondary and postsecondary to adult, come from a variety of sources familiar to teachers and researchers: course evaluations, surveys, questionnaires, portfolios, think-aloud protocols, interviews, focus groups, and discussions both in and outside class. The learner voices give evidence of the learning process in action and show promise both for the continued use of the teaching approaches described and for the future of the students as lifelong learners.

Special Features of the Volume

Several special features are designed to facilitate your reading of this volume. At the beginning of each chapter, you will see two graphic organizers, the first being the familiar interlocking rings of the National Standards (1996). As the Conference Chair, Martha Abbott, and I initially conceptualized the volume, each author was to address a specific goal area. It became clear as the chapters evolved that the 5 C's—Communication, Cultures, Connections, Comparisons, and Communities—are integrated into the best practices in our field. The Communication goal connected with each of the instructional approaches described, and other C's overlapped across chapters, both implicitly and explicitly. The following icon visually highlights the primary goal areas treated in each chapter:

The second icon, a weave pattern, represents an unanticipated component of the chapters. Upon reading the chapter drafts, Marty and I noticed the consistent presence of teaching approaches aimed to develop the critical thinking skills of learners, ranging from knowledge and application to the higher-order skills of analyzing, evaluating, and problem solving. Learning strategies, the steps learners take to enhance their own learning (Oxford, 1990), were another common theme. Relating to the Cultures, Comparisons, and Connections goals were emphases on cultural knowledge and knowledge of content from other subject areas. The use of technology was the focus of one chapter and a component of several others. It became evident that the chapters addressed a part of the Standards document that had not been treated in depth before: the components of the "rich curricular weave," identified as the threads that, when woven together with the goal areas, create the fabric of language learning (p. 28). As presented in the Standards, and in the chapters in this volume, the weave elements include the language system (structures and how they function meaningfully in communication), cultural knowledge, communication strategies (such as paraphrasing, understanding meaning from context, and making and verifying hypotheses), critical thinking skills, learning strategies, other subject areas, and technology. The following symbol summarizes the weave elements addressed in each chapter:

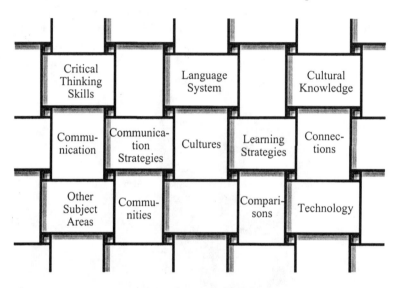

In addition to the icons that introduce each chapter, you will see quotes set off graphically in text boxes. These quotes, which also appear in the text of the chapters, allow you to access key concepts "at a glance." In some cases, the boxes highlight the author's voice, and in others, when identified as such below the quote, they feature the student's voice. As yet another special feature, the authors have included practical classroom guidelines and materials in the figures and appendices.

Suggestions for Reading the 1999 *Reports*

Depending on your interests and needs, you may want to consider some of the suggestions below to help structure your reading of the volume.

By Goal Areas

The chapters in the volume are grouped according to the goal areas they feature, as indicated by the highlighted portion of the 5 C's icon. To lead off, Wenden addresses Communication and Communities. She provides an overview of the field of learner autonomy, illustrating its implications for learners and teachers with comments made by an adult ESL learner who exemplifies the real-world language learner.

Chamot, Barnett, and Lavine speak to Communication and Connections. Chamot describes a six-year grant project in which French, Japanese, and Spanish immersion students in grades 1–6 verbalize the strategies they use as they read and write in the second language. The implications of the children's insights offer guidelines for integrating strategy instruction in programs for early learners. Shifting to the postsecondary classroom, Barnett describes various collaborative approaches that engage learners and encourage them to take more control of their learning. Her students react favorably to outcomes they perceive as resulting from their enhanced involvement and see applications beyond the language classroom. Similarly, Lavine focuses on a particular technique, Student Management Teams, to "give students a voice" in all aspects of their class: curriculum, instruction, and evaluation. She describes challenges and benefits for the teacher, and student management team members discuss their role and the real-world skills they developed.

The next two chapters stress Communication, Cultures, and Comparisons, using examples from the Spanish classroom that can be applied easily to other languages. Lee demonstrates how the use of online newspapers and chats offers students increased opportunities to explore and interact with the Spanish-speaking world beyond the classroom walls. Through portfolios and interviews, her students reflect on what and how they learned from these largely student-directed experiences. Galloway places "growing the cross-cultural mind" at the heart of language instruction and demonstrates how growth can be fostered in our classroom, even at beginning levels. Her students' voices illuminate the process of confronting and acknowledging the boundaries that exist between cultures in order to construct bridges of cross-cultural understanding.

Communication and Comparisons are the central concerns of the chapters by Tulou and Pettigrew and Muccigrosso and Ross, with the former addressing the presentational mode (speaking and writing, standard 1.3 of the Communication goal) and the latter addressing the interpretive mode (reading, standard 1.2). Tulou and Pettigrew provide information about the performance assessment project they have spearheaded in Fair-fax County (VA) Public Schools over the last 4 years, which began as a pilot program in their classes and now encompasses all the secondary-level language teachers in the county. The PALS project promotes in-creased learner awareness of language performance and proficiency by involving learners in the monitoring, problem-solving, and evaluating of oral and written task-based performances. Muccigrosso and Ross describe a reflective model of critical thinking that they apply to the teaching of reading in Latin. In this process, students are encouraged to read for mean-ing using strategies for thinking hierarchically, inferring from context, and assessing recursively. In both these chapters, students make Compari-sons between the language system of English and that of the language they are studying.

Oxford and Carpenter conclude the volume with a synthesis of the eight previous chapters. Oxford, a teacher/researcher, and Carpenter, a university student, dialog with each other, presenting their reactions to and reflections on the broad issues of learner autonomy and National Standards and the approach described in each chapter. The weave of their voices reflects the dynamic nature and rich outcomes of teacher-learner collaborations.

By Weave Elements

If you wish to follow a strand of the weave elements in your reading, consider the following:

- Language system: Chapter 8, Muccigrosso and Ross
- Cultural knowledge: Chapters 5, Lee, and 6, Galloway
- Communication strategies: Chapter 6, Tulou and Pettigrew
- Critical thinking skills: Chapters 1–8
- Learning strategies: Chapters 1, Wenden; 2, Chamot; and 7, Muccigrosso and Ross
- Other subject areas: Chapters 1, Wenden; 2, Chamot; 3, Barnett, and 4, Lavine.
- Technology: Chapter 5, Lee

By Communicative Mode

As characterized in the National Standards, communication can be seen as consisting of three modes, depending on the context and purpose of communication: interpersonal, interpretive, and presentational (1996, pp. 32–35). This framework is the basis of the three standards articulated within the Communications goal, the goal that the chapters all have in common. These modes can also serve as organizing principles to guide your reading of the volume or as the basis for a teaching-methods class.

Interpersonal communication consists of direct, person-to-person interaction through speaking (and listening) and/or writing (and reading) along with the knowledge needed to participate in culturally appropriate ways. In this volume, the following chapters present approaches that highlight the interpersonal mode:

Chapter 1, Wenden
Chapter 3, Barnett
Chapter 4, Lee
Chapter 6, Lavine

The interpretive mode deals with the reception of meaning through reading, listening, and viewing, along with the knowledge of how cultural perspectives are embedded in the texts, products, and images being interpreted. This mode is the focus of the following chapters:

Chapter 2, Chamot
Chapter 3, Barnett
Chapter 5, Lee
Chapter 6, Galloway
Chapter 7, Muccigrosso and Ross

The presentational mode applies to spoken or written communication for an audience that does not have direct contact with the speaker or writer. It includes the cultural knowledge needed to address the needs of the audience or reader. Two chapters address this mode:

Chapter 5, Lee
Chapter 7, Tulou and Pettigrew

By Theme

Yet another approach to reading the chapters is to do so by theme. Three themes emerged from these nine chapters: learner as reflector, learner as collaborator, and learner as assessor. "Learner as reflector" highlights the crucial role that metacognition plays in learning, whether one is a student or a teacher. The chapters that pertain to this theme are:

Chapter 1, Wenden
Chapter 2, Chamot
Chapter 8, Muccigrosso and Ross

Chapter 9, Oxford and Carpenter
"Learner as collaborator" refers to sharing curricular and instructional deci-
sions with the learner. Three chapters deal directly with this topic:
Chapter 3, Barnett
Chapter 4, Lavine
Chapter 6, Galloway
The theme "learner as assessor" is evoked by those approaches that bring
learners into the evaluation process, giving them the opportunity to self- and
peer-assess. Chapters in this strand include:
Chapter 5, Lee
Chapter 7, Tulou and Pettigrew

Final Thoughts

In reflecting on the 1999 *Reports* as a whole, the Conference Chair and
I have come to view the explicit treatment of the weave elements and the
interweaving of teacher and student voices both in the text and in the
classroom as the core contributions of the volume. The joining of teachers
and learners in a partnership is neither an easy undertaking nor a magic
formula that resolves the many issues we face in education today. However, the various collaborative approaches presented in this volume demonstrate how far we as teachers have come in recognizing the central role
that learners play. While there is much yet to be learned about maximizing
learning outcomes, we sincerely hope that you, the readers, will recognize
the potential for enhanced learning depicted in these pages and will be
moved to further the dialog begun here through your own research and
teaching.

Acknowledgments

This volume is the result of a "weave" of many individual and group
efforts. I want to recognize and thank the driving force behind the 1999
theme, Martha Abbott, whose clear vision, expertise in the field of language education, willingness to collaborate and mentor, and sense of humor have resulted in the realization of this volume. The authors themselves, most of whom are close friends and colleagues after our joint efforts on this project, have my utmost respect and appreciation for their
hard work, excellence in teaching, and willingness to share their perspectives with the readership of the Northeast Conference. I am grateful as
well to the NECTFL Board of Directors and Executive Director for their

guidance in developing the theme, feedback on chapter drafts, and ongoing support throughout the project. The fine work of Kurt Müller as long-distance editing consultant and compositor must not be overlooked, for it is he who brought this volume to completion. And finally, I want to thank my family, particularly my husband Craig, for their loving encouragement and patience.

Margaret Ann Kassen, 1999 *Reports* Editor
Catholic University of America

References

Benson, P. (1996). Concepts of autonomy in language learning. In R. Pemberton, E. S. L. Li, W. W. F. Or, & H. D. Pierson (Eds.), *Taking control: Autonomy in language learning* (pp. 27–34). Hong Kong: Hong Kong University Press.

Magnan, S. S. (Ed.). (1990). *Shifting the instructional focus to the learner*. Northeast Conference Reports. Middlebury, VT: Northeast Conference.

National Standards in Foreign Language Education Project. (1996). *Standards for foreign language learning: Preparing for the 21st century*. Yonkers, NY: Author.

Nunan, D. (1996). Towards autonomous learning: Some theoretical, empirical and practical issues. In R. Pemberton, E. S. L. Li, W. W. F. Or, & H. D. Pierson (Eds.), *Taking control: Autonomy in language learning* (pp. 13–26). Hong Kong: Hong Kong University Press.

Oxford, R. L. (1990*). Language learning strategies: What every teacher should know*. New York: Newbury House Publishers.

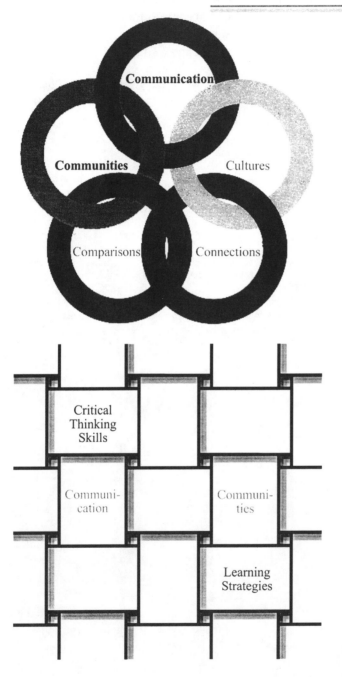

Communication

Communities

Cultures

Comparisons

Connections

Critical
Thinking
Skills

Communi-
cation

Communi-
ties

Learning
Strategies

Developing Autonomous Learners: Defining a New Role for Second Language Teachers in the 21st Century

Anita L. Wenden

York College, City University of New York

The notion of helping learners become more autonomous as language learners is the logical outcome of learner-centered trends that have characterized the field of foreign and second language teaching and learning since the early '70s. As a result of these trends, research on teaching and learning has shifted from trying to discover the best method for teaching to developing an understanding of learner characteristics that might influence the learning process (e.g., Carroll, 1981; Genesee, 1976; Naiman, Frohlich, Stern, & Todesco, 1978; O'Malley, Chamot, Stewner-Manzanares, Küpper, & Russo, 1985; Reid, 1987; Rubin, 1975; Willing, 1988). Humanistic views of learning have replaced behaviorist views in the development of language teaching methodology, and teachers have been urged to include their learners in the decision making about classroom instruction. They have been further encouraged to stress the learners' thinking, feeling, and action in the preparation of tasks and to relate subject matter to their basic needs and lives (McNeil, 1977, as cited in Dubin & Olshtain, 1986, p. 75). Finally, insights from sociolinguistics, specifically the notion of communicative competence, have led to an understanding that the outcome of language teaching should be the ability to use language in a socially appropriate manner in varied settings to accomplish varied purposes, thus calling into question the grammar-focused curriculum that downplays communicative skills and learner needs (e.g., Brumfit & Johnson, 1979; Munby, 1978).

While learner-centered in orientation, all these trends have, in effect, focused on teaching, aiming to change the teacher and the content of foreign and second language instruction. In contrast, learner-centered trends that promote the development of autonomy focus on learning, the hidden underside of teaching, and the learner, acknowledging his/her role in the teaching/learning process. Their aim is to make *learning* the main construct for planning and evaluating foreign and second language instruction and to promote the development of the learner's capacity for a more active, reflective, and self-directed approach to language learning.

In this chapter, therefore, I will focus on the *learning strategies* and *knowledge about learning* that research, theory, and classroom practice in the fields of self-directed language learning and (language) learner strategies have shown to be necessary if learners are to develop their capacity for autonomy (see Cohen, 1990; Dickinson, 1987; Ellis & Sinclair, 1989; Mendelsohn & Rubin, 1995; Naiman et al., 1978; O'Malley & Chamot, 1990; Oxford, 1990; Rubin, 1975; Rubin & Thompson, 1994; Stanchina, 1976; Wenden, 1991). Using excerpts from a learner's account of his experiences learning his foreign language, i.e., English in Germany and the United States, I will first illustrate and describe the strategies and knowledge that are necessary for autonomous learning. Then, I will (1) make suggestions regarding how the roles of both teachers and students will be changed by the promoting of learner autonomy in the foreign language classroom, (2) outline factors underlying the resistance that such a role-change can engender, and (3) provide general suggestions for dealing with it. My concluding remarks will address the social need for autonomous learners, a need which expands the utility of efforts to promote learner autonomy beyond the second language classroom.

A Learner Account

This learner account is excerpted from a larger body of data, consisting of 25 semi-structured interviews of adult learners of English, which sought to identify and describe in a systematic fashion their acquired knowledge and beliefs about language learning. Oshi, the learner whose account follows, was the manager of a New York-based Japanese company with offices in Germany and the United States. Before coming to the United States, he spent two and a half years in Germany. At the time of the interview, he was taking a language class and also preparing to attend business school to pursue an MBA.[1]

Living in Germany

In Germany I did business in English and spoke some German. I got used to speaking English but couldn't improve my TOEFL score or my GMAT score. While in Germany, my score went down. Europe was not good for my English. Europeans don't understand the rules of English. Nobody paid attention to my mistakes, only my friend from London. So I speak according to the order which I think, and everywhere I repeat this. Then I make my own English and always make the same mistakes. Nobody cares.

What happened when your British friend corrected you ?
I tried to learn it by heart or write it down and tried to apply the right English to my sentence or if I say an easier word and I learn a better word, then I try to use it. Of course most people didn't understand what I wanted to say. I went to a language school in Germany…. The English teacher came from England. I tried to use a new word in class, the teacher told me 'you'd better use it in this way' and she wrote it on the blackboard. That was very helpful. The level of the class was not so high. It was for German people—housewives, young girls. I was the second highest. I wanted to come to a country where I could speak English and improve my TOEFL score.

Taking Language Classes in the United States

In the United States, teachers don't teach strictly the rules of English. They try to get the English from the students. That's very good. It was interesting. It was a creative way of teaching. In Japan, the teacher has a book and reads out the main point and explains it…. Teachers first teach the rules and try to let students learn some sentences by heart. I prefer it when students make their own English. Teachers should be passive. Anyhow we must speak English, and when we speak the teacher won't be there.

Why are you taking an English course here in the U.S. ?

I must be able to write essays to complete my admission form to get into an MBA program. After classes I have exercises to do. They teach grammar. That's helpful.... [Another reason is] my job requires that I make telephone contacts and arrange interviews to sell my products. My business clients are not too well educated. They speak very quickly and if I don't understand they become angry and hang up, and I lose a client. The people in the (English) class also have that type of English, and so I have an opportunity to practice.

> I prefer it when students
> make their own English.
> Teachers should be passive.
>
> Oshi, an adult ESL learner

Do you think you need a teacher ?

The teacher keeps asking about my feeling for the United States, and I can speak frankly in the class. The teacher understands me, so I am free to talk. The teacher corrects my understanding.

If I have a job problem, I can discuss this problem with him. It helps me understand the culture.

We are like babies. We don't understand the United States ... the culture. We need to have people we can discuss these problems with.

Talking with His Employee

Does he (the employee) help you improve your English ?

Yes, because I have the opportunity to speak every day, so I can speak spontaneously. I don't have to think what I am going to say first in Japanese and then speak out.

Are you comfortable with him ?

Yes, he speaks slowly, more slowly than others, so it's easier for me. [When we speak] I concentrated on the meaning. I concentrate on his character to decide how he will react to what I say. Will he understand my English ? I am Japanese, and sometimes I might speak wrongly. Others ask me what I mean, but the employee doesn't, he feels my English. There are several ways to say things. I'm very careful because I don't want to disturb relations between people. I don't want to offend them. I also ask him to correct my sentences on important applications. He corrects my grammar and after we finish with business, he corrects me when we talk personal matters.

What do you do when he corrects you ?

I try to understand the reason and check the reason, and if it's not satisfactory, I ask him for the reason. He explains. That discussion is helpful to understand grammar. If he uses new words, I ask the meaning—stop the discussion. Then he uses another word—easier and the discussion continues.

What do you do about the word ?

I am very old. My ability to learn by heart becomes worse. But I'm trying to … it's better to write it down and try to use it.

When you talk, do you worry about making mistakes ?

I never think about if I'm making mistakes. I don't care at all about making mistakes … that's why I came here … why I'm studying....

You don't mind if someone corrects you ?

No. That's one way of improving my English.

Taking Flying Lessons

Let's talk about flying. Is that useful ?

Only to learn English is simple and boring. English is a method for me to do business or to study my MBA and to do business by myself. It's only the means. English by itself is not interesting to me. Through different language I learn some new thing, it will be interesting. I take flying to learn English and flying. I like that very much … to learn something in a different language the fun really increases … I like challenging things.

Reading the *New York Times*

Does reading the Times *help you ?*

It's a good training to improve my English. The summary of the news (in the Sunday issue of the *Times*) is helpful. I read the Japanese newspaper, and then when I read the summary on Sunday, it's easy for me. I know the story. I also keep a scrapbook of newspaper articles and that's helpful to memorize because I have to decide in which category to put the articles. Reading the paper is like an English comprehension test. If I read the questions first and then read the passage, I can complete it in half the time. But if I read first and then look at the questions. It takes longer. It's the same if I read the news first in Japanese and then in English.

Shopping, Restaurants

What about shopping and restaurants ? Is that useful for learning English ?

Not at all. You just order the food and pay the cashier. [When I go shopping or to a restaurant] I just say a word, that's enough. "How much? How do you do?" They answer, and I pick up some words, and if I do not understand, I can imagine what they mean. They don't use hard English. It's too easy.

Taking a GMAT Class

Studying GMAT is good because I must compete with American people, not foreigners. If I get into an MBA class, I must say something. Otherwise, I can't graduate. That's very hard to argue with American people ... to understand the argument going on between American people, and, then, get into the conversation. Very hard but very helpful.

Only something hard is helpful?

Hardness is helpful because the standard of English is higher.

Strategies and Knowledge for Autonomy

What may be inferred from this learner account is the content of a syllabus that aims to develop a learner's capacity for autonomy in second language learning. First, as Oshi illustrates, learners need to know how to use two different kinds of strategies:

- strategies to *manage* their learning
- strategies to *process* their learning

Secondly, if they are to use strategies appropriately, they need to expand and refine their acquired knowledge about:

- the nature of language and language learning
- the specific purposes and demands of a learning task
- personal factors that may inhibit or facilitate learning

The first two of these types of knowledge are referred to as *task knowledge* and the third is known as *person knowledge.*

Self-Management Strategies

There are three self-management strategies: planning, monitoring, and evaluating. As the term suggests, their function is to supervise and regulate learning. They can be applied to any language learning task, such as reading to find the main idea, writing an essay, improving one's oral communication skills, completing a gap-filling exercise. In fact, they are essential to the regulation of any kind of learning, academic or otherwise. Planning, monitoring, and evaluating are also referred to as metacognitive strategies (Brown, Bransford, Ferrara, & Campione, 1983; O'Malley & Chamot, 1990) or as the skills of self-directed learning (Carver, 1984; Dickinson, 1987; Holec, 1981).

Planning

Planning requires *looking ahead* and making decisions about what is to be learned and how best to go about it, i.e., to select objectives. Oshi, for example, had decided that he wanted to (1) be able to speak English like a native, (2) improve his TOEFL score, (3) learn to write essays, and (4) understand the culture. The choice of activities to achieve selected objectives is also a part of the planning process. Oshi chose English classes, a GMAT class as well as a variety of resources in his social environment, his employee, the *New York Times*, flying lessons. In the classroom, these are planning decisions that are typically made by teachers. To be autonomous, learners must be able to take joint responsibility for such decision making in the classroom and individual responsibility for the planning of independent language learning activities.

Monitoring

While planning takes place before a learner engages in a task, monitoring occurs *during* learning. When learners monitor, they note the obstacles they encounter. They assess the causes of these obstacles and measure the progress they are making toward their set objectives (Wenden, 1991; 1997b).

Oshi's account of his learning experience in Germany revealed that he monitored his progress. He noted that nobody paid attention to his mistakes; he "made his own English" and repeated his mistakes; most people didn't understand him. Through monitoring, learners acquire a body of knowledge about their linguistic proficiency, both their strengths and their weaknesses.

Good teachers are characterized by their ability to monitor their students' learning. As they teach, they are careful to see if students are understanding; they note their overall progress. To be autonomous, learners need to learn to do this monitoring for themselves.

> To be autonomous, learners ... must ... evaluate their learning and develop the criteria ... to measure success.

Evaluating

Evaluating involves looking back at a learning task that has been completed to check outcomes and the utility of the strategies and social resources that were intended to promote learning (O'Malley & Chamot, 1990; Thomson, 1996; Wenden, 1991). Oshi notes, for example, that while working in Germany, "I got used to speaking English but couldn't improve my TOEFL score or my GMAT score.... Europe was not good for my English." On the other hand, by talking with his employee, he learned to speak "spontaneously" because he had an opportunity to speak every day. Keeping a scrapbook of newspaper articles helped him remember what he learned because "I have to decide in which category to put the articles." Thus, not only does Oshi check his learning outcomes, but he also can articulate the criteria that serve as the basis for his judgments.

Good teachers also evaluate the effectiveness of their lessons or of a particular task or new materials. Did their learners participate? What kind of questions did they ask? How well did they do the assigned tasks? These questions point to some of the criteria they may use to make a judgment. Similarly, to be autonomous, learners must learn to evaluate their learning and the utility of the activities through which they learn. They need to develop the criteria to measure success.

Processing Strategies

To implement self-selected objectives and remediate problems noted as they monitor or evaluate their learning, learners need processing strategies, more commonly referred to as cognitive strategies (e.g., O'Malley & Chamot, 1990; Oxford, 1990; Rubin, 1987; Wenden, 1991). A review of some of the more common taxonomies reveals the varied ways in which processing strategies may be categorized. Here, I would like to describe them according to their function in learning as

- attending strategies
- elaboration strategies
- practice strategies

When learners read a textbook or listen to a lecture, for example, they cannot deal with all the information that is being provided at one time. They must, therefore, learn to deploy *attending* strategies that focus their attention on some particular aspect of the input. Oshi listened for words he needed when he went to a restaurant and had to order. He concentrated on the meaning when talking with his employee.

Learners also need to make sense of what they attend to; they need to remember it. For this they need to use *elaboration* strategies. These are strategies which enable them to analyze the incoming information and relate it to what they already know so that they can understand it and, at the same time, organize and store what they understand in long-term memory for future use. Oshi categorized articles from the *New York Times*. He asked for explanations of grammar he did not understand and tried to understand the reason for his errors. He inferred the meaning of new words and kept a written record of others.

Finally learners need to retrieve and apply appropriately and fluently what they have learned. For this they require *practice* strategies. Oshi tried to use new words and grammar. His flying lessons helped him develop a more global proficiency as he learned to do new things in English.

Unlike self-management strategies, which can be applied to any learning task, processing strategies are task specific. For example, strategies for writing will be different from strategies for listening. Moreover, while self-management strategies usually require some conscious deliberation, processing strategies can be deployed with or without awareness, depending on the extent to which learners have learned to use them automatically. In other words, just as in the case of language structure and vocabulary, as learners develop skills in the use of a strategy, they must be conscious of their attempts to deploy it. However, with time and practice, less deliberation is required, and in the final stage, when the use of the strategy is automatized, they apply it unconsciously.

Processing strategies are often implicit in the tasks set by teachers or textbook writers in order to engage students in dealing with the topic of learning. For example, when students are asked to do some type of grammar-manipulating exercise, they must use deductive strategies, calling upon the grammar rules they have learned. Depending on the type of questions they are asked about a foreign language text they have read, learners may need to know how to apply such reading strategies as finding the main idea, looking for key words, inferring meaning from context, drawing on background knowledge, and so forth. To be autonomous, learners need to become aware of the need to use processing strategies. They need to learn how to select and apply these strategies appropriately to both the learning and use of their foreign language when needed without the guidance of a teacher.

Knowledge about Learning

Learners' acquired knowledge about the learning process is essential to the appropriate deployment of both self-management strategies and processing strategies; it provides the motivational basis for learners' involvement in their learning (Wenden, in press). Examples of the general knowledge about learning that practitioners recommend learners acquire if they are to be autonomous include knowledge of:

1. the metacognitive and affective factors in learning (Cotterall, 1995; Little, 1994)
2. how language works and how to approach language learning (Cotterall, 1995; Gremmo, 1984, as cited in Gremmo & Riley, 1995; Wenden, 1991; 1995)

3. their own learning processes (Cotterall, 1995; Dam, 1995; Dickinson, 1987; Eriksson, 1993)
4. their learning styles and the expectations they hold about language learning (Cotterall, 1995; Victori & Lockart, 1995)
5. the techniques that they use (Cotterall, 1995; Dickinson, 1987)

The cognitive literature refers to this knowledge as metacognitive knowledge, categorizing it broadly according to whether the content focuses on the task of learning, i.e., *task knowledge*, or the learner, i.e., *person knowledge*.

In his account, Oshi referred to his task knowledge. He understood that there should be a relationship between his language learning activities and his linguistic and professional objectives. Thus, language classes in Germany were not useful as they were geared to the needs of housewives and young girls. On the other hand, the classes he took in New York were useful. The English class provided practice discussing in a style of English he needed for his work, and the GMAT class offered the discussion practice necessary to function in a graduate business course. He had begun to develop a typology of tasks, noting, for example, the similarities between procedures he followed for reading the *New York Times* and for completing an English reading-comprehension test. He also had some basic knowledge about the relationship between language setting and language use. For example, he was concerned about the social appropriateness of his language; he knew there were several ways to say things and did not want to "disturb relations between people ... to offend them." He understood that in certain social situations, such as shopping or eating out, short formulaic expressions were sufficient. He also had views about the best methods for learning. Instead of focusing on grammar rules, teachers should "get the English from the students," i.e., he preferred inductive teaching. He believed that progress in learning requires expert feedback and that for learning to be effective it must be challenging.

Oshi's account also revealed his person knowledge, i.e., general knowledge learners may acquire about cognitive and affective factors that influence learning and more specific knowledge of how these factors apply in their learning. In his account Oshi reflected on age and motivation. He believed that it was because of his age that he could not remember new words easily. He knew that he was motivated to learn English when he was learning something new.

> ## Learners will need an opportunity to become aware of and reflect upon their acquired knowledge and to revise and expand it if they are to take charge of their learning.

Task knowledge is essential to effective teaching. It is implicit in decisions teachers make while preparing a class as they consider:

1. the purpose of the lesson and how it will contribute to the skills/knowledge the student is expected to acquire from the class
2. the prior knowledge and skills students will need to accomplish the task
3. the way to divide and present the content
4. tasks students will be asked to do to understand and master the lesson content
5. the degree of difficulty of the task

Also implicit in these decisions is a teacher's knowledge of cognitive and affective factors that will promote or inhibit learning, i.e., their person knowledge. As Oshi's case illustrates, learners also have acquired task and person knowledge. It may be general (e.g., age affects learning) and/or applied specifically to themselves (I'm old so it will take longer). Based on their perception of their learning experiences, this knowledge may sometimes represent erroneous assumptions about how to learn. Nonetheless, it can influence their approach to learning. Learners will need an opportunity to become aware of and reflect upon their acquired knowledge and to revise and expand it if they are to take charge of their learning.

In summary, Oshi's account illustrates the kinds of strategies and knowledge learners must acquire if they are to approach their language learning more autonomously:

- self-management strategies
- process strategies
- task knowledge
- person knowledge

Furthermore, the account reveals how the exercise of autonomy can vary in scope. On the one hand, it includes self-direction of a *series* of activities undertaken with one or more specific learning objectives in mind. Oshi, for example, had monitored and evaluated his English classes, his many conversations with his employee, and his reading of the *New York Times* on a weekly basis. On the other hand, it also indicates how the strategies and knowledge for self-direction can be focused more narrowly on single tasks, such as those that learners may be expected to complete in a classroom setting. For example, Oshi referred to how he attended to his employee's reaction to the appropriateness of his language, tried to understand the reason for errors that were pointed out, and categorized articles in the *New York Times*. In other words, the knowledge and strategies necessary to promote autonomy are not only applicable to learning in informal settings but also to individual tasks that are the focus of learning in formal settings. Moreover, while this account has featured the experience of an adult learner, the cognitive research has shown that young children and adolescents who aim to take charge of their learning are characterized by their exercise of this capability (e.g., Kreutzer, Leonard, & Flavell, 1975, as cited in Brown et al., 1983; Chamot, 1987; this volume; Chinn & Brewer, 1993; Flavell, 1981; Paris & Byrnes, 1989).

Expanding Curricular Goals

This glimpse into the role learners can play in their language learning highlights the need to include with the goals for foreign language teaching outlined in the Standards for Foreign Language Learning (1996) one standard that refers specifically to *pedagogic autonomy*. As described in this document, goals 1, 3, and 5, *Communication, Connections, and Communities,* emphasize the acquisition of *linguistic autonomy.* Foreign language teachers are expected to help their students acquire the skills necessary to communicate freely about a variety of topics in the classroom and in multilingual settings outside the classroom. In addition, *Cultures* (goal 2) refers to the acquisition of cultural knowledge and *Comparisons* (goal 4) to knowledge about the nature of language and culture. In other words, the Standards do not include an explicit reference to learner autonomy. Still, two of the weave elements, learning strategies and critical thinking skills, which indicate how these goals are to be achieved, do refer to skills basic to autonomous learning described earlier, i.e., processing strategies and self-management strategies. In other words, it appears that the need to promote learner autonomy is, at least, implicitly acknowledged in the document.

> Built in to the present system of education are
> norms about student roles. Students have been
> socialized into these roles from childhood.
> If learners are to become more
> autonomous, these roles will have to change.

Oshi's account as well as the literature on learner training, referred to in the preceding sections, suggest that what is implicit be made explicit. A sixth goal should be added to the Standards, namely self-direction. Such an addition would clearly recognize that language learners also need to acquire the knowledge and strategies that will enable them to take charge of their own learning and that curricula should aim for both linguistic and pedagogic autonomy. It would encourage teachers to develop tasks and materials that would help students learn how to learn in the same coherent and systematic fashion that characterizes their approach to language and culture instruction. Indeed, if language students are to effectively and freely "participate in multilingual communities at home and around the world" (p. 27), it would appear essential that learners' capacity for autonomy be so enhanced.

The literature is now replete with practical models and approaches which readers can refer to for guidance as they devise learning plans to develop and enhance learners' capacity for autonomous learning (see, for example, Brown, 1989; Chamot, Küpper, et al., 1990; Chamot & O'Malley, 1986; Dickinson, 1987; 1992; 1997; Ellis & Sinclair, 1989; Hosenfeld, Arnold, Kirchofer, Laciura, & Wilson, 1981; Hosenfeld, Cavour, et al, 1993; Kelly, 1996; Moulden, 1985; Oxford, 1990; Rubin, McKay, & Mansoor, 1995; Rubin & Thompson, 1994; Victori & Lockart, 1995; Wenden, 1986b; 1991; 1997a; Barnett, Lavine, Tulou & Pettigrew, this volume).[2] However, to be effective, these plans must take into account the major constraint that will be imposed by the traditional roles of students and teachers. Therefore, it is now necessary to consider the impact that promoting autonomy will have on these roles and to understand the factors underlying the resistance it may engender.

Enhancing Learner Roles

Built in to the present system of education are norms about student roles, i.e., what students' contribution to the teaching/learning process should be. Students have been socialized into these roles from childhood. If learners are to become more autonomous, these roles will have to change. That is, students will now be expected to:

1. share the responsibility for learning (Little, 1991)
2. take charge of their own learning (Nunan, 1996)
3. learn on their own and from experience (Eriksson, 1993; Holec, 1981)
4. become partners in the teaching/learning enterprise (Allwright, 1981).

They can no longer be passive and dependent on the teacher but must learn to take on an active role and become independently involved in their learning (Dickinson, 1992; Mendelsohn, 1995). These changes can cause learners to be resistant, unwilling, and uncooperative.

Factors Underlying Learner Resistance to Role Change

The literature suggests that efforts to deal with these attitudes be based on an understanding of how learners are shaped by (1) their cultural values, (2) their beliefs about the role of the teacher and the nature of classroom learning, (3) their goal structure, and (4) their level of self-confidence.

Cultural Values

Holec (1985) refers to the values of a consumer society as a force that can strongly inhibit learners' willingness to change their roles. These values clearly distinguish between the role of consumer and producer. Applied to the educational context, it is the learner who is the passive consumer, whose needs must be completely satisfied as immediately as possible by the producer, who is empowered with the expertise to fulfill these demands. This latter role is assigned to the teacher. Another characteristic of our technological society, which reinforces the role distinction between the learner and the teacher, is the social distribution of knowledge that compartmentalizes different fields of competence and power based on the notions of specialization and expertise. As a result, just as learners would never think of taking over from their doctors when they are ill,[3] it would never occur to them that they might take over or share some of the teacher's functions (Holec, 1985).

Beliefs about the Role of the Teacher

Learners' previous educational experiences will further reinforce their beliefs about role distinctions they have acquired from other settings in their culture. Whatever the culture, years of schooling have socialized learners to view the teacher as the one who knows best (Moulden, 1990) and who must assign tasks, set deadlines, test, and evaluate progress (Abe, Stanchina, & Smith, 1975). They are accustomed to a teacher-centered classroom in which the teacher is active while the students are relatively passive (Mendelsohn, 1995). They have learned to accept the expertise of the teacher and, on that basis, refrain from making choices (Barnett, 1988). These beliefs are sometimes manifested in student reactions to their grades. Anecdotal experience has shown that when they are dissatisfied with their grades, students and sometimes their parents blame the teacher: probably the material was not taught properly, the question was not stated clearly, or the teacher did not correctly understand the student's answer.

Beliefs about Learning

Educational experiences have also shaped students' beliefs and expectations about learning. They may not perceive autonomous learning as "real teaching/learning." As revealed by research on self-directed language learning done at the University of Nancy, learners believe that making their own decisions is a waste of time or just too difficult (Moulden, 1993). Other research, done in Europe, has also reported that when learners work independently, they are insecure about the quality of their learning (Dam, 1995; Huttunen, 1993; Thomson, 1996). Other learners may not realize that learning requires that they engage in the application of their mental skills, and in other cases, they are not even aware that they possess these abilities or of how to use them.

Goal Structure and Motivation

Learners' views of the relevance of learner autonomy to their own goals will also affect their response to this role change. Reporting on one of the first experiments in self-directed language learning conducted at the University of Nancy, Stanchina (1976) noted that learners who remained motivated had clear and immediate goals for learning English which were being served by the experiment, e.g., reading technical engineering texts or giving a keynote address in the United States. It therefore becomes important to understand the nature of the goal structure that learners may bring to learner training.

Huttunen's 1986 analysis of secondary school students' comments about their autonomous language learning provides us with a helpful typology. She identified four types of learners distinguished by their goal structure and general orientation to learning:

- autonomous learners
- competitive learners
- obedient learners
- indifferent learners

Autonomous learners had clear, self-set, personal goals and related their learning to these goals. Moreover, they had their own criteria for evaluating the outcome. Competitive learners, on the other hand, were not interested in their development as learners but only in how they could improve their grade. Obedient learners did the tasks when asked, depending on the teacher for evaluation, i.e., their goals were what the teacher wanted. Indifferent learners did what was asked but with no real sense of intentionality—they had no goals. Thus learners' goal structure will have a clear effect on their motivation to participate in efforts to promote learner independence.

Self-Confidence

Some learners have been brainwashed into believing that they cannot learn on their own (Mendelsohn, 1995); they may have negative feelings about themselves and their ability or skill (Wenden, 1991). Bailey's research on competitiveness in language learning (as cited in Wenden, 1991) has yielded interesting insights regarding how self-image can influence language learning. When learners see themselves as successful vis-à-vis other learners, their learning is enhanced; on the other hand, anxiety results when learners see themselves as less successful, and in some cases, this anxiety can be debilitating, causing the learner to avoid contact with the second language. For some learners with such a self-image, taking on added responsibility for one's learning might be perceived as overwhelming.

Facilitating Change in Learner Attitudes

Helping learners overcome counterproductive attitudes must precede or, at least, accompany efforts to help them learn to learn. First of all, it is necessary to deal with learner beliefs that sustain negative attitudes, e.g., about their role in learning, the teacher's role, and the nature of "real" learning. Tasks that enable learners to bring these beliefs to awareness, articulate, and examine them must be provided. Alternatives to these beliefs must be considered and counterproductive beliefs revised. Secondly, it is important that motivational factors, such as the need for self-confidence, be addressed. Lack of self-confidence can be the result of learners' ignorance of their mental processes and how they work. Learners may not be aware that they can observe, evaluate, and change their own cognitive behavior (Schoenfeld, 1982). Learners need to be made aware of their cognitive capacities and how they function in learning.

A third motivational factor that needs to be addresssed is related to the perceived relevance of learning to learn. Learners may perceive it as an added task that interferes with the main project of language learning. Therefore, they must be led to experience the utility of using strategies and of reflecting on the relationship between erroneous assumptions about learning and their learning behaviors and between these behaviors and learning outcomes. Finally, it is essential that learners experience success in their efforts to apply the knowledge and strategies about learning they acquire. This is one of the most effective ways of demonstrating relevance and raising levels of self-confidence (cf Groteluschuen, Borkowski & Hale, 1990).

Diversifying Teacher Roles

Expanding course goals to include the development of learner's capacity for autonomy in language learning requires that teacher roles be redefined or diversified (Eriksson, 1993; Wenden, 1985; 1991). While they will still need to fill their traditional functions, their added pedagogical challenge will be to find ways of developing their learners' ability to learn, an absolute condition for self-directed learning (Holec, 1990), and this will require a role change.

One of the most fundamental changes will require that teachers learn to view themselves as co-responsible for the learning process with their learners, who must now be accepted as partners in this endeavor, not merely as recipients of linguistic knowledge. This means a change in their perspective on classroom instruction from that of "teaching" to that of "learning." Learning must become the lens through which they view efforts to plan instruction, develop and implement tasks and materials, and evaluate the outcome of their use. The various designations for the teacher's new role point to the new responsibilities:

1. resource person (Dam & Legenhausen, 1996; Ellis & Sinclair, 1989; Vaughan, Guerchon, & Muir, as cited in Wenden, 1991)
2. facilitator (Little, 1994; Tyacke & Mendelsohn, as cited in Wenden, 1991)
3. expert sharing secrets of learning with their learners (Chamot, 1994)
4. helpers (Abe et al., 1975; Dickinson, 1987)
5. ideas or rationale persons (Allwright, 1981)

Teachers' Initial Responses to Role Change

Initially, some teachers may resist the idea of expanding their role to include the promoting of learner autonomy. They may feel that promoting linguistic autonomy is already a sufficient challenge. Moreover, they may question the validity of such a curricular goal, doubting its legitimacy as a teaching objective (Jensen, 1993; Kenny, 1993) or perhaps fearing that it is a threat to their professionalism (Eriksson, 1995). A related reason has to do with how some teachers view their students. They may be uncertain about how students will react (Carver, 1984; Dam, 1995; Lyne, 1993; Smith, 1995) and fear that learner training will lead to anarchy (Kenny, 1993). Or they may lack trust in the learner's ability to cope with the new role (Kohonen, 1991). In other cases, the literature suggests that for some, such questioning results from a personal lack of confidence in their ability to make this change (Carver, 1984; Dam, 1995; Lyne, 1993; Nishitani, 1994; Smith, 1995). In fact, the above stated concerns suggest that teachers may just not be *fully* aware of the significance of promoting learner autonomy and/or that, maybe, they are not certain exactly *how* to meet the demands and fill the responsibilities of their expanded role.

Facilitating Change in Teacher Roles

While this chapter argues for an innovation that focuses on changing the learner, it is clear that, in the case of helping learners learn to learn, key to any progress are the attitudes, beliefs, and approaches of their teachers. These, too, will have to be reexamined and revised as necesssary, for it is the teachers who will be responsible for dealing with curricular and assessment matters. They will have to devise activities that focus on changing learner attitudes. Clearly, therefore, a prerequisite to changing learners is the provision of opportunities for teachers (1) to consider and evaluate how learners may benefit by learning to learn, and (2) to acquire whatever methodological know-how is necessary to help their learners in this way. Teachers may choose to self-direct the organization of these opportunities, working independently or with a small group of colleagues. Alternatively, they may request that their supervisors provide faculty development sessions with these purposes in mind.

Evaluating the Relevance of Promoting Autonomy

While few will disagree with the need to help students become more autonomous, a full appreciation of what this entails will require self-study, reflection, and evaluation.

To completely grasp the relevance of promoting autonomy, teachers will, first of all, have to develop a new understanding about the nature of teaching and the role of learning. Hosenfeld (as cited in Rubin, 1994) proposes that they learn to view teaching as a cognitive apprenticeship and their students as apprentices, learning from them the art of teaching themselves, i.e., of learning. Nunan's experience is illustrative. He writes, "my own interest in seeing things from the learners' point of view developed when I realized that I could not do the learning for my learners—that in the final analysis they would have to do their own learning and the best thing I could do was to help them find ways of doing their own learning" (1996, p. 14).

Teachers will also need to expand and deepen their understanding of the learning process, beginning with an awareness of how they learn. For example, they can reflect on their efforts at learning another language: what were their objectives? what did they do to achieve these objectives? what were their strategies? what problems did they encounter as they learned? how did they deal with them? how did they view the outcome of their learning? and, finally, what assumptions about learning were implicit in the above efforts? In fact, these same questions can be applied to any learning project in which they have engaged. Alternately, teachers can do the tasks they set for their students. What knowledge is necessary to complete the task? How do they divide it? What strategies do they use? They can also analyze their approach to teaching to identify their beliefs about learning. Finally, they need to become more aware of their students' learning processes. How do they approach a task that is easy? that is difficult? what are their beliefs? what strategies do they use? Teachers are expert learners and, therefore, their learning processes often remain below consciousness, being deployed automatically and intuitively. The above suggestions should help them develop a sensitivity to and an appreciation of this neglected underside of teaching.

Methodological Preparation

Teachers will also need to develop the know-how necessary to develop tasks and materials to promote learning to learn within the context of their individual courses. However, as they set out to acquire these methodological skills, it is important that they realize that they are, in fact, their own best resource. That is, in planning *language instruction* and in implementing these plans, they are, typically, required to diagnose and assess students; they must develop tasks and materials, and evaluate their outcome. It is these same skills that they now need to apply to helping students learn to learn, i.e., to the development of learner autonomy. Thus, they will already have a great deal of background knowledge and skill to draw on.

… Incorporating learning to learn … requires an extended process of experimentation, evaluation, and revision.

In addition and as noted earlier, the existing literature, including chapters in this volume, may be referred to for concrete ideas. However, it is important to be cautious in applying the models and procedures described in the literature, for as useful as this practical wisdom may be, it must be applied to one's classroom setting in a discriminating manner. What has worked in one context may need to be adapted for another. Thus, rather than imitation, it is recommended that the models and tasks provided in the literature be analyzed for frameworks to guide the development of procedures specific to one's students and their particular needs. Finally, it must be understood that incorporating learning to learn with language instruction takes time. It requires an extended process of experimentation, evaluation, and revision.

Conclusion

I would like to situate the notion of promoting learner autonomy within the broader social context, pointing to educational and social trends to argue that the value of such efforts will extend beyond the enhancement of foreign language learning. First of all, the need to promote learner autonomy grows out of recognition that the front end model of learning is no longer adequate. The idea that individuals' lives can be divided into three distinct segments, i.e., formal education, work, and retirement and leisure, with all the learning one needs taking place before one moves into the world of work, is a notion that is anachronistic. It is now recognized that educational institutions should prepare learners for lifelong learning. In a world characterized by knowledge explosion and technological change, it is not realistic to believe that the skills acquired by students during their formal schooling will serve them a lifetime. New knowledge will render their learned skills obsolete. They will need to replace them. Moreover, graduates from secondary and postsecondary institutions will need to function effectively both as workers and citizens in an increasingly interdependent world. This will require, for example and at the very least, that they maintain an awareness and understanding of global trends and their local impact. They will need to learn to interact and solve problems with others who are culturally diverse.

Thus the challenges of lifelong learning enhance the relevance of promoting autonomy in the foreign language classroom. For the knowledge and strategies that are so acquired can also be applied to the varied social settings in which learners will find themselves as workers and as citizens in their adult lives. It is by providing their students with the beginning foundation for lifelong learning that teachers can contribute to the grander project of ensuring that learners avoid the risk of remaining prisoners within the narrow perspectives of their cognitive and affective worlds, passive recipients of the consequences of global processes rather than active participants in charting their course.

Notes

[1] The interviews averaged ninety minutes in length. Results of the study, which aimed to discover what learners know about their learning, have been reported in Wenden 1986a, 1987. The account has been edited for syntax and ideas that may not have appeared in sentence form and have been rewritten to facilitate comprehension. Terms used by the learner to express his ideas, however, have not been changed. Another version of the account has been included in Wenden 1997a.

[2] For a more extended list of references, see Wenden 1998a, a monograph that reviews the literature on (1) learner autonomy in language learning, (2) self-directed language learning, and (3) cognitive strategy instruction dating back to the mid '70s.

[3] Of course, it is true that much more information is now available to the general public about health and ways of dealing with illness, in an effort, perhaps, to promote self-direction in "patients." Still, to a large extent, I believe there are not many who are ready to question a doctor's decisions and, certainly, to take over their treatment plan when they are ill.

References

Abe, D., Stanchina, C., & Smith, P. (1975). New approaches to autonomy: Two experiments in self-directed learning. *Mélanges Pédagogiques,* 57–78. Nancy: University of Nancy II, Centre de Recherches et d'Applications Pédagogiques en Langues (CRAPEL).

Allwright, R. (1981). What do we want teaching materials for? *English Language Teaching Journal, 36,* 5–18.

Barnett, L. (1988). *The challenge of integrating learner autonomy into the school.* Unpublished manuscript.

Brown, A., Bransford, J.D., Ferrara, R., & Campione, J.C. (1983). Learning, remembering, and understanding. In J. H. Flavell & E.M. Markman (Eds.), *Carmichael's manual of child psychology: Vol. 1.* New York: Wiley.

Brown, D. H. (1989). *A practical guide to language learning: A fifteen-week program of strategies for success.* New York: McGraw Hill.

Brumfit, C. J., & Johnson, K. (Eds.). (1979). *The communicative approach to language teaching.* Oxford: Oxford University Press.

Carroll, J. B. (1981). Twenty-five years of research on foreign language aptitude. In K. C. Diller (Ed.), *Individual differences and universals in language learning aptitude.* Rowley, MA: Newbury House.

Carver, D. (1984). Plans, learner strategies, and self-direction in language learning. *System: An International Journal of Educational Technology and Applied Linguistics, 12,* 123–131.

Chamot, A. (1987). The learning strategies of ESL students. In A.L. Wenden & J. Rubin (Eds.), *Learner strategies in language learning* (pp. 71–84). London: Prentice Hall International.

Chamot, A. (1994). CALLA: An instructional model for linguistically diverse students. *English Quarterly, 26,* 12–14.

Chamot, A., Küpper, L., Thompson, I., Barrueta, M., & Toth, S. (1990). *Learning strategies in the foreign language classroom: Resource guides for listening comprehension, reading comprehension, speaking, and writing.* ERIC Clearinghouse on Languages and Linguistics.

Chamot, A., & O'Malley, M. (1986). *A cognitive academic language learning approach: An ESL content-based curriculum.* National Clearinghouse for Bilingual Education.

Chinn, C. A., & Brewer, W. (1993) . The role of anomalous data in knowledge acquisition: A theoretical framework and implications for science instruction. *Review of Educational Research, 63*, 1–50.

Cohen, A. (1990). *Language learning: Insights for learners, teachers, and researchers.* New York: Newbury House.

Cotterall, S. (1995). Readiness for autonomy: Investigating learner beliefs. In L. Dickinson & A. Wenden (Eds.), *System: An International Journal of Educational Technology and Applied Linguistics* [Special Issue on Learner Autonomy], *23*, 195–206.

Dam, L. (1995). *Learner autonomy 3: From theory to classroom practice.* Authentik Language Learning Resources Ltd., Dublin: Trinity College.

Dam, L., & Legenhausen, L. (1996). The acquisition of vocabulary in an autonomous learning environment: The first months of beginning English. In R. Pemberton, E. Li, W. Or, & H. Pierson (Eds.), *Taking control: Autonomy in language learning* (pp. 265–280). Hong Kong: Hong Kong University Press.

Dickinson, L. (1987). *Self-instruction in language learning.* London: Cambridge University Press.

Dickinson, L. (1992). *Learner autonomy 2: Learner training for language learning.* Authentik Language Learning Resources Ltd., Dublin: Trinity College.

Dickinson, L. (1997). The use of the G.O.A.L. procedure for learner training. In M. Mueller Verweyen (Ed.), *New developments in foreign language learning, self-management, and autonomy* (pp. 93–102). Munich: Goethe Institute.

Dubin, F., & Olshtain, E. (1986). *Course design: Developing programs and materials for language learning.* Cambridge: Cambridge University Press.

Ellis, G., & Sinclair, B. (1989). *Learning to learn English: A course in learner training.* Cambridge: Cambridge University Press.

Eriksson, R. (1993). *Teaching language learning: Inservice training for communicative teaching and self-directed learning in English as a foreign language.* Goteborg Studies in Educational Sciences 92. Goteborg, Sweden: Acta Universitatis Gothoburgensis.

Eriksson, R. (1995). Learner autonomy. Where have we come from, where are we now? In R. Eriksson & J. Milander (Eds.), *Fourth Nordic conference on developing autonomous learning in the foreign language classroom* (pp. 5–10). Sweden: University of Karlstad.

Flavell, J. H. (1981). Cognitive monitoring. In W. P. Dickson (Ed.), *Children's oral communication skills* (pp. 35–60). New York: Academic Press.

Genessee, F. (1976). The role of intelligence in second language learning. *Language Learning, 26*, 267–280.

Gremmo, M. J., & Riley, P. (1995). Autonomy, self-direction and self-access in language teaching and learning: The history of an idea. In L. Dickinson & A. Wenden (Eds.), *System: An International Journal of Educational Technology and Applied Linguistics* [Special Issue on Learner Autonomy], *23*, 151–164.

Groteleschuen, A. K., Borkowski, J. G., & Hale, C. (1990). Strategy instruction is often insufficient: Addressing the interdependency of executive and attributional processes. In T. E. Scruggs & B. L.Wong (Eds.), *Intervention research in learning disabilities* (pp. 81–101). New York: Springer-Verlag.

Holec, H. (1981). *Autonomy and foreign language learning.* Oxford: Pergamon Press.

Holec, H. (1985). On autonomy: Some elementary concepts. In P. Riley (Ed.), *Discourse and learning.* New York: Longman Inc.

Holec, H. (1990). Qu'est-ce qu'apprendre à apprendre? *Mélanges Pédagogiques, 24*, 75-88. Nancy: University of Nancy II, CRAPEL.

Hosenfeld, C., Arnold, V., Kirchofer, J., Laciura, J., & Wilson, L. (1981). Second language reading: A curricular sequence for teaching reading strategies. *Foreign Language Annals, 4*, 415–422.

Hosenfeld, C., Cavour, I., Bonk, D., Baker, L., & Alcorn, M. (1993). *Activities and materials for implementing adapted versions of reciprocal teaching in beginning, intermediate, and advanced levels of instruction in English, Spanish, and French as a second/foreign language.* Unpublished manuscript. Department of Curriculum and Instruction, SUNY at Buffalo.

Huttunen, I. (1986). *Towards learner autonomy in foreign language learning in senior secondary school.* Department of Teacher Education. Oulu, Finland: University of Oulu Printing Center.

Huttunen, I. (Ed.). (1993). *Learning to learn languages: Investigating learner strategies and learner autonomy: Report on Workshop 2b.* Council for Cultural Cooperation, Strasbourg 6: Council of Europe.

Jensen, B.H. (1995). Learner evaluation and planning and an incident from a presentation. In R. Eriksson & J. Milander (Eds.), *Fourth Nordic conference on developing autonomous learning in the foreign language classroom* (pp. 49-61). Sweden: University of Karlstad.

Kelly, R. (1996). Language counselling for learner autonomy: The skilled helper in self-access language learning. In R. Pemberton, E. Li, W. Or, & H. Pierson (Eds.), *Taking control: Autonomy in language learning* (pp. 93–114). Hong Kong: Hong Kong University Press.

Kenny, B. (1993). For more autonomy. *System: An International Journal of Educational Technology and Applied Linguistics, 21*, 431–442.

Kohonen, V. (1991). *Foreign language learning as learner education: Facilitating self-direction in language learning.* Council of Europe Symposium. Ruschlikong, Switzerland.

Little, D. (1991). *Learner autonomy: Definitions, issues and problems.* Authentik Language Learning Resources Ltd. Dublin: Trinity College.

Little, D. (1994). Learner autonomy: A theoretical construct and its practical application. *Die Neuren Sprachen 93, 5*, 430–442.

Lyne, J. (1993). Feeling socially secure. In R. Eriksson & J. Milander (Eds.), *Fourth Nordic conference on developing autonomous learning in the foreign language classroom* (pp. 33–44). Sweden: University of Karlstad.

Mendelsohn, D. (1995). Applying learning strategies in the second/foreign language listening comprehension lesson. In D. Mendelsohn & J. Rubin (Eds.), *A guide for the teaching of second language listening.* San Diego, CA: Dominie Press.

Mendelsohn, D., & Rubin, J., (Eds.). (1995). *A guide for the teaching of second language listening.* San Diego, CA: Dominie Press.

Moulden, H. (1985). Extending self-directed learning of English in an engineering college. In P. Riley (Ed.), *Discourse and learning.* New York: Longman Inc.

Moulden, H. (1990). Assessing the self-directedness of foreign language learners. *Mélanges Pédagogiques, 24*, 65–74. Nancy: University of Nancy II, CRAPEL.

Moulden, H. (1993). The learner trainer's labours lost? *Mélanges Pédagogiques*, 111–120. Nancy: University of Nancy II, CRAPEL.

Munby, J. (1978). *Communicative syllabus design.* Cambridge: Cambridge University Press.

Naiman, N., Frohlich, M., Stern, H. H., & Todesco, A. (1978). *The good language learner.* Ontario: Ontario Institute for Studies in Education.

National Standards in Foreign Language Education Project. (1996). *Standards for foreign language learning: Preparing for the 21st century.* Yonkers, NY: Author.

Nishitani, M. (1994). On the use of TV programs in self-directed Japanese language learning by immigrants to Japan. *Learning Learning, 1*, 2–4.

Nunan, D. (1996). Towards autonomous learning: Some theoretical, empirical and practical issues. In R. Pemberton, E. Li, W. Or, & H. Pierson (Eds.), *Taking control: Autonomy in language learning*. Hong Kong: Hong Kong University Press.

O'Malley, M., & Chamot, A. (1990). *Learner strategies in second language acquisition*. New York: Cambridge University Press.

O'Malley, M., Chamot, A., Stewner-Manzanares, G., Küpper, L., & Russo, R.P. (1985). Learning strategies used by beginning and intermediate ESL students. *Language Learning, 35*, 21–46.

Oxford, R. (1990). *Language learning strategies: What every teacher should know*. New York: Newbury House.

Paris, S.G., & Byrnes, J.Y. P. (1989). The constructivist approach to self-regulation of learning in the classroom. In B. J. Zimmerman & D. H. Schunk (Eds.), *Self-regulated learning and academic achievement* (pp. 169–200). New York: Springer Verlag.

Reid, J. (1987). Learning style preferences of ESL students. *TESOL Quarterly, 21*, 87–112.

Rubin, J. (1975). What the good language learner can teach us. *TESOL Quarterly, 9*, 41–51.

Rubin, J. (1987). Learner strategies: Theoretical assumptions, research history, and typology. In A. L. Wenden & J. Rubin (Eds.), *Learner strategies in language learning* (pp. 71–84). London: Prentice Hall International.

Rubin, J. (1994). *Components of a teacher education curriculum for learner strategies*. (ERIC Document Reproduction Service No. ED 376 701)

Rubin, J., McKay, S., & Mansoor, I. (1995). *English Works!* New York: Longman.

Rubin, J., & Thompson, I. (1994). *How to be a more successful language learner* (2nd ed.). Boston: Heinle & Heinle.

Schoenfeld, A. (1982). *Beyond the purely cognitive: Metacognition and social cognition as driving forces in intellectual performance*. Paper presented at the annual meeting of the American Educational Research Association. (ERIC Document Reproduction Service No. ED 219 433)

Smith, R. (1995). An interview with Leni Dam. *Learning Learning, 2*, 5–7.

Stanchina, C. (1976). Two years of autonomy: Practice and outlook. *Mélanges Pédagogiques*, 73–82. Nancy: University of Nancy II, CRAPEL.

Thomson, C. K. (1996). Self-assessment in self-directed learning: Issues of learner diversity. In R. Pemberton, E. Li, W. Or, & H. Pierson (Eds.), *Taking control: Autonomy in language learning* (pp. 77–92). Hong Kong: Hong Kong University Press.

Victori, M., & Lockart, W. (1995). Enhancing metacognition in self-directed language learning. In L. Dickinson & A. Wenden (Eds.), *System: An International Journal of Educational Technology and Applied Linguistics* [Special Issue on Learner Autonomy], *23*, 223–234.

Wenden, A. (1985). Facilitating learning competence: Perspectives on expanded role for second language teachers. *Canadian Modern Language Journal, 6*, 981–991.

Wenden, A. (1986a). What do L2 learners know about their language learning ? A second look at retrospective accounts. *Applied Linguistics, 7*, 186–201.

Wenden, A. (1986b). Helping learners think about learning. *ELT Journal, 40*, 3–12.

Wenden, A. (1987). How to be a successful language learner: Insights and prescriptions from L2 learners. In A. L. Wenden & J. Rubin (Eds.), *Learner strategies in language learning* (pp. 103–118). London: Prentice Hall International.

Wenden, A. (1991). *Learner strategies for learner autonomy*. London: Prentice-Hall International.

Wenden, A. (1997a). Developing materials for informed self-learning: Frameworks for planning and intervention. In M. Mueller-Verweyen (Ed.), *New developments in foreign language learning, self-management, and autonomy* (pp. 73–92). Munich: Goethe Institute.

Wenden, A. (1997b, March). *The nature and function of monitoring.* Paper presented at the American Association of Applied Linguistics Annual Conference, Orlando, Florida.

Wenden, A. (1998a). *Learner training in foreign/second language learning: A curricular perspective.* (ERIC Document Reproduction Service No. ED 416 673)

Wenden, A. (in press). Metacognitive knowledge and language learning. *Applied Linguistics.*

Willing, K. (1988). *Learning styles in adult migrant education.* Research Series. Adelaide, Australia: National Curriculum Resource Centre, Adult Migrant Education Program.

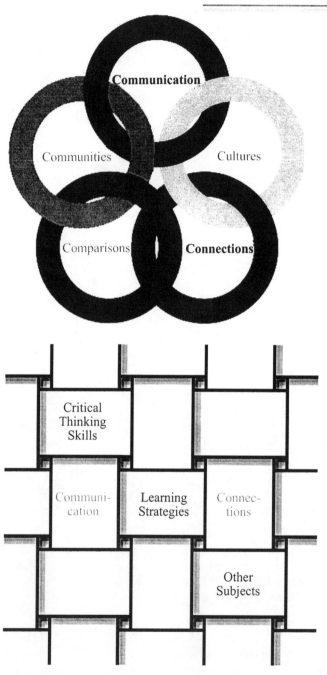

Reading and Writing Processes: Learning Strategies in Immersion Classrooms

Anna Uhl Chamot

The George Washington University

As language teachers we often focus on the product of our students' learning: their proficiency in understanding and using the target language. The processes by which students reach this proficiency are difficult to identify because they are not directly observable. We become aware of learning processes only when our students tell us how they have figured out the meaning of an unfamiliar word, how they have studied for a test, how they have remembered a particular expression, or how they have solved any other type of language learning problem. These types of learning processes which can be recalled consciously and which are used to understand, remember, and produce language are termed learning strategies (Weinstein & Mayer, 1986). Student accounts of their learning strategies can provide valuable information not only for assessing their needs, but also for planning instruction that responds to those needs.

Learning strategies are identified in the National Standards for Foreign Languages as a strand in the "weave of curricular elements" (1996, p. 29). Learning strategies can assist in meeting the standards identified in the five goals of Communication, Cultures, Connections, Comparisons, and Communities. Language teachers who provide explicit instruction in a variety of learning strategies can help their students become more effective and independent language learners. The Connections goal of the Foreign Language Standards identifies the acquisition of information and knowledge across subject areas through the target language. This goal is particularly relevant for language immersion programs, in which the focus of instruction is on curricular content rather than the language itself. In this context, learning strategies can assist students in meeting the dual cognitive demands of processing new information through the medium of a second language.

Language teachers who provide explicit instruction in a variety of learning strategies can help their students become more effective and independent language learners.

This chapter first describes a study that identified the learning strategies of elementary school children in language immersion programs, and then suggests how learning strategies can be integrated into classroom instruction for younger language learners.[1]

Background

Extensive research has been conducted on language immersion programs in Canada, and to a lesser degree, the United States (see, for example, Bernhardt, 1992; Campbell, 1984; Curtain & Pesola, 1988; Genesee, 1987; Lambert & Tucker, 1972; Met & Galloway, 1992; Swain, 1984; Thomas, Collier, & Abbott, 1993). This research has documented the impressive language proficiency levels achieved by children as they study content subjects through the medium of their second language. Immersion research has also revealed that children typically fail to acquire some aspects of grammatical competence, even after five or more years in immersion programs (Swain, 1985), and that older elementary school immersion students begin to avoid using the target language when conversing with their classmates (Tarone & Swain, 1995).

Though the levels of achievement attained by children in language immersion programs are fairly well known, we know less about the processes involved. The learning processes and strategies used by children in foreign language immersion settings are of particular interest because of their potential in identifying children's approaches to language learning, their awareness of their own strengths and weaknesses, and their ability to diagnose and solve their own language learning problems.

The work of Swain and her colleagues has provided insights into the role of language output in making learners more conscious of the gaps between what they want to express in the target language and their current linguistic ability (Swain, 1995; in press). The role of collaborative dialogue in helping learners focus on form and improve their level of accuracy is documented through the taping of student interactions as they work on a language task (Kowal & Swain, 1997; Swain, in press; Swain & Lapkin, 1998). Swain (in press) argues persuasively that when students work collaboratively and discuss problem solutions, they are solving linguistic problems through social interaction. Thus dialogue reveals learners' strategies and problem-solving processes as they work collaboratively.

While we are only beginning to learn about the strategies used by early language learners, learning strategies have been studied extensively with children learning school subjects in their native language. Considerable success has been reported in teaching elementary school children to use learning strategies in first language contexts for a variety of learning tasks, including reading (see Pressley & El-Dinary, 1993; Pressley et al., 1992), writing (see Harris & Graham, 1992), mathematics (see Carpenter, Fennema, Peterson, Chiang, & Loef, 1989; Silver & Marshall, 1990), and for various types of problem-solving (Gagné, Yekovich, & Yekovich, 1993).

Research on language learning strategies has dealt primarily with older students, either secondary school students or adults. Early research identified the characteristics of good language learners (e.g., Rubin, 1975; Naiman, Fröhlich, Stern, & Todesco, 1978; O'Malley, Chamot, Stewner-Manzanares, Küpper, & Russo, 1985a; Wenden, 1983). This research made it possible to develop instruments to measure language learning strategies. Oxford (1986) developed the Strategy Inventory for Language Learning (SILL) on which language learners can indicate the degree to which they use a variety of learning strategies. The SILL can be administered in a number of languages, and a growing body of international research using the SILL has identified correlations between learning strategies and learner characteristics such as learning style, culture, and gender (Bedell & Oxford, 1996; Green & Oxford, 1995; Oxford & Burry-Stock, 1995).

Research with older students has shown that effective language learners use strategies more appropriately than less-effective language learners, and that learning strategies can be taught to both secondary and college-level second language students (Chamot, 1993; Chamot & Küpper, 1989; Cohen, 1990, 1998; Cohen & Aphek, 1981; Cohen, Weaver, & Li, 1995; Hosenfeld, 1984; O'Malley & Chamot, 1990; Rubin, Quinn, & Enos, 1988; Thompson & Rubin, 1996). The application of this research to younger students in language immersion programs holds promise for developing an understanding of their learning processes and ways for helping them learn even more effectively.

Research in second language elementary school contexts has focused on children learning English as a second language (ESL) (Bermudez & Prater, 1990; Jiménez & Gámez, 1998; Muñiz-Swicegood, 1994; Padrón & Waxman, 1988). These studies have investigated the role of learning strategies in reading comprehension, and some have reported success in teaching reading strategies to elementary and middle school ESL students.

Learning Strategies of Immersion Students

In 1993 our research team[2] began working on a six-year longitudinal and cross-sectional study of learning strategies in elementary language immersion programs (Chamot, 1996; Chamot & El-Dinary, in press; Chamot, Keatley, et al., 1996). We were interested in finding out whether children could describe their thinking processes while working in the target language, what learning strategies were used by more-effective and less-effective learners, and how the strategies of younger children might differ from those of older children.

The understanding we have gained of children's metacognitive awareness through their verbal reports on their own thinking and learning processes have provided insights that can be applied to classroom instruction.

Study Participants and Context

The study is being conducted with three immersion programs in the Washington, DC, area. These include a French immersion program, a Spanish immersion program, and a Japanese partial immersion program. The grade levels range from kindergarten through grade six, though not every grade level is included for each of the three languages. Children in the French and Spanish programs are taught all content subjects in the target language, while those in the Japanese program receive instruction in mathematics, science, health, and reading and writing in Japanese for half of each day, and then spend the remainder of the day in English instruction for subjects such as English language arts and social studies.

Most of the students in these programs come from native English-speaking families. A few children in the Japanese program have a Japanese-speaking parent. In the Spanish program, a somewhat larger number of children have a Spanish-speaking parent or parents. In the French program, the majority of students also have native English-speaking backgrounds, but a number of Haitian and francophone African students are also enrolled. Data used in this chapter are from students whose home language is English.

Twelve of the 14 participating immersion teachers are native speakers of the target language, and the two remaining are near-native speakers. All hold either permanent or provisional elementary teaching certificates for the states in which they teach, and many also have teaching credentials and experience from their native countries. Participating teachers have all received considerable preparation and professional development in immersion philosophy and methodology through inservice workshops and/or university course work. The teachers express enthusiasm for immersion education, are rigorous in providing instruction virtually exclusively in the target language, and devote considerable efforts to developing appropriate materials and techniques to assist their students in learning subject matter through the medium of a foreign language.

Procedures

Identifying Subjects

Researchers worked with teachers to develop criteria for evaluating the language learning capabilities of their students. The rating scales developed were then used to identify a random sample of highly effective and less-effective learners in each classroom. Think-aloud interviews were conducted annually with this sample of at least 3 highly effective and 3 less-effective students in each classroom.

Think-Aloud Interviews

Think-aloud procedures were designed to capture children's reported mental processing as they worked on typical school tasks. Researchers worked with teachers to identify appropriate reading and writing tasks for the think-aloud interviews of students in their classrooms. These tasks were designed to contain new and somewhat challenging content, but were structured like familiar classroom tasks. Teachers introduced the concept of thinking aloud to their classes and explained the purpose of the research.

The research team developed a detailed interview guide for data collection, and interviewers participated in training sessions that included watching models of think-aloud interviews and receiving coaching as they conducted mock interviews with the guide.

> # The understanding we have gained of children's metacognitive awareness ... can be applied to classroom instruction.

Individual student interviews were then conducted with each student in the sample. The researcher first explained the purpose of the interview in both the target language and English, telling students they could describe their thoughts as they worked on the tasks in either language.

After explaining how to think aloud, the interviewer modeled thinking aloud while solving a picture puzzle, asked the student to restate what the interviewer had said, and praised the student for identifying the interviewer's verbalized thinking. To practice thinking aloud, students first worked through a logic problem while the interviewer prompted with questions like, "What are you thinking now? How did you figure that out?" Similar prompts were used for the data-collection tasks, which consisted of a reading and a writing task. For the reading task, children read excerpts of level-appropriate authentic children's literature in the second language. Children were told that they could read silently or aloud — or a combination. Most chose to either read aloud or intersperse silent reading with oral reading. It is possible that in choosing to read aloud, children were more likely to focus on decoding. For the writing task, students selected a picture and were asked to write a story about it in the target language. For all think-aloud tasks, interviewers frequently gave open-ended prompts to encourage thinking aloud, and requested clarification and elaboration of children's comments.

Analysis of Think-Alouds

The think-aloud interviews were audio-taped, then transcribed verbatim. Since the focus of the study was on students' thinking rather than on their linguistic production, the research team analyzed data for evidence of cognitive processing and learning strategies using a grounded theory approach (e.g., Strauss & Corbin, 1990).[3] Data were reviewed independently by members of the research team. A preliminary coding scheme of learning strategies was identified, then applied again to the data for confirmation. The coding scheme continued to be revised based on subsequent analysis of additional data. The coding scheme organized learning strategies in three levels. Level 1 identified strategies as either metacognitive or cognitive, Level 2 indicated categories of strategy types within the metacognitive and cognitive categories, and Level 3 further broke down the categories into task-specific applications of the strategies (see Chamot, Keatley, et al., 1996, for complete data analysis).

Researchers then worked in pairs to apply the coding scheme back to the think-aloud data in order to identify and describe the strategies used by each student. First, transcripts were coded independently, then the research pair met to compare their coding, calculating percentage of agreement for reliability and resolving differences through discussion. Coders agreed on the specific level-3 strategy code 79% of the time, and an additional 6% of strategies were coded within the same level-2 category, thus achieving an inter-rater agreement rate of 85% for level-2 strategies. Children's patterns of learning-strategies use were quantified by recording the number and type of strategies as a proportion of the total number of strategies identified. In addition to this quantitative analysis, qualitative profiles of a sample of students are being developed to capture variations and depth in the applications of the strategies reported.

Summary of Results

The think-aloud transcripts indicate that immersion students use a variety of learning strategies, and that more- and less-able students use learning strategies in different ways, as do younger and older students. For example, less-able and younger students used a greater proportion of phonetic decoding, or sounding out words syllable by syllable, than did more-able and older students. More-effective students also used a greater proportion of background-knowledge strategies (including inferences, predictions, and elaborations) than did the less-effective students. Of particular interest was the finding that children in immersion programs develop reading and writing abilities in much the same way that children do in non-immersion native language programs. The language variable may slow down the process at the beginning stages of literacy development, but the developmental progress and use of learning strategies by second language learners appear to be very like that of children learning to read and write in their native language.

We found that many, but not all, immersion students can describe their thinking processes from an early age, and even children who have difficulty in thinking aloud in primary grades are better able to describe their thinking by the middle and upper elementary grades. Of particular interest is the fact that some children exhibit metacognitive awareness through their ability to describe their own thinking in rich detail, often in the second language. As further evidence of metacognition, students often had thoughtful responses about when and why they think in their second language or in their first language. (For additional information on this study, see Chamot, 1996; Chamot & El-Dinary, in press; Chamot, Keatley, et al., 1996.)

The Children Speak

The comments made by children participating in this study provide insights into their metacognitive awareness about their own language learning. The examples that follow in tables 1–5 (from Chamot, 1996) are provided as an overview of the types of comments children made in the think-aloud interviews. In these tables, "I" refers to the interviewer, "S" to the student.

> … children in immersion programs develop reading and writing abilities in much the same way that children do in non-immersion native language programs.

More-able students were capable of describing their thinking processes rather clearly, as in the examples in Table 1.

Table 1. More-Able Students Describe their Thinking Processes	
Examples	Comments
French, Grade 6	
I: Are you thinking in French or in English right now? S: I think in both ... because I have like a picture in my head, but I think in French, but I take ... when I ... my vocabulary was born in English, so..that's why I translate into English.	The student describes what appears to be bilingual processing based on mental imagery. The student realizes that his initial vocabulary developed in English, and gives this as a reason for translating French words into English.
Japanese, Grade 5	
I: Are you thinking in Japanese or in English? S: I'm not thinking in either way, because I'm not saying anything, so ... only pictures.	The student is aware of own use of mental imagery while thinking, and indicates that this imagery is language-independent.
Spanish, Grade 2	
I: When you read, are you thinking completely in Spanish or a little bit in English, too? S: A lot in Spanish ... just a little bit in English. I: When, do you realize when you think in English? S: When it said (referring to the story), "I heard a cheep cheep nearby," I thought a little bit in English ... and all the rest in Spanish.	The student can make an estimate of how much thinking is done in each language, and can identify the point in the story where thinking in English intruded.

In contrast, less-able students often experienced difficulty in thinking aloud, as revealed by the interviewer's notes in Table 2.

Table 2. Less-Able Students Describe their Thinking Processes	
Examples	*Comments*
French, Grade 3	
When D. (the less-effective learner who used the word-by-word strategy) was given the text, he didn't look at the picture. I asked him what he was thinking before he started the text, and he just started reading.	The student did not use cues from the illustration to predict the story, and ignored the interviewer's request to describe his thinking.
Japanese, Grade 3	
The student reads the text aloud, self-correcting occasionally. However, when it comes to reporting about his thoughts while reading, he mostly keeps silent or replies, "I don't know." During the writing task, the student also either keeps silent or says, "I don't know," when asked what he is thinking.	These two students were uncommunicative when the interviewer asked them what they were thinking. Their standard response was "I don't know" or "No."
Japanese, Grade 5	
The student reads the text aloud, but says nothing voluntarily about her thoughts while reading. In response to the interviewer's questions such as, "Did you think about anything here?" she keeps saying "no."	
Spanish, Grades 1–3	
Low-strategy users were less articulate than high-strategy users. The former were frequently silent when asked what they were thinking of or what they usually did to solve a reading/writing problem.	Students seemed to be unable to respond to questions about their thinking processes.

I have one half of my brain that does thinking of stories and the other half does math problems.
First-grade Japanese immersion student

Some students also showed metacognitive awareness through comments in which they talked about their own thinking processes, as shown in the examples in Table 3.

Table 3. Metacognitive Awareness	
Examples	*Comments*
French, Grade 5	
I: And what do you need to do when you see an exercise like this that you need to fill out? S: Me, I think that I need to think about what we did at the beginning of the school year, because this was the first thing that we did in social studies, and then I'm going to look at all the sentences and try to recall what it is. Since there are many that help me and I only need to fill in a word in one place or another, it will be quite easy.	This student has a clear plan for proceeding with the task. The plan is based on her prior knowledge about similar tasks, her analysis of the requirements of the present task, and her confidence that she has the strategies which will make the task easy.
Japanese, Grade 1	
The student listened to the first part of a story and used the illustration to guess what the story was about, since there were so many unfamiliar words. Then the interviewer read a portion of the story without showing the illustration and asked the student to tell what he was thinking. S: I was … I thought of the same thing. I: Okay. You remember the pictures? Okay, is there anything else you were thinking? S: Uh, just a couple of math problems. I: Math problems? You were thinking of math while you listened? S: Uh-huh. I: Oh, that's amazing! S: I know. I have one half of my brain that does thinking of stories and the other half does math problems.	Even without the story's illustration, the student relied on mental imagery while listening to part of the story. However, the student was also reflecting on the math problems completed before the reading task. The student believes that his brain is divided into compartments that either understand stories or process math problems.

Table 3, cont'd.	
Spanish, Grade 2	
I: First, before reading, what are you thinking about at this moment, before starting to read? S: (Student examines the picture) That this story could be a fantasy. I: It could be a fantasy? Why do you say that? S: Because I think (still looking at the picture) that the story is going to be very funny and things are going to happen that can't happen.	This is an example of planning before reading. The student gets ready to read the story by using the illustration to make predictions about what the story will be about.

Some students could describe the strategies they used in some detail, as seen in Table 4.

Table 4. Student Strategies	
Examples	*Comments*
Japanese, Grade 1	
The student notices that the first story includes lots of *ka-ki-ku-ke-ko* (the sequence of the Japanese alphabet/syllabary), and that the first part of each sentence starts with one of these syllables in order. She further mentions that each sentence in the second story starts with a Japanese vowel in sequence (*a-i-u-e-o*).	The teacher uses a large chart of the *hiragana* syllabary to teach the syllables in order, and students are taught to recognize different *hiragana* by going through the sequence.
Spanish, Grade 2	
I: (Shows student a math word problem to solve) When you see a math problem, what do you think about? S: Mm ... that first you need to read the problem and then you think what strategy is easiest to use. Then you solve the problem, using whichever strategy. I: What are your favorite strategies? S: Mm ... drawing ... complete sentence, or a number sentence.	The teacher provides explicit instruction in a process for mathematics problem solving strategies which include understanding the problem, deciding on a plan for solving the problem, carrying out the plan, and checking the answer. This student is focusing on the initial steps in the problem-solving process.

... if I think that this word is important enough, I look it up in the dictionary, but if I can ... understand the sentence and it's clear enough, I don't look it up ... and I deliberately forget about it.

Fifth-grade French immersion student

More-effective students demonstrated that they could use learning strategies appropriately and flexibly, as the examples in Table 5 indicate.

Table 5. More-Effective Students Describe their Strategies	
French, Grade 5	
Examples	*Comments*
(Student did not recognize the word "pastures" in French, and explained what she does when she doesn't know a word in French.) S: ... That depends, if I think that this word is important enough, I look it up in the dictionary, but if I can maybe understand the sentence and it's clear enough, I don't look it up in the dictionary and I deliberately forget about it.	The student makes a judgment about the importance of an unfamiliar word and then chooses which strategy to use.
Japanese, Grade 5	
The student starts by asking questions about the (writing) task. Before writing, she generates content to be written by describing the picture in Japanese. She asks a question about how to say an item in the picture in Japanese. The student writes as she says what she is writing. When asked, she reports that she first constructs what she would write in her head and then writes it. She later reports that there were things that she thought about writing, but she didn't because she couldn't construct them in her head. She reports that when this happens in class, she usually looks the word up in the dictionary. Finally, she indicates metacognitive awareness by saying, "I know a lot of words in English, but unless I know them in Japanese, I cannot do it."	The student appears to have developed useful pre-writing strategies, including imagery, brainstorming prior knowledge, questioning for clarification, mental rehearsal, deletion of unknown words or phrases from the plan or use of a dictionary, and an assessment of her own knowledge.

Table 5, cont'd.
Spanish, Grade 2

The student is asked what he does when he encounters a new word while reading in Spanish. S: Yes, and when I don't understand a word, I have a paper and I can write what page it's on and what sentence, and write the word —and the teacher can tell (me). I: Very good. And if there's no teacher, for example at home, if you're talking with your family and you don't want to use English, what do you do to find a word? S: Like when I want to talk in Spanish? And I don't know a word? I: If there's a word you don't know or can't remember. S: I ask my brother. And if he doesn't know, I look in a book. The student reported a similar set of strategies he used when he couldn't think of a word while writing. He said that first he asked the teacher, but if she wasn't there, then he would write another word that means the same.	This student has a series of strategies for dealing with gaps in his knowledge of the target language. He can describe the circumstances in which each particular strategy can be helpful for him.

These examples of early language learners' comments while working on different school tasks provide important information about the cognitive processes of young language learners. Information gained through think-alouds probably represents only a snapshot of a learner's thinking, as many thoughts may not be retrievable for various reasons. Learners may find it difficult to articulate their thoughts, they may forget some of their rapidly shifting thinking, or they may not be able to bring implicit learning to a conscious level. However, students' descriptions of their thinking are the only way that researchers and teachers can access any part of learners' cognitive processes, and for this reason think-aloud data provide valuable insights into second language acquisition.

Instructional Applications

The importance of learning strategies in language teaching lies in their potential for helping students become better language learners. This potential may be especially strong for language immersion teaching, since children are engaged in the same types of learning tasks (e.g., reading, writing, mathematics, social studies, science) as the children in native language contexts who have shown positive gains in these areas after receiving instruction in learning strategies (for example, Brown, Pressley, Van Meter, & Schuder, 1994; Harris & Graham, 1992; Palincsar & Brown, 1986; Pressley et al., 1992; Pressley et al., 1995; Silver & Marshall, 1990). Since children in this immersion study resembled children in native language contexts in their acquisition of reading and writing skills, it seems reasonable to assume that instruction in the same types of learning strategies could be equally efficacious.

In the course of a series of studies on learning-strategy applications, we have developed a metacognitive model describing the learning process and a framework for learning-strategies instruction (Chamot, 1994; Chamot, Barnhardt, et al., 1996; 1999). This section explores the application of these approaches to learning-strategies instruction in elementary foreign language classrooms.

Metacognitive Model of Strategic Learning

The Metacognitive Model of Strategic Learning is based on extensive learning-strategies research on the learning strategies used by effective elementary, secondary, and college language learners (Chamot, 1993, 1994; Chamot & Küpper, 1989; Chamot & O'Malley, 1993; Chamot et al., 1996; O'Malley & Chamot, 1990; O'Malley, et al., 1985a; 1985b). The learning strategies identified in the model can be used for many different types of tasks and language skills, and all have been used successfully by language teachers.

The model describes the metacognitive processes that learners engage in while completing a task in the target language, and includes *planning, monitoring, problem solving, and evaluating* (see Wenden, this volume). *Planning* involves any type of preparation before a task, such as brainstorming before writing or predicting before reading. *Monitoring* describes the awareness and attention that students direct to the task while it is in progress. *Problem-solving* occurs when learners encounter difficulties as they are working on a task and apply one or more learning strategies to overcome them. *Evaluating* involves checking back after finishing a task or a part of a task, and assessing how well it has been completed. The major learning strategies reported by children in the study are identified in the figure below and are categorized within the Metacognitive Model of Strategic Learning.

Figure. Metacognitive Model of Strategic Learning: Classification of Learning
Strategies Reported by Children During Reading and Writing Tasks

Planning

- Previewing: Identifying main idea, topic
- Predicting from title or illustrations
- Accessing relevant background knowledge
- Organizational Planning: Planning parts and sequence of task; identifying audience
- Self-management: Arranging for conditions that assist learning

Monitoring

- Attending selectively to: known words, key words, text organization, title, picture, linguistic features, pronunciation, skipping, or rereading
- Visualizing while reading
- Monitoring sense, strategy use, sound
- Verifying inference, prediction, or meaning
- Self-correcting online (rather than at end of task)
- Self-questioning online about correctness

Problem-solving

- Making inferences from text, title, pictures, and/or world knowledge
- Predicting upcoming information
- Using background knowledge to elaborate from personal experiences, text features, and/or pictures
- Using knowledge of first and second languages for: deduction (using rules), decoding, semantic awareness, recognizing cognates, translating, borrowing, or language mixing
- Using resource aids such as dictionary, classroom poster charts, or other reference
- Requesting information (spelling, word, sentence, etc.) from teacher, classmate, or other
- Using a sequence to remember needed information
- Making sound associations; recalling auditorially
- Brainstorming needed vocabulary
- Visualizing word or character

- Substituting a known word or circumloqution when the original word or expression is not known or cannot be remembered
- Skipping an unknown word and/or reading on to get meaning

Evaluating
- Retelling a story or other text in own words
- Summarizing the main points
- After a writing task, reading over to revise
- Correcting own errors after completing a task

These metacognitive processes are recursive and can be applied to any learning task. Different learning strategies can facilitate learning and communication at any point. For example, teachers can help children begin to think about their own learning processes by telling them stories that illustrate the metacognitive model described above. With elementary school language learners, we have used an illustrated story about a girl who embarks on a mountain climb (Chamot & O'Malley, 1993; Chamot et al., 1999). In this story, Sophie (or Socorro, or Sachiko, depending on the target language) demonstrates strategic thinking. First, she plans her climb by assembling the equipment and supplies she anticipates needing, such as hiking boots, knapsack, sweater, snack, and water bottle. She monitors her hike by using a variety of strategies, such as visualizing her goal, focusing on the terrain, and encouraging herself. When she encounters a problem (a stream to be crossed), she considers a number of possible solutions, and then picks one to solve the problem. Finally, when she reaches the summit, she evaluates her climb by reflecting on successes, problems, solutions, and strategies used.

Teachers have used this and other stories to show how a character plans, monitors, solves a problem, and evaluates his or her strategic processes to introduce learning-strategy instruction. Later, teachers can refer back to the story to encourage children to identify possible strategies they might use during each process phase of a learning task.

Learning strategies used by children in the immersion study often reflected these four processes for working through a task, as shown in the examples that follow. These examples illustrating the four metacognitive processes are drawn from longitudinal data for a sample of seven students. These data include transcripts for 3 students in French immersion, 2 students in Spanish immersion, and 2 students in Japanese partial immersion.

Grade levels range from Kindergarten to Grade 6, and the longitudinal data for each of the seven students include a minimum of two years to a maximum of five years. The examples are given verbatim and are followed by a translation to English as appropriate. An asterisk (*) precedes incorrect words or usage in the target language.

Planning Strategies

Although most planning strategies occurred during the writing task, some students also used planning strategies for reading, such as previewing a story by making predictions based on its title and illustrations. The following excerpt from the transcript of a think-aloud interview with a fifth-grade student in a French immersion program illustrates the use of several strategies to plan before reading:

> Upon being given a book to read in French, the student immediately reads the title. The interviewer asks why. *"Parce que ... je veux savoir quel livre je vais lire."* [Because I want to know which book I'm going to read.] The interviewer again asks why. *"Parce que sinon ... hm ... je *serai lire à propos des choses et je ne saurais à quoi je lis *à propos de.* [Because otherwise ... hm ... I would be reading about things and I wouldn't know what I was reading about.] The student then begins to look at the cover of the book, and when asked why, explains, *"Et puis je regarde *cet dessin parce que je veux voir ce que ça veut dire, et puis je regarde le nom du chapitre ou quelque chose."* [And then I look at this drawing because I want to see what it means, and then I look at the name of the chapter or something.] After examining and commenting on the map on the book's cover, and relating it to his prior knowledge, the student exclaims excitedly, *"Et puis je vais lire! Et c'est chapitre 1, 'Eléphantine.'"* [And then I'm going to read! And it's chapter 1, "Elephantine."]

This example of planning before reading shows how a strategically oriented student uses background knowledge and text features such as the title and illustrations to preview a book.

Most of the examples of planning occurred with the writing task, in which students had to select a picture as a prompt and then write about it. The example that follows shows how a third grader in the Spanish immersion school describes his approach to planning before writing:

> After the student has decided to write about a picture of a boy leading a dinosaur on a leash, the interviewer asks (in Spanish) what he usually does to write. *"*Escribe el título y *escribe el sentence de tópico."* [Write the title and write the topic sentence.] The interviewer asks from whom he learned about topic sentences, and he identified both his English teacher and his Spanish teacher. When asked if this helps him, he replies, *"¡Sí!*

¡Mucho! Porque no tengo que hacer, '¿Qué estoy escribiendo *sobre, ¿qué estoy escribiendo *sobre?' Tengo mi topic sentence to help me." [Yes, a lot! Because I don't have to go, "What am I writing about, what am I writing about?' I have my topic sentence to help me."] The interviewer asks if this is the first thing he thinks about before writing, and he answers, *"Pienso un poco y estoy pensando qué *está *el cosa más importante y qué dibujo *quiere que yo hable *sobre."* [I think a little, and I am thinking what is the most important thing and what picture I want to talk about.] In describing his approach to writing, the student goes on to say, *"Pienso un poco y *escribe, pienso y *escribe, etcetera."* [I think a little and I write, I think and write, etcetera.] The boy begins to write his story, and after the first sentence (which is a topic sentence!), he stops and asks how much the interviewer wants him to write. She tells him a short story, then asks why he asked this. The student says in English, "That way I know how much to write." The conversation continues mostly in English, with the student explaining that he adds more details if the story has to be longer. When asked about the use of details, he explains, *"Para *los personas que *leelo, *sabe que estoy hablando *sobre."* [For the people who read it, (so) they know what I am talking about.]

This young third grader has developed a system for planning his writing that he has learned from his teachers and that has proven successful.

Monitoring Strategies

Monitoring involves an awareness of how well a task is going while it is in progress. Monitoring is difficult to detect because of its online nature, but some students in this study were able to describe retrospectively how they monitored their performance, as in these examples:

A fourth grade student in the Japanese partial immersion program was decoding a story in Japanese. The interviewer asked, *"Ima nani o kangaete imasu ka?"* [What are you thinking now?] The student answered in English, except for the personal pronoun "I" in Japanese (*watashi*): "Uuh ... well, sometimes *watashi* just sort of read, sort of picture things in my head, like uh ... like pictures, uh ... Like what *watashi* might think about or ... uh or like, like picture that things *watashi* might think look like ..."

While this student appeared to be monitoring by visualizing what was happening in the story she was reading, a fifth grade student in the French immersion program explained his monitoring as follows:

After reading a paragraph aloud, the student says, *"Maintenant je suis un peu confus parce que ... confus. Parce que je suis pas vraiment comme les autres personnes. Je suis pas ... Je ne trouve pas que je *comprendre ça. Parce que maintenant c'est un peu confus parce que ... il y a ça disait l'autre hm phrase ... La tête du serpent du boomerang de bois frappe parmi les volatiles, et puis ça ça dit Tétiki sourit ... Tétiki est la personne*

*(l'homme ou femme) qui a lancé le boomerang, je pense ... [Tétiki] sourit
de fierté parce que le deuxième oiseau qu'il bat (ou déjà battu)* [means
abbattu] *et gagné — je pense ... hm heu ... dans l'après-midi à toujours ...
hm ... le premier coup sur ... du premier coup ... je comprends pas ça et
puis ça dit ..."* [Now I am a little confused because ... confused. Because
I'm not really like other people. I'm not ... I don't find that I understand
that. Because now it's a bit confusing because there was what the other
sentence said.... The snake's head of the wooden boomerang hit among the
birds, and then that ... that says (that) Tétiki smiles.... Tétiki is the person
(the man or woman) who threw the boomerang, I think. (Tétiki) smiles
proudly because it's the second bird he's brought down or already brought
down and won ... I think ... hm ... in the afternoon at still ... hm ... the
first strike ... on the first strike ... I don't understand that, and then it
says...]

This student is obviously struggling to make sense of a text and is very
much aware of what is confusing him. By monitoring the sense of what
he is reading, he is able to identify the moment when he has a comprehension problem.

Problem-Solving Strategies

When students become aware of a problem in comprehension or communication through monitoring, they can then take steps to solve the problem identified. For example, the interview with the fifth grade French
immersion student described above who was struggling to comprehend a
passage went on as follows:

The interviewer asked, *"Si tu ne comprends pas, qu'est-ce que tu fais?"* [If
you don't understand, what do you do?] The student explains, *"Je *va à la
prochaine phrase et je *juste laisse la phrase que je ne comprends pas, et
je *va ..."* [I go to the next sentence and I just leave the sentence that I
don't understand, and I go ...] A few moment later in the interview, the
student explains why he skips sentences that he doesn't understand: *"... si
je vais (*va) à la prochaine chose et si ça n'a rien, je pense, a rien avec
l'autre phrase, je *juste *va et continue ... et *juste laisse la phrase parce
que ce n'est pas vraiment très important juste une phrase, une fois,"* [I go
to the next thing, and if I think that has nothing (to do) with the other
sentence, I just keep going and just leave the sentence, because it's not
really very important — just one sentence, one time.]

This student attempts to solve a comprehension problem by reading on to see
if the next sentence can help him understand, but if it doesn't help, he is willing
to tolerate the ambiguity and continue reading, rather than giving up.

Another example of problem-solving strategies emerged from longitudinal data for a student in the Japanese partial immersion program. In

second grade, this student was struggling to write a sentence in Japanese. She made careful use of the *hiragana* and *katakana* (Japanese syllabary) charts in the classroom to find the character she needed, reciting the order of the syllables until she reached the one she needed. By fourth grade, she describes her approach to figuring out how to spell a word in Japanese by saying that she asks the teacher or a classmate who is a good speller. In fifth grade, she says that when she is trying to figure out how to pronounce a word while reading, she "does the alphabet," meaning that she rehearses the sequence of the Japanese syllabary. In sixth grade, she explains her approach to solving a comprehension problem when there is a word she doesn't know. She says (in English) that first she tries to use a picture, but if there is no picture, she asks a friend or the teacher. If this is not possible, she just goes over the word and then goes on, since "There might be something later on that sort of explains what the word means." This student's approach to figuring out new words in Japanese for either reading or writing seems to develop from a rote approach in the early grades to either asking someone for help or using pictures or the following text to make inferences as she gains in proficiency and maturity.

A second grader in the Spanish immersion program describes a sequence of problem-solving strategies for dealing with new words.

> The interviewer asks in Spanish what the student does when there is a difficult word. She responds, *"*Me trata sound it out."* [I try to sound it out.] After demonstrating with a word, the student continues, *"Después de sounding it out, si eso no sirve, ¿Qué más haces? *Trata *que miro a *los *otros palabras that *está around it y *trata *que guess qué palabra es."* [After sounding it out, if that doesn't work, what else do you do? I try to look at the other words that are around it and guess what the word is.] The student continues to explain that she seeks help from a classmate or an adult, or *"Quizás yo me *lee *este palabra y *lee el resto de la oración, y cuando *puede preguntar a un adulto, *preguntas."* [Maybe I read the word and read the rest of the sentence, and when I can ask an adult, I ask.]

These examples of problem-solving strategies illustrate children's mental activity and their awareness of different ways of making sense of the target language.

Evaluating Strategies

Evaluation is an important part of metacognition because reflecting back on a task helps learners understand both their successes and their shortcomings. Although evaluation did not occur as frequently as problem-solving, some children in the immersion study were able to reflect on their thoughts and actions after completing a task.

> A second grader in Spanish immersion explained, *"Cuando yo *soy escribi-endo y no realize que *soy getting off track, yo read it over cuando *ter-mine. Yo no sé por qué, pero algunos niños no read it over unless it's time para editar o algo.* [When I am writing and don't realize that I'm getting off track, I read it over when I finish. I don't know why, but some children don't read it over unless it's time to edit or something.] The interviewer sought clarification about when the student read over her writing, and the student answered, *"Sí, yo leo inmediatamente después que yo *escribelo para ver si yo got off track y si yo *trata *a borrarlo, porque yo si ... porque yo *trata..porque."* (student mimes ripping her paper). [Yes, I read imme-diately after I write it to see if I got off track and if I try to erase it because I ... because I try ... because] (makes ripping sound).

This young student has already developed the habit of reading over what she writes to check if she has kept on track, whether she needs to erase — or perhaps tear up the paper!

A fifth grade student in the Japanese partial immersion program evalu-ates her oral reading of a story in Japanese in this way:

> After the student reads aloud, the interviewer asks in Japanese why she repeated a word in the text. The student responded (in English), "'Cause I said *[i]mashouta,* but it's *[i]mashita* [was]. The interviewer asked in Eng-lish, "How did you figure that out?" The student answered, "... sometimes I just pronounce things wrong." The interviewer switches back to Japanese to ask the student what she is thinking at that point, and the student replies in English, "I ... just sort of thinking about what it's saying, what's hap-pening in the story."

This student understands that she makes pronunciation mistakes when reading Japanese, and demonstrates her ability to correct a mistake. She also thinks back after reading to what happened in the story.

The examples provided here of immersion students engaging in the processes of planning, monitoring, problem-solving, and evaluating are representative of the comments made by children during the think-aloud sessions. All of the students interviewed used learning strategies, but some children were better able to reflect on their own learning and deploy a range of effective strategies. Some children explained that they had been taught reading or writing strategies, and that they found them useful, lend-ing support to the value of learning strategy instruction.

Learning-Strategies Instruction

Learning strategies can be integrated into any language curriculum. Immersion programs are particularly appropriate for learning-strategies instruction for a number of reasons. First, immersion children can use the learning strategies taught with all content subjects, just as students do when learning in their native language. Second, the strategies can be taught easily in the target language, since immersion teachers generally use the target language exclusively. Third, and most important, learning-strategies instruction helps students become more aware of their own learning and increases their ability to evaluate their own progress.

The guidelines for learning-strategy instruction suggested in this section are based on extensive research and work with teachers in language classrooms (see Chamot, Barnhardt, et al., 1999). Organized planning of learning-strategy instruction is essential because learning strategies, like other skills, need many meaningful practice opportunities before students can use them independently. The following suggestions can assist in planning and implementing learning-strategies instruction:

- Find out what learning strategies your students are already using. This can be accomplished through class discussions, individual or group interviews or questionnaires, or think-alouds such as the ones described earlier in this chapter. By identifying your students' prior knowledge about and use of learning strategies, you can increase their awareness of their own learning and diagnose their learning-strategy needs.
- Practice learning strategies with real learning tasks, rather than applied in isolation. Tasks mediated by learning strategies should be part of the regular curriculum so that students learn how strategies can help them become better language (and content) learners.
- Be explicit in teaching learning strategies. Give each strategy a name, explain to students how and why to use it, and initiate classroom discussions about students' use of learning strategies. Make posters, graphic organizers, and other visuals that display strategy names and applications. The strategies identified in the figure can be rendered in the target language with words appropriate for young language learners.
- Present strategies by modeling them for your students. For example, think aloud about your strategies for reading while you are actually reading. Have your students follow along the text with you (as a handout or on an overhead). Do the

same for writing, solving a math problem, understanding a science phenomenon, or any other learning task in your curriculum.

- Provide many practice opportunities for using learning strategies. Any challenging classroom task or home assignment can be used for practicing strategies.
- Have students evaluate their use of learning strategies so that they can make decisions about which strategies work best for individual learners and tasks. Strategies evaluation can be through class discussions, journals, logs, checklists, questionnaires, and the like. Two questionnaires, one to be used after reading a folktale, and the other after children have written their own folktale, are provided in the Appendix.
- Help students expand their use of learning strategies to new tasks and situations. For example, if students have learned how to make inferences when reading, have them try the same strategy with listening.

These suggestions are drawn from the instructional framework developed for the Cognitive Academic Language Learning Approach (CALLA), which has been applied in both content-ESL and foreign language instruction (Chamot & O'Malley, 1994; Chamot, Barnhardt, et al., 1999). In this framework, teachers plan for five recursive phases of instruction. In the first, *Preparation*, students' prior knowledge about strategies is elicited through a discussion or activity. In the second, *Presentation*, the teacher models how to use a new strategy and explains why it is helpful and when to use it. The third phase is *Practice*, in which students practice one or more learning strategies as they work on a regular classroom task. In the *Evaluation* phase, students reflect on their strategy applications and evaluate their own learning. Finally, in the *Expansion* phase, students are shown how to apply the learning strategies to additional types of learning tasks both in school and at home. The recursive nature of this framework makes it possible for teachers to move in any direction between phases, once the essential first phase of discovering students' prior knowledge has been completed.

Conclusion

This chapter has described how children in three language immersion programs talk about their learning strategies when they read and write in their second language. The examples drawn from children's verbal reports during think-aloud sessions have illustrated a metacognitive learning model comprised of planning, monitoring, problem-solving, and evaluating processes. Children's think-aloud verbalizations as they work on reading and writing tasks can provide insights for teachers into the learning and thinking processes of young language learners. The excerpts from the children's comments indicate that many are active learners who make every effort to construct meaning and are able to reflect on their approaches to language learning. However, less effective language learners in the sample tended to have more difficulty in describing their thinking and appeared to be taking a passive and dependent approach to learning and using a second language. Although the study described in this chapter does not establish a causal relationship between children's metacognitive awareness or use of learning strategies and their second language proficiency, the results are nevertheless suggestive of a possible link. Given the success in native language contexts of improving children's reading comprehension and written composition through explicit learning-strategies instruction, foreign language teachers may wish to consider integrating similar instruction into teaching reading and writing in a second language. At the very least, teachers will discover how their students think about the language learning process, how they solve language-comprehension and -production problems, and how they feel about themselves as language learners.

When students become more aware of their own learning processes and learn how to use effective strategies for language learning tasks, they begin to be self-regulated learners who can identify their own language learning needs and seek opportunities for independent learning.

Notes

[1] I would like to express my appreciation to the students, teachers, and administrators of Fox Mill Elementary School in Fairfax County Public Schools (Virginia) and in Maryvale Elementary School and Rock Creek Forest Elementary School in Montgomery County Public Schools (Maryland) for their time, patience, and willingness to share their insights in participating in this research. I would also like to thank Martha Abbott, Foreign Language Supervisor in Fairfax County, and Dr. Myriam Met, Foreign Language Supervisor in Montgomery County, for all their help, support, and encouragement during the last five years in making it possible to conduct this research in their schools. Finally, Dr. Michael Pressley provided valuable suggestions on the coding scheme developed to analyze the think-aloud protocols.

[2] The study Learning Strategies in Elementary Immersion Programs is being conducted by the National Capital Language Resource Center (NCLRC), a consortium of Georgetown

University, the George Washington University, and the Center for Applied Linguistics. The NCLRC is one of seven Language Resource Centers funded by the U. S. Department of Education to "improve and strengthen the nation's capacity to teach and learn foreign languages." Members of the research team have included: Anna Uhl Chamot, Catharine Keatley, Pamela El-Dinary, Sarah Barnhardt, Jill Robbins, Koichi Nagano, Christine Newman, Alissa Martin, and Susan Dirstine.

[3]A grounded theory approach uses qualitative methods based on data rather than driven by hypothesis-testing. Data are collected, then reviewed by collaborating researchers for evidence of recurring events that suggest a pattern. When potential patterns emerge, they are then tested against the data for validation. The process involves continuing dialogue among researchers and revisiting of the data before arriving at an interpretation.

References

Bedell, D. A., & Oxford, R. L. (1996). Cross-cultural comparisons of language learning strategies in the People's Republic of China and other countries. In R. L. Oxford (Ed.), *Language learning strategies around the world: Cross-cultural perspectives* (pp. 47–60). Honolulu, HI: University of Hawai'i Press.

Bermudez, A.B., & Prater, D. L. (1990). Using brainstorming and clustering with LEP writers to develop elaboration skills. *TESOL Quarterly, 24*, 523–528.

Bernhardt, E. B. (Ed.). (1992). *Life in language immersion classrooms*. Bristol, PA: Multilingual Matters.

Brown, R., Pressley, M., Van Meter, P., & Schuder, T. (1994). *A quasi-experimental validation of transactional strategies instruction with previously low-achieving grade-2 readers*. Amherst, NY: University at Buffalo, SUNY, Department of Educational Psychology.

Campbell, R. N. (1984). The immersion approach to foreign language teaching. In *Studies on immersion education: A collection for United States educators* (pp. 114–143). Sacramento, CA: California State Department of Education.

Carpenter, T., Fennema, E., Peterson, P. L., Chiang, C., & Loef, M. (1989). Using knowledge of children's mathematics thinking in classroom teaching: An experimental study. *American Educational Research Journal, 26*, 499–532.

Chamot, A. U. (1993). Student responses to learning strategy instruction in the foreign language classroom. *Foreign Language Annals, 26*(3), 308–321.

Chamot, A.U. (1994). A model for learning strategy instruction in the foreign language classroom. In J. E. Alatis (Ed.), *Georgetown University Round Table on Languages and Linguistics 1994* (pp. 323–336). Washington, DC: Georgetown University Press.

Chamot, A.U. (1996). Learning strategies of elementary foreign-language-immersion students. In J. E. Alatis (Ed.), *Georgetown University Round Table on Languages and Linguistics 1995* (pp. 300–310). Washington, DC: Georgetown University Press.

Chamot, A. U., Barnhardt, S., El-Dinary, P. B., & Robbins, J. (1996). Methods for teaching learning strategies in the foreign language classroom. In R. L. Oxford (Ed.), *Language learning strategies around the world: Cross-cultural perspectives* (pp. 175–187). Honolulu, HI: University of Hawai'i Press.

Chamot, A. U., Barnhardt, S., El-Dinary, P., & Robbins, J. (1999). *The learning strategies handbook*. White Plains, NY: Addison Wesley Longman.

Chamot, A. U., & El-Dinary, P. B. (in press). Children's learning strategies in immersion classrooms. *Modern Language Journal, 83*(3).

Chamot, A.U., Keatley, C., Barnhardt, S., El-Dinary, P. B., Nagano, K., & Newman, C. (1996). *Learning strategies in elementary language immersion programs.* Final report submitted to Center for International Education, U.S. Department of Education. Available from ERIC Clearinghouse on Languages and Linguistics.

Chamot, A. U., & Küpper, L. (1989). Learning strategies in foreign language instruction. *Foreign Language Annals, 22*(1), 13–24.

Chamot, A. U., & O'Malley, J. M. (1993). Teaching for strategic learning: Theory and practice. In J. E. Alatis (Ed.), *Georgetown University Round Table on Languages and Linguistics 1993* (pp. 36–51). Washington, DC: Georgetown University Press.

Chamot, A. U., & O'Malley, J. M. (1994). *The CALLA handbook: How to implement the Cognitive Academic Language Learning Approach.* White Plains, NY: Addison Wesley Longman.

Cohen, A. D. (1990). *Language learning: Insights for learners, teachers, and researchers.* New York: Newbury House/Harper-Row.

Cohen, A. D. (1998). *Strategies in learning and using a second language.* London: Longman.

Cohen, A. D., & Aphek, E. (1981). Easifying second language learning. *Studies in Second Language Acquisition, 3*(2), 221–235.

Cohen, A. D., Weaver, S. J., & Li, T-Y. (1995). *The impact of strategies-based instruction on speaking a foreign language.* Research Report. Center for Advanced Research on Language Acquisition (CARLA). Minneapolis, MN: University of Minnesota.

Curtain, H. A., & Pesola, C. A. (1988). *Languages and children — Making the match.* Reading, MA: Addison-Wesley.

Gagné, E. D., Yekovich, C. W., & Yekovich, F. R. (1993). *The cognitive psychology of school learning.* New York: HarperCollins.

Genesee, F. (1987). *Learning through two languages.* Rowley, MA: Newbury House.

Green, J. M., & Oxford, R. (1995). A closer look at learning strategies, L2 proficiency, and gender. *TESOL Quarterly, 29*(2), 261–297.

Harris, K. R., & Graham, S. (1992). *Helping young writers master the craft: Strategy instruction and self-regulation in the writing process.* Cambridge, MA: Brookline Books.

Hosenfeld, C. (1984). Case studies of ninth grade readers. In J. C. Alderson & A. H. Urquhart (Eds.), *Reading in a foreign language* (pp. 231–249). London: Longman.

Jiménez, R. T., & Gámez, R. (1998). Literature-based cognitive strategy instruction for middle school Latino students. In R. M. Gersten & R. T. Jiménez (Eds.), *Promoting learning for culturally and linguistically diverse students* (pp. 153–166). Belmont, CA: Wadsworth.

Kowal, M. & Swain, M. (1997). From semantic to syntactic processing: How can we promote metalinguistic awareness in the French immersion classroom? In R. K. Johnson & M. Swain (Eds.), *Immersion education: International perspectives* (pp. 284–309). Cambridge: Cambridge University Press.

Lambert, W. E., & Tucker, G. R. (1972). *Bilingual education of children: The St. Lambert experiment.* Rowley, MA: Newbury House.

Met, M. & Galloway, V. (1992). Research in foreign language curriculum. In P. Jackson (Ed.), *Handbook of research on curriculum* (pp. 852–890). New York: Macmillan.

Muñiz-Swicegood, M. (1994). The effects of metacognitive reading strategy training on the reading performance and student reading analysis strategies of third grade bilingual students. *Bilingual Research Journal, 18*(1&2), 83–97.

Naiman, N., Fröhlich, M., Stern, H. H., & Todesco, A., (1978). *The good language learner.* Toronto: Ontario Institute for Studies in Education. [Re-published 1995. Philadelphia, PA: Multilingual Matters.]

National Standards in Foreign Language Education Project. (1996). *Standards for foreign language learning: Preparing for the 21st century.* Yonkers, NY: Author.

O'Malley, J. M., & Chamot, A. U. (1990). *Learning strategies in second language acquisition.* Cambridge, England: Cambridge University Press.

O'Malley, J. M., Chamot, A. U., Stewner-Manzanares, G., Küpper, L., & Russo, R. P. (1985a). Learning strategies used by beginning and intermediate ESL students. *Language Learning, 35*(1), 21–46.

O'Malley, J. M., Chamot, A. U., Stewner-Manzanares, G., Küpper, L., & Russo, R. P. (1985b). Learning strategy applications with students of English as a second language. *TESOL Quarterly, 19*(3), 557–584.

Oxford, R. L. (1986). *Development and psychometric testing of the Strategy Inventory for Language Learning.* Alexandria, VA: U. S. Army Research Institute for the Behavioral and Social Sciences.

Oxford, R. L., & Burry-Stock, J. A. (1995). Assessing the use of language learning strategies worldwide with the ESL/EFL version of the Strategy Inventory for Language Learning. *System, 23*(2), 153–175.

Padrón, Y. N., & Waxman, H. C. (1988). The effects of ESL students' perceptions of their cognitive strategies on reading achievement. *TESOL Quarterly, 22,* 146–150.

Palincsar, A.S., & Brown, A. L. (1986). Interactive teaching to promote independent learning from text. *The Reading Teacher, 39*(2), 771–777.

Pressley, M., & El-Dinary, P. B. (1993). Introduction (Special issue on strategies instruction). *Elementary School Journal, 94,*105–108.

Pressley, M., El-Dinary, P. B., Gaskins, I., Schuder, T., Bergman, J. L., Almasi, J., & Brown, R. (1992). Beyond direct explanation: Transactional instruction of reading comprehension strategies. *Elementary School Journal, 92*(5), 513–555.

Pressley, M., Woloshyn, V., & Associates (1995). *Cognitive strategy instruction that really improves children's academic performance* (2nd ed.). Cambridge, MA: Brookline Books.

Rubin, J. (1975). What the "good language learner" can teach us. *TESOL Quarterly, 9,* 41–51.

Rubin, J., Quinn, J., & Enos, J. (1988). *Improving foreign language listening comprehension.* Report to U.S. Department of Education, International Research and Studies Program.

Silver, E. A., & Marshall, S.P. (1990). Mathematical and scientific problem solving: Findings, issues, and instructional implications. In B. F. Jones & L. Idol (Eds.), *Dimensions of thinking and cognitive instruction* (pp. 265–290). Hillsdale, NJ: Lawrence Erlbaum.

Strauss, A. L., & Corbin, J. (1990). *Basics of qualitative research: Grounded theory procedures and techniques.* Beverly Hills, CA: Sage Publications.

Swain, M. (1984). A review of immersion education in Canada: Research and evaluation studies. In *Studies on immersion education: A collection for United States educators* (pp. 114–143). Sacramento, CA: California State Department of Education.

Swain, M. (1985). Communicative competence: Some roles of comprehensible input and comprehensible output in its development. In S. Gass & C. Madden (Eds.), *Input in second language acquisition* (pp. 235–253). Rowley, MA: Newbury House.

Swain, M. (1995). Three functions of output in second language learning. In G. Cook & B. Seidlhofer (Eds.), *Principle and practice in applied linguistics: Studies in honor of H. G. Widdowson,* pp. 125–144. Oxford: Oxford University Press.

Swain, M. (in press). The output hypothesis and beyond: Mediating acquisition through collaborative dialogue. In J. Lantolf (Ed.), *Sociocultural theory and second language learning.* Oxford: Oxford University Press.

Swain, M., & Lapkin, S. (1998). Interaction and second language learning: Two adolescent French immersion students working together. *Modern Language Journal, 82*(3), 320–337.

Tarone, E., & Swain, M. (1995). A sociolinguistic perspective on second language use in immersion classrooms. *Modern Language Journal, 79*(2), 166–178.

Thomas, W. P., Collier, V. P., & Abbott, M. (1993). Academic achievement through Japanese, Spanish, or French: The first two years of partial immersion. *Modern Language Journal*, *77*(2), 170–179.

Thompson, I., & Rubin, J. (1996). Can strategy instruction improve listening comprehension? *Foreign Language Annals*, *29*(3), 331–342.

Weinstein, C. E., and Mayer, R. E. (1986). The teaching of learning strategies. In M. R. Wittrock (Ed.), *Handbook of research on teaching* (3rd ed.) (pp. 315–327). New York: Macmillan.

Wenden, A. L. (1983). Literature review: The process of intervention. *Language Learning*, *33*, 103–121.

Appendix. Questionnaire to Evaluate Use of Learning Strategies

This questionnaire was developed to help students reflect on and evaluate the strategies they used for a just-completed reading task (Part A) and after a writing project (Part B). From Chamot, A. U., Barnhardt, S., El-Dinary, P. B., & Robbins, J. (2000). *The learning strategies handbook*, pp. 137–138. White Plains, NY: Addison Wesley Longman.

Reading and Writing Strategies

Part A: We have just read an African folktale about a spider named Anansi. Think about how you read the folktale. Answer the questions about the strategies you used. And remember, there are no right or wrong answers!

1. Before starting to read, I thought about what I already know about stories like Anansi.
   No, I didn't do this.   I did this a little.   I did this a lot!

2. I looked at the title and illustrations and predicted what the story might be about.
   No, I didn't do this.   I did this a little.   I did this a lot!

3. As I was reading, I pronounced each word in my head.
   No, I didn't do this.   I did this a little.   I did this a lot!

4. I used the context (other parts of the story) to make a good guess about the meaning of new words. (Skip this question if there were no new words.)
   No, I didn't do this.   I did this a little.   I did this a lot!

5. As I was reading, I tried to focus on what the characters did and said.
   No, I didn't do this.   I did this a little.   I did this a lot!

6. I made predictions about how Anansi would solve the problem.
   No, I didn't do this.   I did this a little.   I did this a lot!

7. When there were new words in the story, I asked a friend or the teacher what they meant. (Skip this question if there were no new words.)
   No, I didn't do this.   I did this a little.   I did this a lot!

8. After reading the story, I thought about the most important points.
   No, I didn't do this.   I did this a little.   I did this a lot!

9. What other strategies did you use while you were reading the folktale about Anansi the Spider?

Part B: After reading the story about the spider Anansi, we wrote our own folktales. Think about how you wrote your folktale. Answer the questions about the strategies you used. And don't forget, there are no right or wrong answers!

10. Before starting to write I brainstormed ideas for my folktale.
    No, I didn't do this.   I did this a little.   I did this a lot!

11. I planned my story by thinking about (or making notes) of the characters, plot, and where the story would happen.
    No, I didn't do this.   I did this a little.   I did this a lot!

12. I didn't need to brainstorm or plan before writing; I just started writing.
    No, I didn't do this.   I did this a little.   I did this a lot!

13. While I was writing I thought about the people who would read my story.
    No, I didn't do this.   I did this a little.   I did this a lot!

14. While I was writing, I tried to remember what I already know about the parts of a story.
    No, I didn't do this.   I did this a little.   I did this a lot!

15. When I couldn't think of a word I wanted, I looked in the dictionary.
    No, I didn't do this.   I did this a little.   I did this a lot!

16. When I couldn't remember a word I wanted, I just used a different word.
    No, I didn't do this.   I did this a little.   I did this a lot!

17. When I finished my first draft, I asked a classmate to read it and make suggestions.

    No, I didn't do this.　　　I did this a little.　　　I did this a lot!

18. I revised my story to make it better.

    No, I didn't do this.　　　I did this a little.　　　I did this a lot!

19. I made the changes needed for my final draft.

    No, I didn't do this.　　　I did this a little.　　　I did this a lot!

20. What other strategies did you use to write your own folktale?

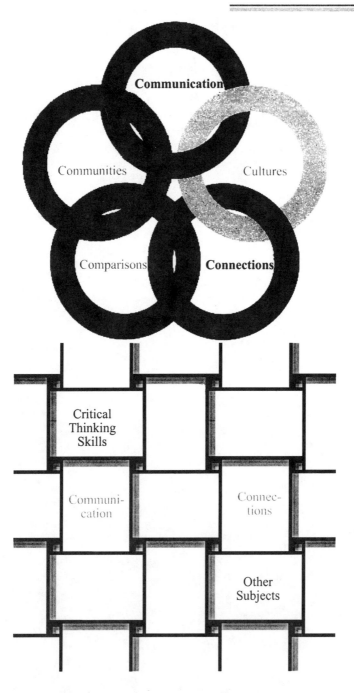

Whose Course Is It? Students as Course Co-Creators

Marva A. Barnett

University of Virginia

When someone asks us what is most frustrating about teaching, we often complain about students' attitudes and the behavior that results from them: students don't care about learning anymore, they don't come to class, or—when they do—they aren't prepared or don't pay attention. All in all, they don't take enough responsibility for their learning! Students' attitudes—determined by many factors, including parents, friends, environment, education, and previous teachers and classes—can change, and by working with our students we can help them grow into responsible, dedicated learners, the learners of tomorrow.[1]

Traditional roles of teacher as expert knower and student as *tabula rasa*, of teacher as leader and student as follower, tend to disengage students from the learning process. When we as teachers assume an overwhelmingly active role, leaving only passivity to the students, it is not surprising that they accept that passive role. Of course, our own expectations and attitudes have been molded by our previous experiences, as both students and teachers: On the one hand, we tend to treat students as we were treated; on the other, having encountered student passivity in the past, we may come to expect it. Thus is recreated the pattern of expectations: Teachers will hand out information, which students hand back on exams and papers.

Because this pattern perpetuates itself, changing it requires a conscious effort to develop more responsible and engaged students. By respecting students for who they are and what they know, by recognizing them as responsible learners and offering them appropriate challenges and support, we can promote better learning through greater student commitment and harder work. This chapter argues the value of shifting one's attitude in this direction, offers techniques and methods for making the shift, and provides students' reactions to the resulting approach.

> It's really good to know that people care about you as a student but also as a person, and that makes a relationship where there's respect, and a lot of times I would just do my homework because I wanted to respect her, not 'cause I really wanted to do it. The only reason that I did it, really, was to keep up that bond. (focus group transcript, 1998)[2]

Why an Attitude Shift?

Who Does Most of the Work?

Consider these questions about course design and implementation:

- Who created the course?
- Who decided what everyone would read?
- Who decided what the workload would be?
- Who decided what counts for how much?
- Who decides how a class meeting will go?
- Who decides what constitutes competent work?
- Who decides what everyone will talk about?
- Who knows just about everything about the topic?

In a typical K–16 course the answer to all these questions is "the teacher." For most of the questions, "the teacher" is the best answer, the one that will lead to a coherent course with a solid content and valid evaluations of students' work. The person who knows the most about the subject and the most about teaching and learning should design the course and make the major decisions. As the teacher, the leader and expert, each of us needs to make final decisions about students' learning and competence; in the end, we need to grade.

If the students' role is as small as the traditional answer to these questions makes it, what stake do students have in most courses—aside from a grade? How can they, and why should they, contemplate taking an active role in making the course work? Without giving up leadership in a course

—and recognizing individual learning styles—we teachers can share the learning and managing with and among our students. We do not always have to determine how a particular class will go. We do not need to define every discussion topic. We can give students some choice about how they learn some information and skills, about how they complete some assignments. As Palmer (1991–92) writes, we can give students a voice.

What's in it for the Students?

Even though the teacher must design and chart the course, setting the basic goals and standards, most students can skillfully take more responsibility for day-to-day activities than we have traditionally encouraged. The various techniques described in the second half of this chapter send a clear message that students have a say in what happens during class and that their ideas matter. Thus they engage more in the course, in the several ways detailed below, and consequently enjoy the course more and learn better.

Greater Confidence in their Ideas

Asking students what they think (both about the subject matter and the way the course is going), listening to their ideas, and responding thoughtfully to them increase students' confidence and willingness to share their ideas.

> She put us at ease, and we felt like she respected our opinions, whether she agreed with them or not.
> I always felt comfortable joining in class discussion—she always welcomed new ideas.
> (two students, final course evaluation, 1998)

Greater Engagement in Courses

One natural, almost immediate, result of greater confidence is students' willingness to engage more fully in our courses. At nearly every level of schooling, students are pulled in many disciplinary and social directions in any one day. They constantly need to set priorities and face frequent deadlines. Since people extend effort in directions they perceive as productive, responding positively to students' work provokes them to care about and focus on our courses.

Conscious Feeling of Responsibility

Student responsibility for making class meetings effective and for learning leads to better preparation, thinking, attendance, and participation. By the time they reach high school, they know what it takes to make a productive discussion; we can develop their sense of responsibility for classroom success in various ways. For example, a few weeks into each course, I ask students to answer anonymously four questions:

- How did the discussion go?
- What could the teacher do to improve class discussions?
- What could the other students do to improve discussions?
- What could you do to improve discussions?

I then consolidate and return their listed answers. Students regularly respond with similar comments, remarks that echo what we teachers repeatedly recommend. Here are sample answers (1996) to the last, most personal, question, answers that I returned to the students:

> Think about analytical questions before coming to class so I don't feel like I'm "on the spot" and pressured to think on my feet—that way I cram up and can't think.
> Maybe read the story twice and try to analyze it before class.
> Try to add more to the discussions.
> It's necessary to really think about the readings before class.
> I could read more closely with a dictionary. I should participate more but I do not feel very comfortable with my French, and I don't feel as if I express my ideas clearly.

Hearing such good suggestions from peers can effectively persuade people to take on their share of the responsibility. Students showed that they recognized their role in learning when, in 1998, 40 percent of them commented on end-of-semester evaluations that a course weakness was their own level of effort.

Community Spirit and Support Network

About peer-editing trios:

> It was also good that we had the same partners [throughout the semester]. I got to be good friends with them and got used to calling them, like, every night [laughter]. But it was good.
> Uh-huh.
> (two students; focus group transcript, 1998)

Students who take responsibility for learning spend more time creating, refining, and developing their ideas without our intervention (for a summary of the theory and research on student responsibility in college, see Davis & Murrell, 1993). As social creatures, we naturally feel more responsible toward people we know than toward strangers. A very simple way to build community, and hence responsibility, is to make sure students get to know each other as soon as possible. Throughout the semester, we can continue to build community spirit by structuring cooperative groups or teams in which students not only work but also develop interpersonal rapport and support networks. This kind of community within the classroom can extend beyond the classroom as well, as when one student used the class listserve to invite classmates to lunch at the French House. As recommended by the Communities National Standard for Foreign Language Learning 5.1, "Students use the language both within and beyond the school setting," sharing "their knowledge of language and culture with classmates" (1996, p. 60).

In answer to the final course evaluation question, How effective were the student-student interactions and teacher-student interactions? one student wrote, "*Extremely effective!* There was just *amazing* interaction between students and teacher and it was definitely the most effective aspect," Another wrote, "Wonderful—we feel 'bonded' in this class—students + teacher" (1998).

Better Intellectual Development

> She always stressed that we could present as many new ideas as we wanted, as long as we had something logical to support that. And that helped a lot, not only just writing for French, but it helps you think about other things the same way.
> Yeah, I think so.
> Taking an argument and having solid things to back it up ... , it's going to help, you know, if you go into law, if you're going to do the literature stuff, if you're just going to have a conversation with somebody.
> (three students; focus group transcript, 1998)

The greatest good that stems from this approach—a good for both students and society—is the deeper intellectual development that results from students truly engaging with their own ideas and those of others in a supportive community (see the summary of Swedish research results in Rhem, 1995). It has become axiomatic that people who study for tests soon forget most of what they could produce in the testing situation. It is through taking on ideas and trying them out for a while, arguing with them, analyzing and synthesizing them, supporting them with evidence from the course, and finally working them into the texture of one's understanding that people learn. By listening patiently to students' ideas and diligently questioning unsupported opinions, we can successfully move students to higher levels of critical thinking. They come to understand that solid thinking involves more than receiving knowledge from perceived authorities or believing one opinion to be as good as another; they recognize that good opinions are supported with reason and facts and that individuals must commit to their beliefs, taking into account what they have learned (Perry, 1970, 1981; Belenky et al., 1986; see Kurfiss, 1988, for summary). And one of the most important aspects of teaching critical thinking is providing an atmosphere "wherein students can let go of some of the personal moorings that impose limitations on the ways they think" (Meyers, 1986, p. 99).

> ## Traditional roles of teacher as expert knower and student as *tabula rasa* ... tend to disengage students from the learning process.

As the Connections goal of the National Standards states, "Students reinforce and further their knowledge of other disciplines through the foreign language" (1996, p. 50). Thinking skills developed through foreign language study further students' learning in other fields of study, even though disciplinary conventions can be somewhat distinct from each other. For instance, interpretive skills developed through analyzing figures of speech can be adapted to explain anthropological phenomena; the ability to organize a detailed argument to persuade readers that Phèdre was literally a monster is analogous to the skill needed to debate whether Andrew Johnson should have been impeached. Critical thinking skills are one of the weave elements underlying the curriculum (National Standards, 1996, p. 29).

Greater Student Satisfaction

Finally, we should not dismiss the importance of students' satisfaction with their academic experience and with their own successes. We are all heartened to see comments such as the following in response to the question, What sort of effort did you put into this class? "*A lot*. More than most other classes. I feel like I've improved a lot." When asked for course improvement suggestions, the same student responded, "None. She took all our suggestions to heart. She changed the final exam because of our suggestions" (1998). Given such students' self-perceived effort and improvement, their happiness about the course and teacher's flexibility does not result from pandering to the "student as consumer." On the contrary, such students recognize that the course proved challenging and beneficial, while responding to their needs and desires. Everyone wins in a big way. For example, upon majority student vote, we revised the final exam from a pencil-and-paper test of the same skills and knowledge that students had already shown they had mastered into a student-organized, -directed, and -produced tour of the university grounds. In using their research, composition, editing, and speaking skills to create a French tour designed for francophone visitors, the students took another step toward fulfilling the National Standards Communication goal.

For the Teacher: Are the Challenges Worth the Benefits?

These abundant advantages for student learning make worthwhile our tackling a potentially demanding challenge: being flexible and relinquishing some control. Students will accept the responsibility that comes from helping define class meetings only if we share with them some decision-making and if we respond nimbly to their ideas. In giving up some control, we gain freedom, intellectual stimulation, student responsiveness, and interpersonal connections. Moreover, Boice (1996) provides evidence that college teachers who show their students that they care (what he calls "being immediate") experience far less classroom incivility. Students who might shy away from taking on responsibility may change their minds when faced with engagement on the part of their peers or when we orchestrate greater levels of responsibility into their cooperative group work (see Johnson et al., 1991a, for practical suggestions). Certainly, not every student will respond to this approach in every course; we must wonder, however, whether those who do not take responsibility when offered it would be any more engaged in a less interactive course.

New Ideas

> When you're working together, it helps to be in a group, because you can learn from each other.
> Plus, each person has something different to offer.... We all read the same poem, but we came up with different analyses, and I think that's also kind

of what happens with poetry, because everyone has a different idea of what
it is. I think it's not just the teacher spitting out *what it should be* to you.
(two students, focus group transcript, 1998)·

Students offered these responses to my standard practice of asking
them to choose poems to study in depth. Their choices complement the
required readings on the syllabus, and their group presentations define
class activities for two weeks. Involving students in selecting some readings requires a teacher to take some risk and be open-minded. Yet what
might occasionally be lost in their choosing a relatively slight poem (a
rare occurrence, actually) is more than matched by the vigor with which
they study and explicate *their* poem. Stimulated to produce their own
ideas, they are struck by what they can learn, and we also benefit from
their thinking. It can be tantalizing, provoking, vexing; their ideas make
us think more, just as working through ideas teaches students to know pertinent facts and think about them. As Wayne Booth notes, "Responding to
students' rival readings actually changed my opinions about how to appreciate a given novel or work of criticism" (Boyer Commission, 1998, p. 16).

In language courses, students working in groups may produce grammar and pronunciation mistakes. As we know, however, their errors, or
learner talk, are a window into their understanding of the target language
that give us insights into their learning processes (Brooks et al., 1997) and
learning strategies (Oxford, 1990). Moreover, even as they make target
language errors, they are most likely hearing others' ideas and learning
something, as long as the work is challenging, interesting, and clearly
defined. If, on the other hand, they speak English during group work, we
need to investigate why:

- Did they not understand the directions?
- Have they finished the assignment?
- Was it easier or more difficult than we'd thought?
- Are they bored and thus not as engaged as we'd like? If so, what would be best
  to do in the future?

Powerful Positive Peer Pressure

People who work in well-organized groups come to expect and rely on
support from each other. The structure inherent in cooperative learning tasks and
projects (detailed below) encourages students to monitor themselves and each
other (Johnson et al., 1991b, pp. 30–38) and thus more likely become lifelong

learners. We simply need to meet the challenges of defining tasks clearly, giving necessary support, and trusting students to work conscientiously.

Better Student Preparation

> What impeded your learning?
> Workload too heavy. (Teaching Analysis Poll, 1995)
> What most helped you learn in this course?
> Each class we are accountable for something. (Teaching Analysis Poll, 1996
> Work each night. (Teaching Analysis Poll, 1998)

In fact, the 1995 workload in French 332 did not vary much from that in 1996 and 1998. Yet students' perception of the workload and of the value of preparation became more positive as I made clearer how their work affected their learning; students can recognize their own hard work and acknowledge its value. Better student preparation will result from our clear directions, openness to students' ideas, and class activities that cannot work without students' serious preparation (see Millis, 1998). Hand in hand with a high level of student engagement are two demands on us: being flexible and knowing our subject very well (see Harper & Lively, 1987, for applications of this perspective to high school and community college conversation classes). When we give students more responsibility, when we challenge them to bring knowledge and ideas to class, they need to perform. Since we must respond to their work, we control totally neither the information brought nor how it is managed. Yet when we respond thoughtfully to students' ideas, questions, and experience—giving them our full attention and engagement—they take our assignments seriously, realizing that they are accountable:

> I definitely tried at the beginning, like, not to read. You know, in a lot of classes you can skim a couple of pages just so you have one thing to say and then, "Good job; you spoke." And then that didn't work. So then I started really reading, took time, looked up the words I didn't know. (focus group transcript, 1998)

How Do We Make our Attitude Shift Visible?

Deciding to shift our attitude as teachers to one more respectful of students as people and thinkers will not work until they understand our perspective. Typically trained to be passive, students do not usually expect this new attitude. But they will respond to our challenge to take a central role and thus enhance their learning when we show them clearly that *they* matter in the course. We can do so in three different ways:

- by defining clear, challenging expectations
- by teaching to engage students directly
- by stepping back frequently to see how the course is going.

Enunciating Clear, Challenging Expectations

Because students have mostly been trained to receive knowledge passively, we must counter their natural expectations with explicit expectations of our own. We can show that we count on their active engagement by lifting the veil of secrecy over why we conduct class as we do, by challenging and supporting them as necessary, by offering them clear criteria for what constitutes good work (including models of students' achievements), and by giving clear, quick feedback on their performance.

Lifting the Veil

Traditionally, teachers have carefully veiled the reasons for specific assignments and classroom activities and have avoided discussing course objectives after listing them in a description or syllabus. They might have said, as did the Wizard of Oz, "Pay no attention to the man behind the curtain!" It was as though the students would somehow learn better if they did not know the point of the lesson. For instance, a standard language course goal is reading-skill development. Yet traditional activities center on asking students what happened in the text, with the seemingly implicit assumption that answering questions spontaneously teaches students how to read, or that, knowing already how to read, students can answer comprehension questions. It was not until the 1980s that we began teaching reading strategies explicitly, letting students in on some secrets of learning (see, for example, Phillips, 1984; Barnett, 1988).

As responsible thinkers, students will more likely buy into a course when they know why they are asked to invest and what they should expect to reap. On the first day of a course, we need to ask students what they expect from the course. This works best when they think individually, then discuss in small groups before sharing with everyone their answers to questions such as: What do you expect to learn in this course? How do you expect this course to expand on the one you just finished? Why did you enroll in this course? Explicitly juxtaposing our expectations with theirs makes the course much more meaningful for them and sets the stage for us to cue them in on the "whys" of various teaching and learning activities. It also helps us close the gap between what students and teachers traditionally expect from a course (Teeples & Wichman, 1997–98).

... students' perception of the workload and of the value of preparation became more positive as I made clearer how their work affected their learning.

For example, I currently aim to help students develop their critical thinking skills, including their ability to find and analyze provocative rhetorical figures of speech in literary texts, which we call *figures de style* (e.g., metaphor, oxymoron, euphemism, antiphrasis). Thus I frankly tell the students with each rhetorical-figure exercise that memorizing definitions is just the first step; in reality, they need to learn how to discover important rhetorical figures of speech in a text and explain why they are powerful. During the focus group (1998), one student noted that having to find the *figures de style* in a citation from a familiar reading made the students really appreciate French writing. Another student added, "And she made you figure them out, like why is it there, what is the point, the significance? I guess we have to do that if we'll ever start understanding the subtleties." Thus, although students groaned on seeing yet another *figure de style* exercise sheet, they acknowledged the value of the exercises because they knew why they were doing them and because they found they learned from them. (For a succinct summary of several effective techniques for teaching thinking, see Weiss, 1992–93).

Maybe if she'd just said, 'this is the reason why we're doing it, this is what I want you to get out of it,' then maybe we'd probably think about it a little more.
Student in French 332 focus group, 1998

Perhaps the most telling argument for removing the veil of secrecy comes from a focus group recommendation (1998). Proud of my technique of requiring students to share in class two or three questions about the short stories we read, believing that it engaged the students in discussing what *they* wanted or needed to know, I had asked the facilitator to discuss this technique specifically. Although one student noted her gratitude for these chances to discuss what they had not understood from readings, another said,

> I didn't know that those [questions] were that important, though. Maybe she should have stressed that this is why we're doing it. Cause I didn't really do it.... Maybe if she'd just said, "this is the reason why we're doing it, this is what I want you to get out of it," then maybe we'd probably think about it a little more.

Her comment confirms many students' willingness to work for the intrinsic goal of learning, of "getting something out of it."

Offering Challenges and Support

Challenging students without demanding too much can be difficult, but we can offer students support of various sorts. The value of community support and cooperative study is well documented; for example, Treisman found at the University of California-Berkeley that minority students who were organized into supportive, cooperative study groups in a challenging honors program were substantially more successful in calculus than were students who studied on their own (1985). Also, scaffolding, giving students help where and when they need it, helps them accomplish more challenging tasks than their level of expertise would seem able to sustain (Shrum & Glisan, 1994). We can build scaffolding into the course ahead of time (as in the case of model answers, described below), but we can also set up a scaffold quickly, when students let us know that it is necessary.

> Another thing that she did one time that really helped—'cause we weren't doing very well on the structure of our papers—we were just throwing down words and ideas. So she made us write an outline, and that was really, really helpful. And it made us really think about our thesis and how to back it up, and that was, really, that was a good paper.
> I was going to say the same thing.
> (one among the best students in the course and the other the weakest; focus group transcript, 1998)

The "outline" mentioned was the requirement that each student submit—before writing the next paper—preliminary ideas and thesis statement, together with supporting arguments and evidence. As a model of both the process and the product, together in class we created such an outline.

Essential support also comes simply from our willingness to meet students where they are and help them progress. Students easily perceive such support and often note it on end-of-semester evaluations: "strengths:

enthusiasm for the material but especially for teaching, and a willingness to do whatever necessary to help us." "The instructor furthered my interest in the subject [by being] enthusiastic, made me confident in my ability, pushed us to our limits" (1998). People thrive on facing and meeting reasonable challenges.

Giving Clear Criteria and Models

> We had a syllabus that told us what was due during the whole semester, and we never got off of it, which was nice.
> We turned in something [to be] graded just about every class and got it back quickly.
> Overall, every little thing that we did fit in somewhere.
> (three students, focus group transcript, 1998)

The teacher is the leader, and the students want to know where they are going and how to get there. The syllabus is the first road sign, and it needs to guide dependably. Among other things, a syllabus should pin down major assignments and tests, making clear that details will come in good time and will depend, to some extent, on how students respond to materials as they meet them. Even when first teaching a new course, we should be able to define in course packets or on web sites clear guidelines and grading criteria for assignments, in-class work, and exams. Two examples appear in Appendices B and C; see also Tulou and Pettigrew in this volume.

Beyond theoretical guidelines, however, concrete models of good work help students understand what they are to do, while inspiring them with what is possible. Students are remarkably willing to permit us to offer their work anonymously as models for future students, and even for their classmates. After all, what could be a greater sign of their success than having their work chosen as a good example? For instance, the first time my students analyzed rhetorical figures of speech in writing, few of them went beyond definitions, even though we had discussed numerous analyses in class. In returning their graded work, then, I added a sheet of sample "A" answers from students who had succeeded. Armed with these models and the realization that some of their classmates were already at this level, more students analyzed better on the next assignment.

On peer-editing guidelines (see Appendix D), one student noted:

> She had specific expectations for what we would say. She gave us an outline, didn't she, in the packet. This was what she expected us to write and what would help us, and so I think this will help me in revising papers [in future courses]. (focus group transcript, 1998)

Giving Clear Feedback

> All my classes have a percent for participation, but you never have a clue,
> like whether that's a joke or not. But, like early in the semester, she gave
> us an indication of what our participation grade was, an idea of what to
> work on. So you knew that she was really paying attention. So we knew
> that it actually mattered. (focus group transcript, 1998)

Combining models with individual feedback gives students clear paths
toward success. After they have tried to follow a model, they need to know
what is good about their work and how to improve it. The student quoted
above notes that people work harder when they know their work is noticed
and when they learn how well they are doing. It takes just a few seconds
per student to complete the Participation Feedback Form (Appendix E);
I distribute these about a month into the course and then again, if necessary, a month later. Whenever students see their current grade and my
suggestions, their participation improves perceptibly for the next several
class meetings.

Similarly, grading students' peer-editing efforts may seem like a waste
of time, and for years I simply labeled their editing with check-plus,
check, check-minus. Noting students' end-of-semester complaints that
peer editing was busy work and that peers' comments were not very helpful, I began giving their editing more detailed, individual feedback and
assigning it letter grades. The grade book shows that editing skills improved, and students' comments are positive: "We got graded on how we
evaluated other people's drafts, and so we wanted to do a good job; we
wanted to make comments that would really help them, so we would get
a good grade on that" (focus group transcript, 1998). This student's frank
avowal of the reciprocal effect of receiving a "good grade" on her desire
to do a "good job" to help others is particularly telling given her stellar
performance in the course, 100% attendance, consistently thoughtful discussion comments, and subsequent admission into the College honors
program. Because most students' ingrained concern about their grades
cannot be denied, we may as well use it to their advantage. The value of
clear feedback and well-founded grades on students' willingness to put
forth the effort they need to learn cannot be overestimated.

**Combining models with individual feedback
gives students clear paths toward success.**

Teaching for Direct Student Engagement:
A Variety of Techniques

Along with making our expectations clear, we need to teach in ways that directly engage students in learning and explicitly show them that we, as well as the other students, need and depend on their ideas and work. Doing so requires recognizing different learning styles and differing contributions. The following techniques are not meant to be inclusive, but, rather, appropriate to foreign language and literature courses, as well as representative of the wide range of active learning techniques that promote students' engagement and responsibility (for other suggestions, in a wide range of disciplines, see Bean, 1996; Bonwell & Eison, 1991; Campbell & Smith, 1997; Kraft, 1990; Meyers & Jones, 1993; Silberman, 1996).

Cooperative Learning

Cooperative learning (similar to collaborative learning [Bruffee, 1993], although considered by some to be different) has enjoyed wide support among specialists in both K–12 education (Kagan, 1988, for example) and college education (e.g., Johnson et al., 1991a; Millis & Cottell, 1998; Cooper, 1990). Sometimes misunderstood to mean simply having students work in groups, cooperative learning is, in fact, a highly structured approach to teaching that includes five basic elements (Johnson et al., 1991a, pp. 6–8):

1. positive interdependence: students' belief that they all sink or swim together
2. face-to-face promotive interaction: students helping, encouraging, and supporting each other's efforts to learn
3. individual accountability: students' recognition that they are responsible for their own learning and for that of group members because individuals' learning represents that of the group
4. social skills necessary to group success, including leadership, decision-making, trust-building, communicating, and managing conflict
5. group processing: activities that enable groups to determine how well they are working together and what they can do to improve.

Clearly, structured cooperative learning is one way to work consciously toward building a class of students into a team that works together, taking responsibility for their own and others' learning. Cooperative learning activities that influenced students' positive response to

French 332 include team-building activities undertaken at the beginning of the course to help them meet each other, think-pair-share, student-initiated discussions, peer editing, and group projects. Traditional lecturing can also prove more engaging for students when it includes cooperative learning techniques, some of which are presented below.

> When you're working together, it helps to be in a group, because you can learn from each other. (focus group transcript, 1998)

Team-Building Activities. Some of the earliest (and shortest) activities in French 332 have multiple objectives: to familiarize students with each other, promote group bonding, establish cooperative groups, and introduce students to simple aspects of cooperative learning, such as the roles of leader, notetaker/reporter, and encourager. Often, before giving the class an assignment, such as clarifying what they expect to learn in the course or comparing their answers to identifications of theatrical terms, I rearrange them into groups of three or four. One can quickly do this by asking students to count off from 1 to 6 (in a class of 20, to arrange groups of 3 or 4); they then move to meet with others who counted the same number, thus meeting people in a different part of the room. I ask them to discover something interesting and not too personal about everyone in the group: for example, "Find out one thing you all like and one thing you dislike." "Find out who got up the earliest this morning." "Find out who lives the farthest away." In answering such simple questions, students get to know each other and relax more. Students *always* appreciate this personal connection, as summarized by one focus group comment (1998): "I have discussion sections that are smaller than this, and I don't know everybody's name. [Here] we all know each other. The first day of class, or the first week, whatever, everyone learned each other's names."

Think-Pair-Share. The think-pair-share technique is a mainstay of informal cooperative learning groups, in which students come together briefly during class to accomplish a task (as opposed to formal cooperative learning, in which students work on a larger project over a relatively long period of time) (Johnson et al., 1991a, pp. 4:2, 5:10). Easy to set up and requiring as little as three minutes of class time, this technique asks students to think individually, exchange ideas with a partner, and share the results with the rest of the class and the teacher. For example, when we begin the unit on poetry, I ask students to spend thirty seconds thinking about how they would describe poetry and then to compare and contrast their ideas with those of someone nearby to see whether they can synthesize them together (a two-minute task). When they indicate by a show of hands which pairs came to a synthesis, I ask those to share first, knowing that people who agree have added strength of conviction and willingness to speak up. Think-pair-share activities give every student quiet thinking time followed by a relatively safe, private opportunity to voice their ideas. Before announcing their thoughts to everyone, they can explain and fine-tune them. More students have ideas; more are willing to share them; ideas are generally better for having been contemplated. Using think-pair-share to kick off discussions may be one reason why French 332 students regularly cite them in answer to the Teaching Analysis Poll question: "What most helps you learn in this course?": "Discussion in class a plus." (1998) "Class discussions are engaging." (1997) "Discussions." (1996) "Class discussions are going really well." (1995)

Group Projects. Projects that students complete in groups can be the best or the worst of a course, depending on how carefully and clearly we structure them. Learning how to structure and grade them well pays off in increased student motivation, enthusiasm, and hard work, as these two students' focus group comments about group poetry presentations (1998) indicate:

> We made it fun, but it was serious. Everybody had to read and just about everyone researched their poem. It wasn't like a joke, but it wasn't "another paper."
> You really got a better knowledge, having to present it and teach the class.

For a full explanation of the procedures used, see the Poetry Presentation Guidelines in Appendix C. (For a thorough discussion of peer teaching, see Whitman, 1988.)

Student-Initiated Discussion. Student-initiated discussion is another productive discussion-starter that has its roots in cooperative learning. Here is one student's focus group comment about this technique (1998):

> Typically, the discussion just kind of took off wherever we wanted it to go, which is kind of cool.... She would bring out certain things to stimulate our thought or whatever, but she never made us talk about one thing and only that thing. Like, if we had other ideas, we could go off on that, too.

At first reading, this comment might sound as though discussions were disorganized or somewhat sporadic. On the contrary, not only did I find student-initiated discussions to follow logical threads of thought, students in courses taught with this technique practically never complain that discussions go off on tangents or are disorganized. In addition, over the years I have found that students' serious questions about a text typically lead to a discussion of topics similar to those I would have proposed had I determined the direction of the discussion (for corroboration, see Campbell & Smith, 1997, pp. v–vi). Of course, in order to prepare for this more open-ended sort of discussion, we need to prepare more carefully, thinking not only about what we find to be the key discussion points but also imagining different ways to approach them from the issues students raise.

Orchestrating student-initiated discussion also requires convincing students that their questions about the assigned text are essential. Usually, I simply ask them to bring two or three questions that they cannot answer or that they find interesting, but we can also define the type of questions we would like (for instance, comprehension questions, analytical questions, questions the asker cannot answer, opinion questions, and so on). In class, students work in cooperative groups of three or four to answer as many of each other's questions as possible in 5–10 minutes. Of course, I circulate among groups, getting an idea of what types of questions they have raised, and on what topics. The questions that remain after their discussion are often ones that no one in their group can answer.

Students next organize their remaining questions logically: for example, comprehension questions vs. analytical questions, fact questions vs. opinion questions, or questions that can be answered from the text vs. questions that require additional information. I write the categories on the board and invite a student from each group to write the most interesting questions of each type for the class. Students remaining in the group begin thinking about new questions as they appear on the board; I check to ensure accurate question categorization. The number of questions from each group depends on time available for this discussion.

After 8–10 questions are on the board, I decide in what order to take the questions to create a logical discussion and number them. For example, I often treat the simpler or more concrete questions first, then the more analytical or complex. The discussion then evolves from students' questions, as I ask students to clarify questions when necessary and challenge them to answer them. I work to ensure that as many essential ideas as possible are discussed critically and to weave students' questions and comments into coherent discourse. Variations on this technique appear in Appendix F.

Peer Editing

> It really helped to have her input and [other students'] input, and then we
> had adequate time to go back and do another draft; that was good. (focus
> group transcript, 1998)

A main focus of French 332 is composition, and students can constructively edit their colleagues' essays by working in cooperative groups. In fact, giving three-person peer-editing groups time to build group connections may well avoid students' natural reluctance to criticize others' papers (a reluctance noted by Diane Birckbichler, cited in Omaggio Hadley, 1993, p. 339). Both to symbolize our mutual team effort and to help students write better, I edit all students' first drafts using the peer-editing guidelines in Appendix D; thus we all focus on helping writers make the best arguments possible by commenting mainly on purpose, organization, and clarity. Since students at this advanced-intermediate level often create as many errors as they correct when asked to edit for grammar, I encourage editors only to point out patterns of errors, and many do so accurately. I mark and grade grammatical accuracy on the final draft, although I explain how to handle complex structures that students include on first drafts.

Peer-editing is an activity that allows students to develop their analytical and critical reading skills, which they can apply in many realms. As such, it is one of the "rich curricular experiences" that foreign language teachers can weave into the fabric of language learning (Standards for Foreign Language Learning, 1996, pp. 28–30). Along with providing appropriately detailed peer-editing guidelines, we need to give students models of good editing (gathered from previous classes or from our own work) and a chance to practice editing at least once in class. Spending class time on an activity clearly conveys its importance; having students try out editing guidelines when we are there to answer questions and track their progress saves false starts and wrong turns when they later edit on their own. The day the first paper draft is due, therefore, students spend thirty minutes in their peer-editing groups reading and commenting on others' drafts. Two students work on the third student's paper (who reads another's paper), which generates comparative editorial comments when they voice main comments to the writer. I randomly select which student's paper becomes the focus of the group by having each group discover an arbitrary fact (for example, who most recently saw a movie or who has the next birthday) and then choosing the person to the left or right of that person. Students seem to appreciate the fairness of such a random selection process. Listening in on various groups, I gain a good sense of how well editors follow the guidelines, how clearly they explain their reactions, and how willingly students engage in the process. If necessary, I can review certain points for individuals or, later, for the entire class.

Throughout the semester, when all drafts are submitted along with the final paper, I grade individual students' editorial comments, taking into account thoroughness, clarity, and tone. I make sure the editor's comments take into account most of the points suggested on the Peer-Editing Guide-lines (Appendix D); I applaud particularly insightful and helpful comments; I suggest ways to improve general or vague remarks. I also tell editors when they need to be more critical in order to help writers improve their papers. (For a more lengthy cooperative peer-editing structure, see Johnson et al., 1991b, pp. 71–72.)

> What have you learned in this course?
>   How to write.
>   You actually need to write your French papers like your English papers, not just put a bunch of words down on the page and not have them make sense.
> (two students, focus group transcript, 1998)

Engaging Students during Presentations. Literature and civilization courses often require us to present a wealth of information to students not only through readings but also through classroom presentations and lectures. Since attention spans average no more than 15 minutes, and classes typically last at least 50 minutes, we need techniques to re-engage students' attention. Used thoughtfully, such activities tell students that their ideas matter and that they need to assimilate what they are hearing and seeing. We can use questions and other activities at the beginning and throughout a presentation to keep students intellectually engaged (Sarkisian, 1994; see Appendix G). Students' work with such questions may be treated individually or cooperatively.

One specific cooperative learning technique uses focused discussions as "bookends" before and after the lecture, with pair discussions interspersed throughout (Johnson et al., 1991a, pp. 5: 10–12). As always, it is important to make the task and instructions explicit and precise and to require a specific product (such as a written answer). In summary, this technique works as follows. Students next to each other first complete a task designed to organize their thoughts about the upcoming lecture: for instance, they might note and share answers to the question, "What do you already know about the predominant religions in France?" After a 10–15-minute lecture, paired students undertake a think-pair-share task designed to involve them with the information they just heard. In our example, they might compare what they had already known with what has been presented and note new information. Or they might give a reaction to the theory, concept, or information presented or relate the new material to past learning. After this three-or four-minute discussion, two or three randomly selected students share their answers with the class. This process repeats after each lecture segment. The class ends with a four- to five-minute pair discussion to summarize the material covered, a discussion that should result in students' integrating new information into their existing conceptual frameworks, or schemata (for a summary of schema theory as it applies to foreign language reading, see Barnett, 1989). Students will develop skill in responding to lectures thoughtfully if we give them opportunities to process these tasks by asking questions such as, "How well prepared were you to complete these discussion tasks?" and "How could you come even better prepared tomorrow?" The question types in Appendix G may be used in the bookend lecture format.

Using Instructional Technology

Some technological innovations can help us give our students more responsibility, help them engage more directly with the course and course material, and help them recognize the importance of their work (see Warschauer, 1995, for practical ideas about implementing technology in courses). Electronic mail is now reasonably easily accessible to students at a number of schools and colleges, and some teachers require e-mail discussions outside class as part of their participation, along with offering to answer students' questions via e-mail. When they can quickly and regularly use e-mail to communicate, students generally appreciate this closer contact with their teachers, the fact that they can ask at any moment a question (even a so-called "dumb question") and may well have an answer within 24 hours. Some seem more willing to communicate through e-mail about how the course is going for them and what else in their lives is affecting their ability to succeed. In fact, e-mail can be so appealing that teachers with many students may need to limit its use in order to avoid a flood of messages. Likely advantages of e-mail discussion, however, include our seeing deeper analyses and more participation from students who are shy in person and from those who write more easily than they speak. Kern (1995), for instance, found that students exchange ideas more during class via computer than via oral discussion, but with perhaps less coherence and less grammatical accuracy. Students who have e-mailed comments and questions about a text before coming to class—and who have taken the time to read others' remarks—are farther along in their thinking than those who read the text at the last minute (Ramazani, 1994). As for community-building, teachers who set up course-wide lists may find that students use them to set up target-language lunches and review sessions for the final exam; the list seems to make them feel more a part of that particular group.

Since e-mail does take time for both teacher and students, we need to make sure that our e-mail assignments are not overwhelming. If our syllabus is already full, we must realize that writing and reading e-mail is yet another requirement that should be added only in place of something else. Students need to have easy, frequent access to e-mail; if they do not, we must recognize the extra time needed to get to a terminal. Finally, we need to grade e-mail participation explicitly if we want students to engage in it as reliably as in other assignments (see Appendix B for criteria).

The World Wide Web offers another opportunity to show students that their work really matters. Elsewhere in this volume, Lee discusses using a web home page and chat room to engage students with current events in the target-language countries. Gaspar (1998) explains how foreign language students can research through the web, as well as through traditional sources, to create group projects. The web also offers the advantage that publication there exposes "student writing to an outside readership who will deliver real-world feedback and response straight to the author's e-mail account" (Kirschenbaum, 1996). Thus students' presentations made available on the web are real work for a real audience.[3]

Stepping Back to Take a Look

In various ways, we need to involve our students throughout our course, reminding them of their central role, their goals, their successes, and their potential. By invoking their metacognitive skills, their ability to think about what they are doing and why, we can regularly help them step back a moment to become aware of what they are learning, how they are learning, and how well the course is working for them. They thus learn more about how to learn and get to know themselves as learners, which is a key element of their success (Rhem, 1995; Carrell, 1989). We can do this subtly, or we can focus explicitly on metacognitive strategies, using, for instance, scenarios or mini-case studies that illustrate productive metacognitive strategies (Loring, 1997, writing of first language reading at the K–12 levels). Several techniques that relate to the various aspects of metacognition are detailed below.

What They're Learning

Angelo and Cross, in *Classroom Assessment Techniques* (1993), present a plethora of techniques designed to engage students' metacognitive awareness on several fronts: course-related knowledge and skills; learners' attitudes, values, and self-awareness; learners' reactions to instruction. In this volume Lavine discusses the philosophy and methodology of these techniques, with a focus on student management teams. Two other techniques particularly appropriate to foreign language and literature courses are student-generated test questions (#25, pp. 240–243) and word journals (#14, pp. 188–192). When students create possible test questions, they show us what they consider the most important or memorable content, what they understand as fair and useful test questions, and what answers they give to questions they have posed. Thus, if we ask for these questions at least three weeks before the test date, we know more about what to teach and/or review, and we can also re-educate students who have unrealistic expectations about tests (Angelo & Cross, 1993, p. 240). Students very much appreciate as well the opportunity to discuss test format and expectations ahead of time. To use this technique, we write specifications about the kinds of questions we want. Students need to know what they are to do, how their questions will be used, what sort of feedback they will receive, and how this activity will help them perform better (p. 242). To use the data they give us, we can roughly tally the types of questions students propose. For example, how many require only a knowledge of facts? How many require only paraphrasing a text read; how many require synthesis or analysis? We can use some of their questions as examples in giving feedback and others as review questions. It is important to state clearly at the beginning of this process what will be done with students' questions, whether any will actually appear on the test, for instance, in order to avoid misunderstandings.

Word journals can help us assess students' ability to read carefully and their skill and creativity at summarizing a short text in a single word, as well as their proficiency in explaining and defending, in a paragraph or two, why they chose that word (Angelo & Cross, 1993, p. 188). Practicing this classroom assessment technique helps students become more adept at writing highly condensed abstracts and at storing large amounts of information in memory by "chunks." To use the word-journal process, teachers must make sure the exercise works with a particular text by following the proposed directions before giving them to the students. We also need to tell our students that the choice of a specific word is less important than the quality of their explanation, and we need to give them some ideas about what their explanations should contain (p. 190). By sharing with students several different good approaches submitted, we can help them develop their range of responses to texts.

When we offer students such thought-provoking exercises and tell them why, we also give them the opportunity to learn more about how they are developing skills and about why we teach as we do. Classroom assessment techniques such as student-generated test questions and word journals are less about finding out how well students have mastered the material and more about discovering—for both us and them—how they are grappling with the material and skills of the course. By provoking metacognitive thinking, they help us all understand better the learning process.

How They're Learning

People are more likely to take responsibility for things under their control. Thus helping students recognize that they have a great deal to say about what and how they learn—that this is, in fact, more their province than that of the teacher—empowers them to take more initiative to learn well (see Wenden in this volume). As noted earlier, requesting students' comments about the course should go beyond asking how well we are doing as teachers to ask the students to contemplate their own contributions. For courses that include a significant amount of discussion, asking students what their colleagues can do to improve the level of discussion, as well as what they can do individually, and then reporting their answers back to them typically results in a noticeably increased quality in preparation and participation (Loevinger, 1993). Similarly, asking students to rate their preparation for lectures shows them how essential their thinking is to their understanding and remembering and gives them clear criteria by which to judge their involvement and resulting success (McAllister, 1997) (see Appendix H). We can also help students take more responsibility by directly giving them useful information about strategies relevant to foreign-language learning in general (see, for example, Oxford, 1990; Rubin & Thompson, 1994) or to specific aspects of the course, for instance, memorizing and taking tests (Learning Skills Center, n.d.) or reading a foreign language (Phillips, 1984). For a discussion of elementary school children's learning strategies and ways to integrate them into the classroom, see Chamot in this volume.

How Well the Course Is Working for Them

> Every single thing we said in the evaluation [Teaching Analysis Poll]—and we were, like, scraping to find bad things to say—she changed. They weren't even like really bad things.
> She changed the room, she brought in a speaker, she changed her final exam. I think those were the only things we ever mentioned that we would kinda want to be changed.
> (two students; focus group transcript, 1998)

As noted throughout this chapter, we have many and varied ways to ask students how well the course is helping them learn (see Appendix A and Lavine in this volume for details). By soliciting and responding to students' comments about how well they are learning in the course, we not only get new ideas (often quite good ones); we also promote students' commitment to the course. By replacing the final exam with a student-requested tour of the university, in French, we reinvigorated our flagging end-of-semester energies in a demanding composition course, discovered French connections at the university, and produced an amusing and enlightening videotaped tour from students' perspectives. At the same time, students wrote, edited, and revised another paper, something they would not have accomplished with a final exam.

Conclusion

On balance, the mutual respect, novel ideas, hard thinking, and caring engagement engendered by treating students as responsible adults more than outweighs the value of any control we relinquish in acknowledging that the course belongs to them as well as to us. In order to succeed with this approach, we must make our attitude clear to our students, leading them to recognize that our attitude is "not like, 'I'm your teacher, and I can make you do this.' It's helpful." (student comment during focus group transcript, 1998). People most often commit themselves to endeavors in which they are interested and have a personal stake. And, as Richard Light's work in assessment confirms, such a commitment to academic work is productive and frequently leads to happiness in students' college careers (1992). As teachers, we play a significant role in determining how committed our students are to foreign language, culture, literature, civilization, and history. And success partly comes from a "strength" a student noted on the 1998 French 332 final course evaluation: "caring about us, working with us."

Notes

[1]Dedicated to my students of French 332, in appreciation of their patience, ideas, and ever increasing levels of engagement. French 332 (The Writing and Reading of Texts), a University of Virginia French composition course that also serves as an introduction to the study of literature, is prerequisite for nearly all succeeding courses, required of majors and minors, and enrolls primarily first- and second-year students (enrollment limited to 15). The course is designed to prepare students to take higher-level courses on francophone literature,

civilization, and history while helping them improve their communication skills (see the National Standards Communication goal). Specific goals include improving students' abilities to read and discuss texts analytically (including understanding and interpreting rhetorical figures of speech) and to write persuasive essays. Toward these course-wide goals, I help my students work on improving their abilities to recognize what they do not understand and ask about it, to ask and answer interpretative questions, to define, recognize and then analyze figures of speech, and to read and comment judiciously on others' writing.

[2]Quotations come from students enrolled in French 332 (The Writing and Reading of Texts). I developed the approach presented in this chapter over four spring semesters, from 1995 through 1998. Students' comments are solicited in a variety of ways: mid-semester questionnaires, specific questions about class activities, Teaching Analysis Polls, end-of-semester evaluations, end-of-semester focus group (quotations are unedited transcriptions of students' oral remarks; for details, see Appendix A). Given my administrative responsibilities in faculty development, I teach only one semester each year.

[3]Details are beyond the scope of this chapter, but sample student publications are available at the following URLs:
English essays:
> http://www.engl.virginia.edu/~enwr1016/index.h tml
> http://www.engl.virginia.edu/~enwr1013/Art/
compilations and analyses of data about the American Civil War:
> http://jefferson.village.virginia.edu/vshadow2/cwprojects.html
African art exhibitions:
> http://cti.itc.virginia.edu/~bcr/rela345_98.html

References

Angelo, T.A., & Cross, K.P. (1993). *Classroom assessment techniques: A handbook for college teachers* (2nd ed.). San Francisco: Jossey-Bass.

Barnett, M.A. (1988). Teaching reading strategies: How methodology affects language course articulation. *Foreign Language Annals, 21*, 109–119.

Barnett, M.A. (1989). *More than meets the eye: Foreign language reading, theory and practice.* Washington, DC: Center for Applied Linguistics/Prentice-Hall.

Bean, J.C. (1996). *Engaging ideas: The professor's guide to integrating writing, critical thinking, and active learning in the classroom.* San Francisco: Jossey-Bass.

Belenky, M. F., Clinchy, B. V., Goldberg, N. R., & Tarule, J. M. (1986). *Women's ways of knowing: The development of self, voice, and mind.* New York: Basic Books.

Boice, R. (1996). *First-order principles of college teachers: Ten basic ways to improve the teaching process.* Bolton, MA: Anker.

Bonwell, C.C., & Eison, J.A. (1991). *Active learning: Creating excitement in the classroom.* (ASHE-ERIC Higher Education Report, No. 1). Washington, DC: The George Washington University, School of Education and Human Development (hereafter SEHD).

The Boyer Commission on Educating Undergraduates in the Research University. (1998). *Reinventing undergraduate education: A blueprint for America's research universities.* Stony Brook, NY: State University of New York. Retrieved January 15, 1999, from the World Wide Web: http://www.sunysb.edu/ boyerreport

Brooks, F.B., Donato, R., & McGlone, J.V. (1997). When are they going to say "it" right? Understanding learner talk during pair-work activity. *Foreign Language Annals, 30*, 524–541.

Bruffee, K.A. (1993). *Collaborative learning: Higher education, interdependence, and the authority of knowledge.* Baltimore, MD: The Johns Hopkins University Press.

Campbell, W.E., & Smith, K.A. (Eds.). (1997). *New paradigms for college teaching.* Edina, MN: Interaction Book Co.

Carrell, P.L. (1989). Metacognitive awareness and second language reading. *The Modern Language Journal, 73,* 121–134.

Chickering, A.W., & Gamson, Z.F. (Eds.). (1991). *Applying the seven principles for good practice in undergraduate education.* New Directions for Teaching and Learning, No. 47. San Francisco: Jossey-Bass.

Cooper, J. (1990, May). Cooperative learning and college teaching: Tips from the trenches. *The Teaching Professor, 4* (5), 1–2.

Davis, T.M., & Murrell, P.H. (1993). *Turning teaching into learning: The role of student responsibility in the collegiate experience.* (ASHE-ERIC Higher Education Report, No. 8). Washington, DC: The George Washington University, SEHD.

Gaspar, C. (1998). Situating French language teaching and learning in the age of the internet. *The French Review, 72,* 69–80.

Harper, J., & Lively, M. (1987). Conversation classes: Activities and materials that encourage participation. *Foreign Language Annals, 20,* 337–344.

Johnson, D.W., Johnson, R.T., & Smith, K.A. (1991a). *Active learning: Cooperation in the college classoom.* Edina, MN: Interaction Book Co.

Johnson, D.W., Johnson, R.T., & Smith, K A. (1991b). *Cooperative learning: Increasing college faculty instructional productivity.* (ASHE-ERIC Higher Education Report, No. 4). Washington, DC: The George Washington University, SEHD.

Kagan, S. (1988). *Cooperative learning.* San Juan Capistrano, CA: Resources for Teachers.

Kern, R. (1995). Restructuring classroom interaction with networked computers: Effects on quantity and characteristics of language production. *The Modern Language Journal, 79,* 457–76.

Kirschenbaum, M.G. (1996). Once upon a time in ENWR: The world-wide web as a publication medium for student essays. *Teaching Concerns,* Fall, 1–2. Charlottesville, VA: Univ. of Virginia Teaching Resource Center newsletter. Retrieved January 15, 1999, from the World Wide Web: http://www.virginia.edu/~trc/tc96fmk.htm

Kraft, R.G. (1990). Group-inquiry turns passive students active. In R.A. Neff & M. Weimer (Eds.), *Teaching college: Collected readings for the new instructor* (pp. 99–104). Madison, WI: Magna.

Kurfiss, J.G. (1988). *Critical thinking: Theory, research, practice, and possibilities.* (ASHE-ERIC Higher Education Report, No. 2). Washington, DC: The George Washington University, SEHD.

Learning Skills Center. (n.d.). *Taking tests: General tips.* Unpublished handout, The University of Texas at Austin.

Learning Skills Center. (n.d.). *Principles of memory.* Unpublished handout, The University of Texas at Austin.

Light, R.J. (1992). *The Harvard assessment seminars: Second report.* Cambridge, MA: Harvard University.

Loevinger, N. (1993). Using mid-term evaluations to give students responsibility for the course. *Teaching Concerns,* January, 1. Charlottesville, VA: Univ. of Virginia Teaching Resource Center newsletter. Retrieved January 15, 1999, from the World Wide Web: http://minerva.acc.Virginia.EDU:80/~trc/ tcmideval.htm

Loring, R.M. (1997). Reading as a thinking process. In A.L. Costa & R.M. Liebmann (Eds.), *Envisioning process as content: Toward a Renaissance curriculum* (pp. 76–94). Thousand Oaks, CA: Corwin Press / Sage.

McAllister, W. (1997). *Self-assessment form for HIEU [European History] 202*. Unpublished handout, Teaching Resource Center, University of Virginia.

Meyers, C. (1986). *Teaching students to think critically: A guide for faculty in all disciplines*. San Franciso: Jossey-Bass.

Meyers, C., & Jones, T.B. (1993). *Promoting active learning: Strategies for the college classroom*. San Francisco: Jossey-Bass.

Millis, B.J. (1998). Helping students learn through guided peer questioning. *USAFA Educator, 6* (2), 4–5.

Millis, B.J., & Cottell, Jr., P.G. (1998). *Cooperative learning for higher education faculty*. Phoenix, AZ: Oryx Press / American Council on Education.

National Standards in Foreign Language Education Project. (1996). *Standards for foreign language learning: Preparing for the 21st century*. Yonkers, NY: Author.

Omaggio Hadley, A. (1993). *Teaching language in context* (2nd ed.). Boston: Heinle & Heinle.

Oxford, R. (1990). *Language learning strategies: What every teacher should know*. New York: Newbury House/HarperCollins.

Palmer, P.J. (1991–92). Good teaching: A matter of living the mystery. *Essays on Teaching Excellence, 3* (3), 1–2. A publication of The Professional and Organizational Development Network in Higher Education (POD Network).

Perry, W. G., Jr. (1970). *Forms of intellectual and ethical development in the college years: A scheme*. New York: Holt, Rinehart, & Winston.

Perry, W. G., Jr. (1981). Cognitive and ethical growth: The making of meaning. In A. M. Chickering et al., *The modern American college: Responding to the new realities of diverse students and a changing society*. (pp. 76–116). San Francisco: Jossey-Bass.

Phillips, J. (1984). Practical implications of recent research in reading. *Foreign Language Annals, 17*, 285–296.

Ramazani, J. (1994). Student writing by e-mail: Connecting classmates, texts, instructors. *Teaching Concerns* (September). A publication of the Teaching Resource Center, University of Virginia. Retrieved January 15, 1999, from the World Wide Web: http://minerva.acc.Virginia.EDU:80/~trc/tcemail.htm

Rhem, J. (1995). Deep/surface approaches to learning: An introduction. *The National Teaching and Learning Forum, 5* (1), 1–4.

Rubin, J., & Thompson, I. (1994). *How to be a more successful language learner* (2nd ed.). Boston: Heinle & Heinle.

Sarkisian, E. (1994). Information sheet on participatory lectures. Available from the Derek Bok Center for Teaching and Learning, Harvard University, Cambridge, MA.

Shrum, J.L., & Glisan, E.W. (1994). *Teacher's handbook: Contextualized language instruction*. Boston: Heinle & Heinle.

Silberman, M. (1996). *Active learning: 101 strategies to teach any subject*. Boston: Allyn and Bacon.

Teeples, R., & Wichman, H. (1997–98). The critical match between motivation to learn and motivation to teach. *Essays on Teaching Excellence, 9* (2), 5–6. A publication of The Professional and Organizational Development Network in Higher Education (POD Network).

Thinking together: Collaborative learning in science. (1992). [Video]. (Available from Cambridge, MA: Derek Bok Center for Teaching and Learning)

Treisman, U. (1985). A Study of the mathematical performance of black students at the University of California, Berkeley. Unpublished manuscript, 71 pp.

Valdés, G., Dvorak, T., & Hannum, T. (1989). *Composición: Proceso y síntesis* (2nd ed.). San Francisco: Random House.

Warschauer, M. (1995). *Virtual connections*. (Tech. Rep. No. 8). Honolulu: Univ. of Hawai'i Press.

Weiss, C.A. (1992–93). But how do we get them to *think? Essays on Teaching Excellence, 4* (5), 1–2. A publication of The Professional and Organizational Development Network in Higher Education (POD Network).

Whitman, N.A. (1988). *Peer teaching: To teach is to learn twice.* (ASHE-ERIC Higher Education Report, No. 4). Washington, DC: The George Washington University, SEHD.

Appendix A. Soliciting Students' Comments

Students very much appreciate having an opportunity before the end of the semester to comment on how well a course is working for them. Depending on their comments, we can make reasonable changes in the course to accommodate their needs, or we can explain again why we have assigned "such difficult" readings, why there are "so many" quizzes, why class participation counts. This appendix includes three methods of gathering students' comments well before the course ends (Mid-Semester Questionnaires, specific questions, Teaching Analysis Polls) and two end-of-semester methods (evaluation forms and focus groups).

A-1: Mid-Semester Questionnaires

Mid-semester questionnaires can be as long or short, as general or specific, as we like. Here are the questions I typically use for French 332, a course taught almost entirely through discussion:

- How did the discussion go?
- What could the teacher do to improve class discussions?
- What could the other students do to improve discussions?
- What could you do to improve discussions?

Students answer such questions anonymously during five minutes at the end of a class period before the middle of the semester. It is important to summarize or itemize the comments and discuss them with the students either during the next class or via an e-mail message to all students.

A-2: Specific Questions about Class Activities

At times when we would like to know how students respond to a specific activity, we can simply ask them. To keep this activity brief, I hand out quarter-sheets of paper at the end of class and ask only one or two questions. For instance, to discover students' perceptions about the group poetry presentations, I have asked (in French), "What do you think about the system we used to discuss poetry? (That is, you chose the poems to study, you prepared them in groups, you gave oral presentations, and you discussed together.)" In order to see how well students were understanding readings and discussions, I have asked (in French), "What was the most important point you learned from the discussion today? What questions do you still have about the story we read for today?" Similar to the one-minute paper and muddiest point classroom assessment techniques (Angelo & Cross, 1993), these questions elicit answers that give me insights I would otherwise rarely get. I can then adjust my assignments and discussion-leading the next class, reviewing if necessary.

A-3: Teaching Analysis Polls

Teaching Analysis Polls (TAPs) are offered by the Teaching Resource Center at the University of Virginia and, under other titles, by faculty development programs around the country. But a faculty developer is not necessary, since colleagues can easily act as consultants to do TAPs for each other. The process begins when the consultant visits the teacher's classroom for 25–30 minutes to poll the students about their perceptions of the course. (After introducing the consultant, the teacher leaves.)

The consultant gives groups of four or five students five minutes to answer three questions:
- What most helps you learn in this class?
- What impedes your learning?
- How can improvements be made?

One student in each group writes on the board the answer that the majority of group members agree about. The consultant monitors responses to verify that a proposed solution accompanies any problem.

With the whole class, the consultant reviews these comments, clarifying ambiguities and keeping only those observations a majority of students approve.

The consultant thanks the students and reiterates that the instructor will receive the summary of reactions remaining on the board.

During the follow-up meeting, the consultant gives this information to the instructor, and they discuss ways of responding to the comments. Here are some of the benefits:
- The TAP gives more details than do written evaluations because students discuss the course in a confidential and interactive setting, while the consultant monitors responses to eliminate vagueness.
- Students learn from each other, as they debate their various perceptions of the course.
- Students appreciate having this chance to share their ideas about the course.
- Because only responses that have been agreed upon by a majority vote are reported, the teacher can focus on the main issues.
- A TAP requires no more than 30 minutes of class time, and an additional half-hour outside of class to review the results.
- What is learned from a TAP, especially one done in the first six weeks of the semester, helps both teacher and the students get more from the course immediately.

A-4: End-of-Semester Evaluations

End-of-semester evaluations at colleges and universities are frequently required and are created either within individual departments or formulated and distributed centrally. The

U.Va. French Department form contains standard questions about the course and instructor. I add specific questions focused on activities pertinent to our course:

- What did you learn in this course?
- How effective were the following aspects of the course, and how could they be improved in the future?
  - peer editing
  - class discussion
  - student-student interactions and teacher-student interactions
  - e-mail communication

A-5: Student Focus Groups

Prompted by the editor of this volume, in 1998 for the first time I asked my students to spend about 45 minutes talking about the course with an objective consultant trained to lead focus groups (my thanks to Jennifer Chylack and Jennifer Secki, University of Virginia, for leading and videotaping the focus group). Students did not object to having this focus group videotaped, and I promised not to view the tape until after submitting final grades. Of course, I was not present at the focus group, which took place on our final exam day, after the students' tour of the University Grounds (which was also videotaped). Like the Teaching Analysis Poll, the focus group provided thoughtful, detailed, finely tuned feedback about the course. Quotations attributed to "focus group transcript" are unedited transcriptions of students' oral comments during this focus group. Students not only responded to the consultant's questions (see below) but also added comments about aspects of the course important to them. Here are the focus group goals and prompting questions that the consultants and I created:

Goals:

- Determine learner reaction to
  - teacher's approach to course
  - various exercises
- Determine which exercises were most helpful/effective in developing skills
- Determine how engaged and connected to the course the students felt
- Determine how responsible to the course the students felt.

Questions:
1. Describe the course activities:
    a. What did you do in class?
    - What types of exercises?
    - What did you think of the student-generated questions about short stories?
    - What did you think of the poetry presentations and tour?
    - What kinds of interactions were there?
    - Which did you find to be the most helpful in learning how to think clearly and express yourself well in French?
    - How important did you think it was to attend class and participate? Why?

b. What types of homework assignments did you have?
  • How was homework integrated into the course?
  • How important did you think it was to do the homework? Why?
2. Attitudes about the course:
  • How comfortable were you in this class?
  • How would you define Ms. Barnett's attitude about the course and the students?
3. Have you used the material / knowledge from this course in other areas / classes / places? Please specify.
4. How did the workload in this course compare to that of other 300-level French courses? Would you recommend this course to other students? Why or why not?

Appendix B. Participation Grading Guidelines

(Adapted from the work of Edmund P. Russell, Department of Technology, Culture, & Communication, School of Engineering and Applied Science, which was itself adapted from the work of Martha L. Maznevski, McIntire School of Commerce, University of Virginia. Used with their kind permission.)

Grading stresses quality of participation, not quantity per se. The key to quality is preparation before class or before writing on e-mail. I expect that average participation will be in the B range. Before mid-semester, I will let you know what your participation grade is so far, and how to improve it.

A Shows excellent preparation. Analyzes readings and synthesizes new information with other knowledge (from other readings, course material, discussions, experiences, etc.) Makes original points. Synthesizes pieces of discussion to develop new approaches that take the class further. Responds thoughtfully to other students' comments. Builds convincing arguments by working with what other students say, but may question the majority view. Stays focused on topic. Volunteers regularly in class and on e-mail but does not dominate.
B Shows good preparation. Interprets and analyzes course material. Volunteers regularly and participates on e-mail in a timely fashion. Thinks through own points, responds to others' points, questions others in constructive way, may question majority view, raises good questions about readings. Stays on topic.
C Shows adequate preparation. Understands readings but shows little analysis. Responds moderately when called upon but rarely volunteers, or talks without advancing the discussion. Writes short, non-analytical e-mail messages.
D Present. Shows little evidence of preparation or comprehension. Responds when called on but offers little or distracts the discussion.
F Absent, or non-responding via e-mail.

Appendix C. Poetry Presentation Guidelines

(translated from French to English)

C-1: How to Present a Poem to the Class

Outside Class:
Read the poem, discuss it with your group, and explicate (analyze) it. Remember that it's very important to specify the principal theme or atmosphere of the poem and to support your thesis statement. Depending on which poem you analyze, you will find that different aspects of the poem are more or less essential to your analysis; but don't forget to consider scansion, rhythm, rhyme, images, narration (if any), atmosphere, emotions, etc. Speak about the poet if necessary; but don't repeat the information in the text, and don't give the poet's biography. Discuss the poem and your ideas with your teammates; feel free to write the presentation together or to write parts of it individually, as you prefer.

Share the work of the oral presentation. In your group, decide who will present which part. Create as imaginative a presentation as you like.

Practice your presentation to be certain that it's clear. Your group will have *30 minutes* to present your analysis. Be sure not to read your presentation to the class; remember that *you're speaking to your colleagues.*

In Class:
Before the beginning of class, write on the board the vocabulary that you expect others won't know. Pronounce and explain these words before beginning your presentation.

Present the poem. It's certainly best to memorize the poem. In any case, you need to present the poem in a way that immediately indicates your interpretation of it. You might use music or pictures, for example. Use your analysis of the poem to decide what changes of voice are necessary, and practice your poem presentation out loud several times. I recommend that you record and analyze it before doing it in class.

Present your analysis. Decide in advance how you will orchestrate your presentation, and remember not to read it.

Be open to questions and new interpretations that will help you improve your final, written analysis.

Lead the discussion. It's up to you, as group presenters, to entertain questions and lead the discussion. I'm part of the audience, as are the other students. We'll spend the entire class discussing each poem.

C-2: How to React to Presentations

Outside Class:
First, study the poem before coming to class, and note your interpretation.

In Class:
Remember that you are responsible for helping your colleagues perfect this analysis before they write it in its final form. Therefore, make sure that they support their thesis statement(s). Ask questions to get more information if necessary. If you have another interpretation that you still find logical after having heard the presenters', offer it (with your supporting arguments). As a result, we'll discuss other possibilities, and you'll give your colleagues new ideas.

Take notes during the presentation. Contribute to the discussion. Two types of contributions are very useful: questions that oblige the presenters to think more deeply and comments that offer a new interpretation or that support it. Questions of clarification are often necessary, but less useful to the presenters. *Be sure to ask a probing question or offer a useful commentary.*

C-3: How These Exercises are Graded

The presentation:
Your presentation grade will count as four individual class participation grades. Since half the grade will be *a grade for the entire group,* it's worthwhile helping your partners to prepare as well as possible; the other half of the grade rates what you do as an individual. The two grades will depend on your ability to explain and support your ideas and on the quality of your French.

Your reaction to presentations: This individual grade will count as a class participation grade and will depend on the quality of your comments and questions. Work toward engaging in a true discussion.

Appendix D. Peer-Editing Guidelines

(translated from French to English) (Adapted from Valdés et al. (1989). *Composición: Proceso y síntesis* (2nd ed.). San Francisco: Random House.)

Use these questions to analyze your colleagues' essays and to help them fine-tune them. (In addition, you will learn how to ask yourself questions about your own essays.) Take notes on another sheet of paper, or on each essay itself, and save this handout.

First impressions
What is the thesis of this essay, the main point?
How does the author support the thesis?
Are you convinced of the value and exactness of the arguments?
What pleases you about this essay?
More detail: Are there places where
you need more information or more proof?
what's written adds nothing (or almost nothing) to the thesis or to the essay?
the organization is not clear?
the author should add more details?
the details are …
very well chosen?
superfluous?
uninteresting?
weak?
the language or tone is inappropriate to the purpose or to the readers?
the language is …

particularly interesting or powerful?
difficult to understand?
ambiguous or confusing?
redundant?
incorrect?
Are the quotations well chosen to support the thesis? Are they well analyzed?

Summary
Does the essay achieve its purpose? Are you convinced by the arguments, the examples, the reasoning?

How could the author improve the essay? Where should the author work hardest to revise?

Appendix E. Participation Feedback Form

Name: _____
Your participation grade in class so far: ___
How can you improve this grade? Follow the suggestions checked below:
__ Come to all the classes.
__ Volunteer when you have a chance to.
__ Show that you have well prepared the text or the lesson by offering good questions or good comments.
__ Push yourself a bit by trying to say something more difficult, analytical, or imaginative than usual.
__ Comment via e-mail in a more detailed and analytical way.
__ Try to move the discussion forward by responding to your colleagues' ideas.

Appendix F. Variations on Student-Initiated Discussion Techniques

1. Student groups can present the most interesting question and their answer to the entire class.
2. We can ask student groups to synthesize and prioritize their remaining questions.
3. After getting comfortable with this activity by working in small groups, students may prefer to raise their questions before the entire class.
4. We can invite individual students to write their most interesting question on the board before class begins. Of course, with this system, the students who arrive early are most likely to have a chance to ask their questions.
5. Students can send their questions to classmates (and the teacher) over e-mail ahead of the class meeting. This method is most suited to larger projects with a longer time frame, since students need time to prepare their questions, reach a networked computer and send them, read colleagues' questions. Because of these multiple steps, fewer students may be prepared for class than with the simpler method.

Appendix G. Engaging Students during Presentations

(Adapted with the kind permission of Ellen Sarkisian, Derek Bok Center for Teaching and Learning, Harvard University, from her adaptation of *Participatory Lectures*, 1994.)

Begin with a question or questions that help you understand what your listeners are thinking or what their relevant experiences are. For example: What is the historical context of *War and Peace*? Why might we be interested in the origins of Spanish? How many of you have traveled outside the United States?

If background reading or preparation has been assigned, ask questions about it to review and integrate that information. For example: During World War II, how was the French Underground formed? What were some of the economic and sociological factors that contributed to the rise of Naturalism?

Pose a problem (perhaps at the beginning of your talk) and elicit several answers or solutions. You can then explore and build on these. For example: Why do you think it's so hard to develop a native accent? Why might so many people from other countries have fought in the Spanish Civil War?

Ask students to raise their hands to answer, to vote, in effect. For example,: What is the direction of the data? Who thinks it's increasing? decreasing?

Use questions with surprising answers or with answers that are counter-intuitive. For example: What is the probability that two people in this room have the same birthday? How many Muslims live in France?

Use thought-provoking questions and questions without a right answer. For example: Do you think U.S. policy toward Haiti has become more or less strict in the last twenty years? Which references could you use to support your position?

After making a major point, ask a question that allows listeners to apply that information. If you have time and the information warrants it, ask them to vote on the right answer, then turn to their neighbors and persuade them of the answer within the space of two minutes. When the time is up, ask them to vote again (you should get more correct answers). (See Mazur's involvement of students in lectures on the videotape "Thinking Together," 1992). For example: Now that we've studied the effect of velocity on the driver of a car suddenly stopped from 40 miles per hour, what do you think would happen to the driver stopped while going backward? Would she feel pushed forward, backward, or neither?

Give your listeners opportunities, when appropriate, to write down answers before discussing them.

Solicit questions throughout the presentation, when appropriate, and at the end.

Appendix H. Self-Assessment

Self-Assessment Form

(Slightly adapted and used with the kind permission of William McAllister, Teaching Resource Center, University of Virginia, who adapted his from the work of Patrick Rael, Bowdoin College)

Please check those items that are applicable to your work in this course so far this semester.

—- Before Lecture —-
__ I read assignments *before* the corresponding lecture.
__ I re-read at least some assignments before the corresponding lecture.
__ I take notes while reading the assignments.
__ I try to make connections between the reading assignments, looking for agreement, disagreement, and/or differing emphases.
__ I organize my thoughts about the material in advance of the corresponding lecture.
__ If I do not understand the material, I write out questions in order to quiz myself or I ask questions in lecture.

— During Lecture —
__ I have attended every lecture.
__ I have attended almost every lecture.
__ If I am unable to attend lecture, I secure class notes from a reliable source.
__ I have asked a question during lecture.
__ I have participated in large-group discussion, usually responding to questions asked by the instructor.
__ I take notes regularly during lecture.
__ I always participate in the (sometimes offbeat) activities during lecture.

— Before Discussion Section —
__ I read assignments *before* the corresponding discussion section.
__ I re-read at least some assignments before the corresponding section.
__ I prepare a list of talking points I might wish to discuss during section.
__ I prepare a list of questions about material I do not understand or about which I would like to have more information.

— During Discussion Section —
__ I have attended every discussion section.
__ If I am unable to attend the section, I secure class notes from a reliable source.
__ I participate in discussion every week, either by raising an interesting question, responding to a point made by someone else, or making some other substantive contribution that facilitates learning for myself and my colleagues (the other students).

—Contact, Communications, and Continuing to Think about the Course—
__ I think about issues raised in this class at some time when I am not dealing directly with work related to the class.
__ I have talked with others about issues raised by the course.
__ I read carefully the comments on my graded assignments.
__ I have sought out my TA or instructor (whether in person, during office hours, by phone, or by e-mail) for some purpose other than to complain or ask some routine question concerning course assignments.

After reading over this list, one thing I can do to facilitate my own learning is: (please turn over and write on other side if necessary)

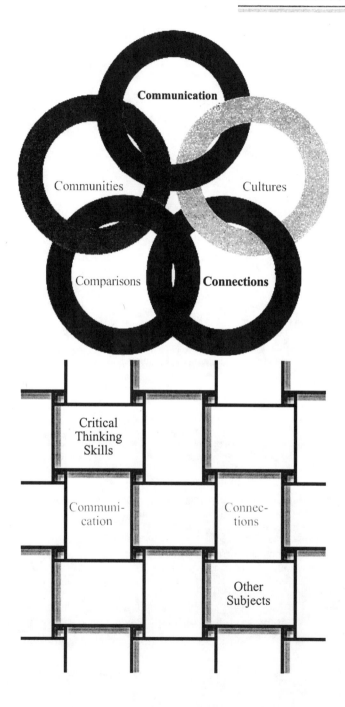

Student Voices: Changing the Teaching–Learning Paradigm using a Student Management Team

Roberta Z. Lavine

University of Maryland

"The Student Management Team ... was a new idea for me, allowing students to voice their opinions on class projects, homework, and the overall success of the class."

Kasey Gronau, Senior, University of Maryland

Changing the Teaching–Learning Paradigm

Shifting the educational paradigm from an emphasis on teaching to a focus on learning is one of the most intensely discussed topics in academia. With so many universities examining the quality of their programs for undergraduates, there are frequent debates about what constitutes good instruction, how to maximize learning, and how to facilitate change. Placing greater emphasis on learning requires a complex and collaborative effort by administrators, faculty, and students. Real change involves not only classroom practices and curricular adjustments, but a myriad of other transformations, including rethinking and redesigning the following: the mission and purpose of an institution, the way success is measured at a university, the teaching–learning structures employed, the underlying theories of learning applied, the notions of productivity and funding, and the nature of faculty and student roles. Many experts agree that in order to create powerful educational environments learning should be student-centered, with instruction that is cooperative, collaborative, and constructed by participants. Communication should not follow the traditional one-way flow from teacher to students, but rather be a two-way exchange between learners and the instructor. Establishing clear learning outcomes and utilizing varied assessment tools at the institutional as well as the classroom level are also integral components of change (Barr & Tagg, 1995).

Researchers and practitioners alike have suggested a myriad of techniques and approaches to facilitate an emphasis on learning, empower the learner, and develop learner-centered curricula (Marzano, 1992; Myers, 1993; Nunan, 1988). These include task-based learning (Nunan, 1989), problem-based learning (Engel, 1991; Stepien & Gallagher, 1993; Wilkerson & Gijselaers, 1996), cooperative learning (Cooper et al., 1990; Johnson et al., 1991), resource-based learning (Cohen, 1995), and simulation (Crookall & Oxford, 1990; Greenblat & Duke, 1981; McKeachie, 1986). In addition, it is essential to teach students to recognize how they learn, so as to enhance their own learning potential and develop lifelong learning skills (Stevick, 1989). Working with learning styles (Ehrman, 1990; McCarthy, 1980; Oxford, 1990b; Oxford et al., 1990) and learning strategies (Chamot & O'Malley, 1994; Cohen, 1990; Oxford, 1990a; Weaver & Cohen, 1994), exploring gender differences (Belenky et al., 1986; Clinchy, 1990; Cross, 1983; Nyikos, 1990; Oxford, 1993), as well as relying upon approaches that foster creativity and diversity, such as multiple intelligences (Gardner, 1983), are only some of the possible avenues available to educators.

As we modify classroom orientations and practices, we must also change our approach to assessment. Relying mainly on one type of assessment (e.g., written tests) or focusing primarily on summative evaluations (e.g., end-of-semester evaluations) that often come too late to effect change and are questionable at best, restricts both students and instructors to minimal opportunities to improve learning. In contrast, systematically utilizing authentic assessments and formative evaluations, like the many classroom assessment techniques developed and compiled by Angelo and Cross (1993), furnish all participants in the educational process with timely and detailed feedback that can have an immediate impact on learning (Angelo & Cross, 1993; Maloney, 1994; Nuhfer, 1992).

Classroom Assessment Techniques

"How could I possibly learn anything from my students?"

John A. Krogman, University of Colorado, *before* experimenting
with a Student Management Team (Nuhfer, 1992, p. 10)

Angelo and Cross (1993) define classroom assessment as an approach
that contributes information about what and how well students are learning in a particular class. They characterize classroom assessment as: (1)
learner-centered, because it focuses attention on improving learning, not
on teaching; (2) teacher-directed, since each teacher decides what, when,
and how to assess; and (3) mutually beneficial, as it requires the active
participation of both learners and the teacher and often results in improving learning and teaching skills (p. 4). In addition, Angelo and Cross maintain that Classroom Assessment Techniques (CATs) are "formative, con-
text-specific, ongoing, and firmly rooted in good practice" (pp. 5–6).

Classroom Assessment Techniques can be divided into three general
categories: techniques for assessing course-related knowledge and skills;
activities for determining learner attitudes, values, and self-awareness;
and tasks for evaluating learner reactions to instruction. While it is beyond
the scope of this chapter to explore all fifty of Angelo and Cross's suggestions, a short description of a few examples will be useful. Two of their
easiest and most productive CATs are the *Minute Paper* (pp. 148–153)
and the *Muddiest Point* (pp. 154–158). Both are designed to evaluate
course-related knowledge and simply require the student to answer one
or two questions in less than five minutes. To use the *Minute Paper*, also
commonly known as the *One-Minute Paper* or the *Half-Sheet Response*,
the teacher should allow two or three minutes at the end of the class for
the students to write answers to the following questions: (1) What was the
most important thing you learned during this class? and (2) What important questions remain unanswered? The teacher then can review the responses after class, quickly see what the learners do and do not understand, deal with doubts during the next session, as well as make any adjustments to the course. Similarly, the *Muddiest Point* poses the question,
What was the muddiest point in _____? (e.g., a reading assignment, a
video, or a class session). As with the *Minute Paper*, the *Muddiest Point*
requires students to analyze information and use critical thinking skills.
These two CATs are often combined into one, and are valuable tools for
eliciting feedback on any subject, from any size class, at any level.

Another CAT recommended by Angelo and Cross, *Group-Work Evaluations* (pp. 349–351), gauges learner reactions to instruction. The *Group-Work Evaluations* are very simple questionnaires constituting a systematic method to gather reactions to group tasks, and are especially useful for courses regularly utilizing small-group work, cooperative learning activities, or prolonged collaborative projects. Angelo and Cross suggest the following questions (p. 350):

1. Overall, how effectively did your group work together on this assignment?

   Poorly   Adequately   Well   Extremely Well

2. Out of the group members, how many participated actively most of the time?

   None   One   Two   Three   Four

3. Out of the group members, how many were fully prepared for the activity?

   None   One   Two   Three   Four

4. Give one specific example of *something you learned from the group* that you probably wouldn't have learned working alone.

5. Give one specific example of *something the other group members learned from you* that they probably wouldn't have learned otherwise.

6. Suggest one change the group could make to improve its performance.

When using this kind of evaluation, it is essential that students be assured confidentiality, and that the teacher stress that all learners are accountable for honest input. To guarantee that students take the evaluation seriously, teachers may use the data as part of a grade or as a point of discussion within the group.

Classroom Assessment Quality Circles

The Classroom Assessment Technique most relevant to this discussion is the *Classroom Assessment Quality Circle*. Angelo and Cross (1993) describe Quality Circles as teams of students and the teacher, working together for two main purposes: to offer an avenue for feedback and input about a particular class, and to create structured and positive ways for students to become involved in their own learning (p. 339). The teacher may form several Quality Circles in a class and ask each group to concentrate on specific aspects of the course. In fact, all students may be encouraged to participate in a Quality Circle resulting in multiple circles in a particular class. Quality Circles have been used successfully in a variety of classes and have been particularly effective with large groups (Angelo & Cross, 1993).

One variation of Classroom Assessment Quality Circles is the LEARN (Locate-Establish-Assess-Research-Nominate) model described by Andrews (1997). The LEARN system focuses on identifying opportunities for improving learning. The teacher and a student team brainstorm about the class to pinpoint any obstacles to student progress. Based on their observations, the team writes a survey and administers it to their classmates; changes are then made according to the data. A final step is the assessment of the modifications.

Another form of Quality Circles, and the technique that I have chosen to focus on here, is the Student Management Team (SMT), which Edward Nuhfer and his colleagues (1992) systematically developed at the University of Colorado.

Student Management Teams

"... I did learn from my students! ... Together we discovered what worked best for that class – not for every class. All of us completed the course with a true sense of accomplishment."

John A. Krogman, University of Colorado, *after* experimenting
with a Student Management Team (Nuhfer, 1992, p. 10)

What Are Student Management Teams?

Student Management Teams are collaborative efforts among the students on the team, all the learners in a particular course, and the teacher.[1] The team functions as a vehicle that encourages students to take responsibility for the overall success of their class. As an independent agent, as well as an integral part of the larger classroom, the SMT provides ongoing assessment and suggestions, evaluates specific activities and materials, reflects on the situation of the class in general, and actively modifies and improves instruction. The essence of the SMT is that the teacher and the students all cooperate to produce the best educational experience possible. According to Nuhfer (1992), this technique should not be viewed as a license to criticize, nor should the term *management* be understood as giving students free rein to *manage* the class environment as they see fit, but as a way to build community:

> What is ultimately being "managed" in the student management team is the improved quality of community. The professor is *not* being "bossed" by students. Instead professor and students are coming together to discover how teaching and learning might be improved and to define positive actions that will reap immediate and long-term benefits. If a contest over power and control develops, it is likely because the ultimate function has been temporarily forgotten by involved parties. (p. iii)

Student Management Teams, Total Quality Management, and Education

Student Management Teams are based on the theory of Total Quality Management (TQM) originally developed by W. Edwards Deming (1986, 1993). TQM advocates the implementation of a vision of excellence shared by all levels of an organization. Quality is defined by meeting or exceeding customer expectations and must be measured to enable continuous improvement. TQM therefore calls for continuous feedback and discussion between management and workers throughout the entire business process. Through the systematic and early detection of potential problems, improved quality control can be achieved. This approach results in an opportunity to correct defects before the completion of a particular job or product as well as the possibility of successfully serving the client. It also allows for increased creativity and communication among all levels of the organization. Adapting these ideas to education, Wolverton (1994) points out that "students become the focus, classroom effectiveness the concern, and assessment the means by which educators gain feedback about what works and what needs to be improved.... The ultimate goal is to enhance classroom effectiveness in order to improve student learning" (p. 1).

... this technique should not be viewed as a license to criticize ... but as a way to build community.

According to McDaniel (1994), TQM principles implemented in educational systems cause significant changes in the way students are perceived. In the TQM view, students are consumers and must be empowered, not merely graded; they are associates who contribute to the learning process, not empty vessels waiting to be filled. In addition, these learners function as part of a cooperative team, not a competitive group, and are motivated contributors to education, not the receivers of predetermined content. McDaniel also offers the following observations on the impact of TQM on the teacher's role (p. 28), stating that in the new, or learner-centered, paradigm, educators must:

- Correlate curricular aims to fit into their students' needs and into other aspects of the college's educational system
- Coach and counsel more than teach or lecture
- Create comfort and trust in the classroom
- Eliminate barriers and obstacles that interfere with the joy of learning
- Monitor for continuous improvement but reduce or eliminate formal testing
- Adjust teaching strategies to promote cooperation, teamwork, and success
- Think in terms of "talent development" rather than "deficit reduction"
- Arrange instruction so that it allows students to learn "just in time"—when it meets an actual "need to know"
- Provide increasing opportunities for student choice, individually or in groups.

TQM has been adapted to the realities of education in a variety of positive and productive ways (Andrews, 1997; Chizmar, 1994; Corensky, McCool et al., 1991; Corensky, Baker et al., 1990; King, 1993; Peak, 1995). For example, the focus of this chapter, the Student Management Team, is one approach that traces its roots to Total Quality Management. Both research and anecdotal evidence suggest that such adaptations of TQM are growing in popularity due to their benefits to the classroom (Andrews, 1997; Angelo & Cross, 1993; Greenberg, 1998; Nuhfer, 1992).

While most pedagogical specialists stress the value of quality control concepts for the classroom, it is important to be cognizant of the criticisms advanced in regard to implementing TQM in education. For example, Beaver (1994) and Andrews (1997) summarize the most salient difficulties in modifying TQM for educational arenas as follows: general resistance to the idea of students as customers since they may be at odds with one another in their view of quality instruction or may not have enough knowledge about course content to make valid recommendations; faculty opposition to interference in course content and instructional methods; inconsistencies between faculty and TQM reward systems; perceived threats to academic freedom due to pressure to conform to a particular program or to meeting specific performance standards; and the costs of TQM training.

In spite of these objections, critics do not dismiss TQM completely, but affirm that certain aspects can benefit current pedagogy, as expressed by Beaver (1994), "Higher education should borrow from that program [TQM] what is appropriate, based on moderation and common sense: listening to the customer when prudent, attempting to measure the quality of our service for the purpose of improvement, and integrating some total quality management techniques with the traditions and practices of the academy" (p. 114).

Key Issues in Creating and Implementing Student Management Teams

The major issues in developing and using student management teams will be discussed in this section. For a step-by-step overview of the process, see the Appendix.

Presenting the Concept to the Class

The Student Management Team is a collaborative effort by learners and the teacher. To be fully successful, the entire class must understand the goals of the team, the feedback process, and the roles of all members of the class and the team. For these reasons, the teacher should clearly explain all aspects of the SMT early in the semester, and provide students with written information, such as this short description from my Business Spanish syllabus:

> In this class, we will also have a Student Management Team (SMT). This is a small group of students who will act as representatives of the entire class and as advisors to the teacher during the semester. The idea of the SMT is based on Total Quality Management: providing continuous and varied input to address problems and offer solutions throughout the process, not just at the end, results in a better product. In this case, the product is our class. Note that I say our class; everyone is this class shares in the responsibility for the course's ultimate impact and success. We will discuss the SMT further in class.

Another example of an introduction to the idea of the SMT is the one Maloney includes in his syllabus for a civil engineering class:

> I am making a commitment to working with you to make this course the best one you will take.... To do this, we will work together with a knowledge of communication and learning processes to employ Total Quality Management or Continuous Process Improvement principles to improve the quality of learning and teaching in the course. You will be required to take a much more active role in this course than you have in your previous courses. (cited in Portnoy, 1994, p. 1)

Instructors may also elect to give more detailed written background information to the team or the entire class. Suggestions for documents include *Care and Feeding of Your Professor* (Nuhfer, 1992, pp. 14–43) and *Improving the Quality of Learning and Teaching through Student Involvement* (Maloney, 1994).

Fully empowered to criticize, the team must always offer an alternative, thus emphasizing a shared sense of responsibility.

To further clarify such oral and written explanations, Nuhfer (1992) suggests the following specific charge to help ensure that both the team and the class clearly comprehend the SMT's managerial role:

> Students, in conjunction with their instructor, are responsible for the success of any course. As student managers, your special responsibility is to monitor this course through your own experience, to receive comments from other students, to work as a team with your instructor on a regular basis, and to make recommendations to the instructor about how this course can be improved. (p. 3)

Forming the Team

A Student Management Team generally consists of three to five students. There are many different ways to form the team. The teacher may ask for student volunteers, pick students randomly, select participants nominated by others, or designate participants according to specific criteria. For example, one semester I picked any interested students, and another term, I selected students who had already taken a class with me and whom I knew well. Yet another time, I requested volunteers and offered extra credit for participation. All these models had positive results.

Frequency of Meetings

The Student Management Team and the teacher must have regular communication to be successful. Nuhfer (1992) recommends that students have a face-to-face meeting each week, consulting the professor every two to three weeks (pp. 6–7). While an excellent suggestion, this model may not be feasible for every institution. It was unrealistic for my students, many of whom worked at least 20 hours a week in addition to taking a full load of courses, so the team and I devised alternative methods of communication. We used e-mail, mail reflectors, telephone calls, and written notes. We also developed a variation on full team face-to-face meetings. At least two students would meet together, and afterwards they would follow up with the other team members. Once a consensus was reached, approximately every three weeks, I would personally consult as many members of the team as were able to attend a meeting. Thus, through creative thinking and flexibility, we were able to achieve our goals despite conflicting schedules.

Location of Meetings

Another concern in implementing the SMT deals with the location of meetings. Nuhfer (1992) advises that meetings take place in a neutral place, away from both the classroom and the professor's office (p. 7). This arrangement is essential to maintain a sense of impartiality and to foster creativity. Students are less likely to feel empowered in the professor's physical domain.

Keeping a Journal

To facilitate the entire process, Nuhfer advises that the team keep a log or journal of their suggestions and the general progress of the class (1992, p. 7). The journal should be rotated among the members of the team so each student serves as recorder; keeping only one journal has the advantage of providing a quick and explicit reference point and of fostering collaboration. I have tried this several times without much success. When consulted about this issue, the team opted to form a rotation to write summaries of our meetings and send these through e-mail. The information was also forwarded to the class to achieve the widest communication possible.

The Team Focus

The Student Management Team can focus on any aspects of the class that the team and the teacher feel are important. Nuhfer (1992) proposes that the team concentrate their efforts on either the teacher (to address the teaching style and general pedagogy) or on the content of the course (to improve the syllabus, texts, activities, attendance policies, testing, etc.) (pp. 3–4). In my experience, the two are so often intertwined that it is impossible to make a clear distinction. For example, the Spring 1998 team approached me about a variety of issues including the workload, our use of technology, activities, the class's anxiety about presentations, and my learner-centered approach. Given the freedom to have a say in the class process, they did not criticize everything, but rather were focused and reflective in their comments, often acknowledging that some of their classmates' ideas (e.g., elimination of all projects) were capricious and unrealistic. Their comments usually focused on a particular concern, for instance, the number of questions they were assigned for a specific reading, the date an oral presentation was due, or how they were to carry out an activity.

Whether the emphasis of the team is on the class, the instructor, or a combination of the two, the job of the SMT is to assess and evaluate the efficacy of the class. Fully empowered to criticize, the team must always offer an alternative, thus negating any focus on negatives and emphasizing the positive aspects of a shared sense of responsibility. The team is ultimately accountable to both the class and the teacher, who may select specific areas to be examined or exclude aspects of the class from its purview. In addition, the teacher retains the option of acting on individual recommendations, either at the time they are made or in the future. In order to preserve a sense of accountability, it is essential that the teacher explain to the team and, at times the class, why certain changes will or will not be implemented (Nuhfer, 1992).

The Importance of Commitment

Commitment is a crucial component of the SMT approach. Research as well as personal experience confirms that a high degree of personal involvement by all participants, but especially by the teacher, is essential for the team to succeed (Angelo & Cross, 1993; Greenberg, 1998; Nuhfer, 1992). Teaching assistants (TAs) and others may participate in the group, but it is still essential that the teacher be an active force for the students to maintain their commitment. A case in point occurred one semester during which my Undergraduate Teaching Assistant (UTA) assumed a major role in the team, acting as an intermediary between the students and me. While an excellent experience for the UTA, this model was less successful because of the lack of direct communication between the student team and the teacher. In subsequent semesters, both the UTA and I were integral members of the team, significantly improving cohesion and effectiveness.

The teacher's commitment is apparent not only to the team, but to the entire class as well. Angelo and Cross (1993) confirm, "This clear commitment sends the message to the members of the Quality Circles and to the rest of the class that their assessments do matter. This message encourages students to assess the course more thoughtfully and responsibly" (p. 342). Losing interest midway in the process or not making time to meet with the team will guarantee failure.

Group Dynamics

As a final point, Nuhfer (1992) notes that the team should rely on the group dynamics approach of researchers and industry quality circles (p. 5). This is an extremely important recommendation, and the teacher should be aware that an orientation toward, and training in, group dynamics is likely to be necessary, especially if the students have not had any experience in collaborative ventures. Students should be made aware of issues affecting group behaviors such as the impact of external influences on the group, the importance of heterogeneity of input, factors affecting fear, trust, and participation, the establishment of interdependence, the role of the leader, and the importance of closure (Billson, 1992). Another essential point to stress is the evolution of the group, including these stages: (1) forming (beginning moments during which group members first come together); (2) storming (the time when members seek to establish their roles in the group through inter-group discussion and conflict); (3) norming (the moment when the group becomes a cohesive unit and develops a unity of purpose); and, (4) performing (the final step, in which attention is focused on the task) (Nuhfer, 1992, p. 42).

The Teacher's Voice

"A professor at the University felt he wasn't communicating with the students. He was getting very mixed reviews. He used the SMT pretty much as the model calls for. Two semesters later, he won a teaching award!"

James Greenberg, Center for Teaching Excellence, University of Maryland

General Considerations

I generally employ a Student Management Team in all my classes and have experimented with this technique for at least four years. Having a team provided a perfect opportunity to fully integrate the business content and practices with language learning and active pedagogical models. While most of my classes are in Business Spanish, the team need not be tied to a business environment. The SMT functions well in such diverse areas as engineering, education, business, languages, language pedagogy, English literature, or cross-cultural communication. I have even successfully experimented with such a team while working with university professors in Ecuador on two occasions. Although it may not be for everyone, once implemented, the potential for positive gain can be astounding. For the SMT to be effective, professors must view the experience as a process and an opportunity to solve problems and be creative, not as a personal assault. It is difficult to validate complaints and criticisms, but the students' viewpoint generally proves extremely helpful, even if it takes a little getting used to!

When using a team, teachers should keep in mind that the implementation guidelines are suggestions and should be adapted to their individual situations. It is also important to remember that the ultimate goals — improved communication between students and the teacher and a successful learning experience — may be achieved in many ways, as noted by Greenberg (1998), "My sense is that it is providing a dedicated time to talk with the SMT about the success of the class itself that is the key, not so much how many students, or frequency of meetings, etc."

Benefits

I have benefited from the input of SMTs in many ways. Like Nuhfer and his colleagues (1992), with the assistance of the SMT, I have solved problems and improved overall course organization, assignments, assessment methods, and presentation and discussion techniques. In addition, I have had the benefit of the creativity, fresh ideas, and multiple perspectives of my students. For instance, they have helped me develop task-based activities, suggested changes to my guidelines for group presentations based on what they felt to be the class's weakness in formal public speaking, and devised interesting and collaborative ways of reviewing material for exams.

Challenges

Student Management Teams may not always function as hoped. As noted earlier in this chapter, students sometimes feel at a loss about how to advise the teacher. Focusing on the educational process and not the content of the class, as well as asking specific questions, can be extremely helpful in guiding the team. Instead of posing general questions that promote negativity such as "What is wrong in this class?" it is more productive to frame the query in specific and proactive terms such as: "I have noticed that students seem confused about *x* although we have reviewed it several different ways. Here are some ideas I have…. What do you think will be most productive? What other suggestions do you have?" Students can offer valuable suggestions when given a clearly defined task. As I wrote this chapter, I consulted with my current Student Management Team, expressing concern about the amount of English that was spoken during group activities and asking them to help me address this particular issue. In response to this task, they devised the following: students would be able to earn *dolaresos*, a currency already familiar to one member of the team, which I had created by combining U.S. dollars and Mexican pesos. The *dolaresos* could later be exchanged for points on the final exam, according to a scheme the team devised and I approved. The team suggested that I give students *dolaresos* only if I felt learners performed extraordinarily well and were working at top capacity. Students would also lose *dolaresos* for speaking English or not doing their work. All members of the team were excited about this idea, and we tried it out in class the following day. I must say that the frequency and level of Spanish increased considerably!

Instead of posing general questions that promote negativity ..., it is more productive to frame the query in ... proactive terms.

Nuhfer (1992) cautions that after employing a student management team in a particular course over several semesters, there really may not be a need for the team's input since the major problems have already been resolved. I have not found this to be so for two reasons. First, many instructors constantly modify courses they have previously taught, and second, the dynamics of each class transforms it into a new and unique entity. I believe that the success of the Student Management Team is greatly related to paving the way for students to understand the shift in the teaching–learning paradigm. I have found that many learners need time to adjust to the idea of the SMT. In fact, initially students may react with confusion, even alarm, at the idea of being responsible for part of the learning process. At the beginning of a semester, I have even heard students comment that the entire idea is "silly and crazy," yet, they have called the idea of the SMT "fantastic" and "exciting" at the end of the term. "It is unfair," states Greenberg, "to expect students to take responsibility willingly when their educational experience has not taught them how to do it" (1998; also, see Wenden, this volume.) Fabián Faccio, who has been both an Undergraduate Teaching Assistant and a student management team member, stresses the relationship between adequate preparation and the success of the SMT. He describes the reactions of his classmates to a team in a situation in which there was only minimal preparation: "Most of the people felt very uncomfortable with the situation (including the SMT) because it was so new.... In that sense, the students didn't know what we were going to be doing, so I don't think that we used the Student Management Team that well."[2] However, once learners clearly understand the mechanism for change and input that the SMT provides, as well as the part they play in the process, they generally embrace the opportunity to effect their own learning.

The Student's Voice

"We represent the best interests of each student on issues of work, assignments, lectures, or level of understanding."

William Ibarra, Student Management Team member, University of Maryland

General Considerations

The Student Management Team gives participants a unique perspective on the teaching–learning process. All students, but most especially the members of the team, cross the traditional line between teacher and learner and develop a sense of responsibility and accountability. I have been informally gathering reflections from team members for several years. In the Spring 1998 semester, I gathered reactions more formally, soliciting open-ended and unguided written reflections and conducting a videotaped round-table discussion with the SMT. Students responded to specific questions but also elaborated on their experiences, adding personal comments and observations as they saw fit. Many interesting themes and insights emerged in these documents.[3]

Giving the Students a Voice

All members of the SMT agreed that the team members gave each student in the class an important voice. As pointed out by one of the team members, the students were surprised initially at being asked to provide feedback on the class. After a while, the key role played by the SMT became a source of pride, and the participants began to relish their roles as class spokespersons. "The Student Management Team can function as a strong voice for the entire class," stated William Ibarra, one member of the team. Kaladi Josephs also confirmed the importance of the SMT's presence and input, explaining, "It kind of feels really nice ... to be the voice of the class, because being student management, you are all voices, and we are like mirrors, so we are reflecting what we see, and each person sees things differently."

The SMT was especially proud of the way the team acted as a catalyst for increasing the involvement of all students in the course. All four members of the team commented that they believed that the class developed a feeling of collaboration and mutual trust. One of the team members explored this point in depth:

In my eyes, the Student Management Team permitted our class to become more involved and made the professor more approachable. Through representatives like me, the students of the class could give direct feedback of their opinions without the fear of approaching a professor by themselves. In this way, students really loosened up and discussed with me often what they thought was successful in the class, what could be improved, and what they would like to change.... It was very interesting to see how the class reacted to having their own personal "lobbyists," as one might call us. Initially they were unaccustomed to the feeling of having a voice in the work that they are required to do. As time went on, though, they incessantly pursued the SMT with new ideas, suggestions, or complaints. They became actively involved in improving the course that they were currently taking and interested in the class as I have seen in no other. Truly the students seemed to have gained a more personal relationship with all the other students as well as the professor through their own involvement in the course's outcome.

Offering Alternatives

The SMT felt that all students responded exceptionally well to the ability to offer alternatives. They thought that having the ability to suggest new ways to fulfill tasks not only empowered them and allowed them to work to their strengths, but also helped relieve stress. One incident in particular serves as an excellent example of creative cooperation. Toward the end of the semester, students had to answer fifteen questions about a book they were required to read. The team responded to the class's anxiety about the assignment by brainstorming alternatives with the entire class. They presented the teacher with a plan in which groups of students would answer different questions and post the answers to the class Web Chat. Thus, through a collaborative effort, all the information would be available to the entire group. Speaking for the team, Rachelle Lewis stated, "It reduced the stress to have that kind of choice."

> ... the management team prepared us for the business world.... Our professor created a challenging environment where we had to become leaders, managers, and problem solvers.
>
> William Ibarra, Student Management Team Member

Developing Real-World Skills

Another idea that emerged in the comments of the SMT was that the experience of participating in this type of group afforded students the opportunity to use skills perceived to be valuable for the real world. Ibarra comments, "… being a member of the management team prepared us for the business world. What I acquired were the necessary problem solving skills regarding important matters of the class. Our professor created a challenging environment where we had to become leaders, managers, and problem solvers."

Effective Communication

The members of the team considered the establishment of effective communication of prime importance. Ibarra stressed the significance of keeping everyone informed:

> We held meetings twice a month to inform our progress to the professor. Through the use of the Internet, we had a good communication level with the students to relay any important information concerning class projects or class assignments. Without effective communication, the management team will not function properly and it will be a waste of class time.

Although there seemed to be successful communication channels, both the team and I agreed that even better interactions could be achieved by having periodic meetings of the team and the students during class time, without the teacher present.

The SMT also initiated several surveys to elicit feedback from the students. These surveys, designed and administered by the team, resembled a typical feedback instrument in that they contained questions about homework, testing, classroom practices, etc. However, the survey clearly indicated that the students knew that they shared responsibility for the class and that in order to criticize they were required to offer alternative ideas, as is evident in the following questions:

Spanish 315
Student Management Team
Questionnaire

- Are you generally satisfied with the amount of material that is being covered? If not, why? What would you recommend?
- Do you find the lectures helpful and informative? If not, why? What would you recommend?
- Do you find the homework helpful? If not, why? What would you recommend?
- Do you think you are participating enough in the activities during the class? If not, why? What would you recommend?
- Are you doing all the homework that the teacher is assigning? Are you putting in the necessary amount of work outside of class?
- Are there specific problems that you are having with this class? If so, what would you do to correct them?

Team Members and Relationships to Peers

The Student Management Team gave voice to a final and very interesting theme, its relationship to both the class and the teacher. All the team members initially felt uncertain and anxious about how their classmates might perceive them. "Sometimes students [in the class] presume that the members of the management team are the 'teacher's pets' because we are constantly exchanging communication with the professor. One of the challenges is how to earn the respect and confidence of the classmates," clarified Ibarra. Gronau, too, explained the team's feeling of crossing the traditional student / teacher line:

> The students [in the class] were not sure where to put us...[At first,] they didn't understand that we are students, completely equal as they are, and that we are trying to be their voices, and that the biggest challenge [was] really to make them understand...that we don't have special privileges....

In response to these concerns, the team ultimately suggested gaining the students' confidence by having an introductory meeting with the class early in the semester to explain its function and responsibilities. The team advised the teacher not to attend this session.

Positive Feedback

The Student Management Team expressed delight at receiving positive feedback from both the students and the teacher. The entire team made it clear that the class was very close and like a "family." Perhaps Ibarra summarized the participant's feelings best when he exclaimed, "Some of the best times are when the professor offers to buy lunch for the management team; then you know you're doing a good job!"

The Student Management Team, Language Learning, and the National Standards

Using a Student Management Team has a myriad of implications for the educational and personal development of both the students and the teacher. In this chapter I have discussed the impact this technique can have on changing the teaching–learning paradigm, on fostering active participation in all aspects of the pedagogical process, and in improving both teaching and learning. This collaborative approach between teachers and students can also be viewed in light of the Standards for Foreign Language Learning (1996); the Student Management Team has a direct relationship to the Communication, Connections, and Communities goals.

The Student Management Team addresses the Communication goal and each of its targeted standards (1.1 Interpersonal Communication, 1.2 Interpretative Communication, and 1.3 Presentational Communication). The team is involved in real communication and negotiation of meaning as members speak with the teacher and their classmates to discover and solve problems, read and analyze all forms of written input from the class and instructor, and synthesize and present information either to their classmates or the instructor in both formal or informal venues. In fact, working in a situation that had real consequences acted as a motivator; the team often asked for help in different discourse and communication strategies and appropriate style in order to "sound more Spanish" and convey exactly what they wanted to say. Of course, it is clear that the actions of the SMT are linked to the Communication goal only if the foreign language is the mode of communication. Most of the time, the Student Management Teams I have worked with have used the target language in their communications, especially when presenting information or consulting students in class. In addition, the team and I generally use Spanish in our meetings, although students sometimes use English, as in the questionnaire above.

The Connections goal calls for expanding instruction by making connections with other disciplines (1996, p. 49). As noted earlier, the SMT is a concept adapted from actual business practices in which student members use quality management principles in realistic ways. Additional bridges connect the language and business worlds both inside and outside the classroom: The SMT can be an integral part of an interdisciplinary approach, in this instance, Spanish for Business and Cross-Cultural Communication.

A Student Management Team exemplifies standard 5.2 of the Communities goal, Lifelong Learning. Learners clearly expressed that participation in the team helped them develop or enhance such prized real-world abilities as leadership, organization, management, problem solving, and critical thinking. These skills, whether implemented in English or Spanish, clearly assist the learner to be proactive in the learning process and make the most of his or her environment.

In describing the "weave" of curricular elements, the National Standards (1996) confirm, "Students should be given ample opportunities to explore, develop, and use communication strategies, learning strategies, critical thinking skills, and skills in technology, as well as the appropriate elements of the language system and culture" (p. 28). While the Student Management Team by itself cannot address all these aspects, as part of a language class in which students work in and with the target language in realistic contexts, the SMT clearly facilitates the development of critical thinking as well as communication and learning strategies.

Conclusion

A Student Management Team can be a beneficial and innovative means of involving students in their own learning and of effecting change in educational environments. It is a classroom assessment technique that is relatively easy to implement, and can be adapted by the teacher to address the specific needs and concerns of a particular course at any level, but is especially suited to secondary and university classes. Utilizing Student Management Teams can have a positive impact not only on the classroom and the teacher, but on the students and the instructional process as well. This structure fosters the development of group cohesiveness, collaboration, and creativity. It also helps participants learn such important real-world skills as problem solving, organization, and communication techniques. Finally, the investment of time and commitment can lead to significant gains in shifting the focus from the teacher to the learner.

Notes

[1] I owe a debt of gratitude to the members of all the Student Management Teams I have worked with during the past few years; however, I would particularly like to thank Fabián Faccio, Kasey Gronau, William Ibarra, Rachelle Lewis, and Fernando Pegado, the members of the team from my Spanish class, Cross-cultural Communication, in Spring 1998, who participated in the research for this chapter.

[2] This class was conducted in a technology-enhanced classroom that contained 20 computers, access to many kinds of software, including specialized software for anonymous input, and Internet and video access. Many students did not have a high degree of computer literacy and the learning curve was very high. This resulted in anxiety among some learners.

[3] I would like to thank the editor of this volume, Margaret Ann Kassen, for her assistance in this process. I also would like to thank Elizabeth Lewis who transcribed the video.

References

Andrews, H. A. (1997). TQM and faculty evaluation: Ever the twain shall meet? (ERIC Document Reproduction Service No. ED 408 004).

Angelo, T. A., & Cross, P. K. (1993). *Classroom assessment techniques: A handbook for college teachers*. San Francisco: Jossey-Bass.

Barr, R. B., & Tagg, J. (1995). From teaching to learning: A new paradigm for undergraduate education. *Change*, Nov.-Dec., 13–25.

Beaver, W. (1994). Is TQM appropriate for the classroom? *College Teaching 42*(3), 111–114.

Belenky, M. F., Clinchy, B. M., Goldberger, N. R., & Tarule, J. M. (1986). *Women's ways of knowing: The development of self, voice, and mind*. New York: Basic Books.

Billson. J. M. (1992). Group process in the college classroom: Building relationships for learning. In M. Maher & V. Tinto (Eds.) with B. L. Smith & J. MacGregor, *Collaborative learning: A sourcebook for higher education*, *Vol. II* (pp. 21–41). University Park, PA: The Pennsylvania State University, the National Center on Postsecondary Teaching, Learning, and Assessment (NCTLA).

Chamot, A. U., & O'Malley, J. M. (1994). *The CALLA handbook: Implementing the Cognitive Academic Language Learning Approach*. Reading, MA: Addison-Wesley.

Chizmar, J. F. (1994). Total Quality Management (TQM) of teaching and learning. *The Journal of Economic Education, 25*(2), 179–190.

Clinchy, B. M. (1990). Issues of gender in teaching and learning. *Journal on Excellence in College Teaching, 1*, 52–67.

Cohen, A. D. (1990). *Insights for learners, researchers, and teachers*. Boston: Heinle & Heinle.

Cohen, P. (1995). Putting resource-based learning to work. *Education Update, 37 (3)*. Retrieved January 15, 1999, from the World Wide Web: http://www.ascd.org/pubs/eu/march95.html.

Cooper, J., Prescott, S., Cook, L., Smith, L., Mueck, R., & Cuseo, J. (1990). *Cooperative learning and college instruction: Effective use of student learning teams*. Long Beach, CA: California State University Foundation.

Corensky, R., Baker, R., Cavanaugh, C., Etling, W., Lukert, M., McCool, S., McKay, B., Min, A., Paul, C., Thomas, P., Wagner, D., & Darling, J. (1990). *Using Deming to improve quality in colleges and universities*. Madison, WI: Magna.

Corensky, R., McCool, S., Byrnes, L., & Weber, R. (1991). *Implementing total quality management in higher education*. Madison, WI: Magna.

Crookall, D., & Oxford, R. L. (1990). *Simulation, gaming and language learning*. New York: Newbury House.

Cross, D. (1983). Sex differences in achievement. *System, 11*, 159–162.

Deming, W. E. (1986). *Out of the crisis*. Cambridge, MA: Institute of Technology, Center for Advanced Engineering Study.

Deming, W. E. (1993). *The new economics for industry, government, education*. Cambridge MA: Institute of Technology, Center for Advanced Engineering Study.

Ehrman, M. (1990). The role of personality type in adult language learning: An ongoing investigation. In T. S. Parry & C. W. Stansfield (Eds.), *Language aptitude reconsidered* (pp. 126–178). Englewood Cliffs, NJ: Prentice Hall Regents.

Engel, J. (1991). Not just a method, but a way of learning. In D. J. Boud & G. Feletti (Eds.), *The challenge of problem-based learning* (pp. 21–31). New York: St. Martin's Press.

Gardner, H. (1983). *Frames of mind: The theory of multiple intelligences*. New York: Basic Books.

Greenberg, J. (Director, Center for Teaching Excellence, University of Maryland), personal communication, June 25, 1998.

Greenblat, C. S., & Duke, R.D. (Eds.). (1981). *Principles and practices of gaming-simulation*. Beverly Hills, CA: Sage.

Johnson, D. W., Johnson, R. T., & Smith, K. A. (1991). *Cooperative learning: Increasing college faculty instructional productivity*. ASHE-ERIC Higher Education Report No. 4. Washington D.C.: The George Washington University, School of Education and Human Development.

King, A. (1993). From sage on the stage to guide on the side. *College Training, 41*, 30–35.

Maloney, W. F. (1994). *Improving the quality of learning and teaching through student involvement*. College Park, MD: University of Maryland, Center for Teaching Excellence.

Marzano, R. J. (1992). *A different kind of classroom*. Alexandria,VA: Association for Supervision and Curriculum Development.

McCarthy, B. (1980). *The 4MAT system*. Oakbrook, IL: Excel.

McDaniel, T. R. (1994). College classrooms of the future. *College Teaching*, 42 (1), 27–31.

McKeachie, W. J. (1986). *Teaching tips: A guidebook for the beginning college teacher* (8th ed.). Lexington, MA: DC Heath.

Myers, C. (1993). *Promoting active learning strategies for the college classroom*. San Francisco: Jossey-Bass.

National Standards in Foreign Language Education Project. (1996). *Standards for foreign language learning: Preparing for the 21st century*. Yonkers, NY: Author.

Nuhfer, E. (1992). *A handbook for student management teams*. Denver: University of Colorado at Denver, Office of Teaching Effectiveness.

Nunan, D. (1988). *The learner-centered curriculum*. New York: Cambridge University.

Nunan, D. (1989). *Designing tasks for the communicative classroom*. New York: Cambridge University.

Nyikos, M. (1990). Sex-related differences in adult language learning: Socialization and memory factors. *Modern Language Journal, 74*(3), 273–287.

Oxford, R. L. (1990a). *Language learning strategies: What every teacher should know.* New York: Newbury House.

Oxford, R. L. (1990b). Styles, strategies and aptitude: Connections for language learning. In T.S. Parry & C.W. Stansfield (Eds.), *Language aptitude reconsidered* (pp. 67–125). Englewood Cliffs, NJ: Prentice Hall Regents.

Oxford, R. L. (1993). *La différence continue* ...: Gender differences in second/foreign language learning styles and strategies. In J. Sutherland (Ed.), *Exploring gender* (pp. 140–147). Englewood Cliffs, NJ: Prentice Hall.

Oxford, R. L., Ehrman, M. E., & Lavine, R. Z. (1990). Style wars: Teacher-student style conflicts in the language classroom. In S. S. Magnan (Ed.), *Challenges in the 1990s for college foreign language programs* (pp. 1–25). Boston: Heinle & Heinle.

Peak, M. H. (1995). TQM transforms the classroom. *Management Review, 84,* 13–18.

Portnoy, Alisse. (1994, December). What works in college teaching: Improving the quality of learning and teaching through student involvement. In J. Greenberg (Ed.), *Teaching and Learning News* 4(2). College Park, MD: University of Maryland, Center for Teaching Excellence.

Stepien, W., & Gallagher, S. (1993). Problem-based learning: As authentic as it gets. *Educational Leadership: Journal of the Department of Supervision and Curriculum Development, N.E.A.,* 50(7), 25–28.

Stevick, E. W. (1989). *Success with foreign languages: Seven who achieved it and what worked for them.* New York: Prentice Hall.

Weaver, S. J., & Cohen, A. D. (1994). Making strategy instruction a reality in the foreign language curriculum. In C. A. Klee (Ed.), *Faces in a crowd: The individual learner in multisection courses* (pp. 285–323). Boston: Heinle & Heinle.

Wilkerson, L. & Gijselaers, W. H. (Eds.). (1996). *Bringing problem-based learning to higher education: Theory and practice.* San Francisco: Jossey-Bass.

Wolverton, M. (1994). *A new alliance: Continuous quality and classroom effectiveness.* (ERIC Document Reproduction Service No. ED 392 368).

Appendix. Sample Plan for Implementing a Student Management Team

Introduce the concept to the class: I usually introduce the idea of the Student Management Team during the second or third class session. I repeatedly mention the concept until I actually form the team. Students may be initially surprised or even fearful of the idea of providing input.

Form the team: I recommend waiting until the third week of class to form the Student Management Team. In my institution, this is the end, or almost the end, of the add-drop period, so that I have a stable class population at this time. Waiting until the third week also gives me time to get to know the students. Unless I form the team with students whom I already know, I generally try to approach one or two learners whom I think will be assets to the team based upon their enthusiasm and motivation, their organizational capacity, or their intellectual promise. I complete the team by asking for volunteers.

Charge the team and clarify their mission and focus: This is an essential step. Students are sometimes unclear about what they are supposed to do. I usually give them a written statement of their responsibilities, such as Nuhfer's charge as noted earlier in the chapter. I then provide them with a possible agenda for our first meeting. Clearly stating which areas are off limits is also important at this time.

Agree on meeting frequency, times, and dates, as well as other means of communication: This is often a difficult step since students' schedules are so hectic. I have found that evening works best for my students. Often I treat the team to dinner. With the last two Student Management Teams, the team made extensive use of e-mail to communicate. I generally ask the team to meet every week, but I find that they communicate informally after or before each class, and meet formally less frequently.

Instruct the team in keeping the journal: When talking about the journal, it is important to stress that the team keep notes and reflect upon the process. Ideally, the journal should be shared among all participants. I have found that often one person takes charge of the journal and it functions less as a reflective method than as a record of team ideas.

Listen to the students and keep an open mind! Perhaps, this is the most challenging aspect of working with a Student Management Team. Often the students will present ideas that you consider very farfetched, or criticize and offer alternatives for something you think is wonderful. At these times it is essential to explain why you cannot agree with a particular suggestion. Remember, students and teachers interpret class tasks and requirements in very different ways! For example, while educators may look at the entire learning process, students often focus almost exclusively on the amount of work a specific task requires.

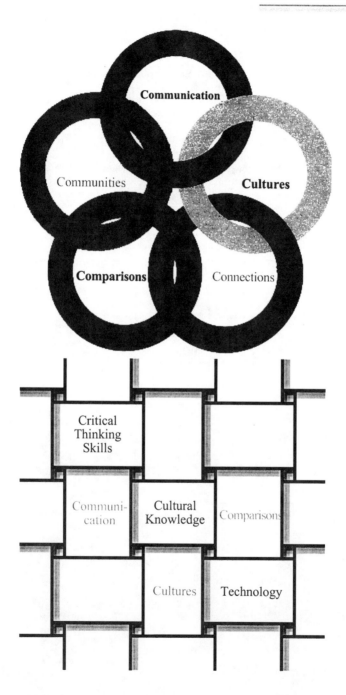

Student Perspectives on the Internet: The Promise and Process of Online Newspapers and Chats

Lina Lee

University of New Hampshire

As Internet technology has progressively become a powerful instructional tool for foreign language learning, more and more language professionals are interested in incorporating online resources into their teaching. The Internet enables students both to access authentic, up-to-date cultural information and to communicate with others. Furthermore, the World Wide Web creates many opportunities for students to read and use the target language both inside and outside the classroom. Yet as teachers explore the potential of the Internet, some fundamental questions arise: What processes facilitate the use of the Internet by learners? How do learners react to this promising new resource? What impact does the Internet have on students' learning outcomes?

This chapter responds to these questions by examining the integration of various Internet resources into an advanced Spanish course. In this course, the use of online newspapers was combined with online chats in order to engage students actively in learning and to increase interest and motivation in foreign language learning. Student learning outcomes were explored through portfolios, student questionnaires, and interviews.

First, I will provide an overview of Internet-based instruction for foreign language teaching. Second, I will address the use of online newspapers and online chats to make connections to National Standards for Foreign Language Learning (1996). Third, I will describe in detail the current project using the FACE model—Facilitation, Access, Collaboration, and Evaluation—as a framework for designing online activities. Then, I will report on students' perceptions of themselves as language learners when using Internet technology. Finally, I will conclude with pedagogical implications for online technology for enhancing learner self-direction.

Internet-Based Instruction for Foreign Language Teaching and Learning

Internet technology offers many innovative opportunities to engage students in their language acquisition. Not only can students explore target cultural resources using browsers such as Netscape or Internet Explorer but they may also interact with native speakers around the world via online communication such as e-mail, newsgroups, and chat rooms. Previous studies in a variety of settings have shown that Internet technology facilitates teaching and enhances learning (e.g., Chun, 1994; Kelm, 1992; Kern, 1995b; Kuttenberg & Zeller, 1997; Lee 1997b; Oliva & Pollastrini, 1995; Sullivan & Pratt, 1996; Sutherland et al., 1995; Warschauer, 1996). Among these studies, both the use of synchronous (real-time) and asynchronous (non-real-time) online discussion supported the development of students' language skills. In addition, the process of using online technologies fostered students' interest and motivation in learning both language and culture.

> ... computer-mediated communication
> allowed all students to participate ...

Studies showed that electronic writing for communication on a local area network facilitated classroom discussion and helped students improve their oral skills (Beauvois, 1992). For instance, Beauvois (1998) found that the students of intermediate French who used the electronic synchronous communication software program Deadalus InterChange for class discussion did better on their oral exams than those who spent the same amount of time in oral discussion in the classroom. Using an electronic network also enhanced students' communication skills and strategies. Another Beauvois study (1997) showed that "students do communicate better as a general rule in the computer lab, if better means using longer, more complete utterances, expressing less superficial ideas, and communicating generally more openly about any given subject" (p. 180). She further commented that computer-mediated communication allowed all students to participate rather than some students as in a traditional classroom.

E-mail and newsgroups are used for non-real-time electronic conferencing. Oliva and Pollastrini (1995) conducted a study using native speakers to communicate with advanced Italian students via e-mail and newsgroups. The results of the study indicated that "computer network resources help students improve their language skills in a manner similar to full immersion or study abroad, but are based more heavily on written communication" (p. 552).

Other studies describing the use of e-mail and newsgroups reported an impact on students' motivation and attitude toward language learning (e.g., Cononelos & Oliva, 1993; Lee, 1997b; Lunde, 1990; Sanaoui & Lapkin, 1992). For instance, Barson, Frommer, and Schwartz (1993) carried out a cooperative research project among students in intermediate-level French at Stanford, Pittsburgh, and Harvard via e-mail. Their results indicated that learners gained confidence in their use of French and increased their motivation through the use of electronic communication. Other researchers observed that the use of e-mail or other online networks creates a relatively non-threatening atmosphere in which students can express, negotiate, and interpret meaning within a meaningful context (Beauvois, 1992; 1994; Lee, 1997b; Sutherland, et al., 1995). In sum, the research suggests that the Internet can have a positive impact on the development of linguistic skills and can enhance learner's positive feelings about the learning process.

Understanding the diversity of the target culture is important in foreign language learning (Savignon, 1983; Canale & Swain, 1980). The use of the World Wide Web affords endless opportunities for gaining exposure to the target culture. For instance, Arizona State University has implemented Web-based assignments throughout the semester in several French, Portuguese, and Spanish classes (Lafford & Lafford, 1997). In the case of the French classes, students browsed the Web for aspects of francophone culture that interested them, such as music and tourist sites, and they were asked to write summaries of the information they found. Students at the advanced level of Spanish were required to prepare oral reports on topics in Spanish culture using Web materials. Questionnaires given at the end of the semester revealed very positive student response to the use of the Web. Students also indicated that they enjoyed reading cultural information in the target language and "their attitude toward the use of Spanish about the target culture was positively affected by their experiences with the World Wide Web" (Lafford & Lafford, 1997, p. 238).

Without a doubt, online technology provides immediate access to cross-cultural information exchanges among learners. For example, Kern (1998) showed that the use of e-mail and MOOs (Multiple user domains Object Oriented) promoted the development of cultural literacy among users, enriched their knowledge of the target culture, and helped them gain a better understanding of their own culture from another culture's perspective. Overall, the Internet affects students' learning of communication skills and their development of cultural knowledge and understanding. Online interaction also motivates students to participate actively in the use of the target language.

Online Newspapers and Chats with Advanced Language Learners

Most students in my fifth-semester course at the University of New Hampshire major or minor in Spanish; they are motivated and have a good attitude toward foreign language learning. The goals of the culture project that I developed are (1) to create opportunities for advanced language students to read authentic materials and gain cultural knowledge and (2) to enhance communication and intercultural exchanges. Current events are particularly appropriate for the advanced level (ACTFL Proficiency Guidelines, 1986), as learners at this level have acquired the grammatical structures and vocabulary needed to support their understanding of written authentic materials, although they may have difficulty in comprehending technical terms from specialized fields. In order to achieve these goals, I have chosen to combine two Internet resources, online newspapers and online chats.

Online Newspapers

Using a browser, such as Netscape or Internet Explorer, students can easily access a large number of online newspapers such as *Clarín Digital* from Buenos Aires, *La Jornada* from Mexico, and *ABC* from Madrid. Students can choose to read articles on politics, economics, art, music, etc., according to their personal or professional interests and needs, a particular plus for students who double major in Spanish and another field, such as international affairs, political science, Latin American studies, or foreign language education. Daily newspapers also allow students to advance their knowledge of current lexical items and idiomatic expressions in the target language. In addition, the process of interpreting, analyzing, synthesizing, and evaluating the cultural texts goes beyond the comprehension of simple facts. Students have the opportunity to develop their reading skills and strategies.

Online Chats

Online chats create a "virtual community" where students discuss topics of interest and interact with others. Once students log into the chat room, they type their comments, click to send them, and their words appear immediately on the screens of all those who are connected. Unlike the asynchronous interaction among e-mail users, the online chat engages users in a real-time conversation in which they receive immediate responses and feedback. According to Savignon (1983), having opportunities to "use the target language to express, interpret, and negotiate meaning with others" is essential to acquire functional language skills (p.11). The chat dialogues, therefore, create such opportunities for students to use their language skills. Indeed, the use of online chats as a medium for communication is an individualized, interpersonal, and interactive task that allows students to experience "active" learning beyond the traditional classroom.

I have chosen to use two different chatrooms for this project, one for students to communicate with each other, and another for them to interact with native speakers. An easy and user-friendly private chatroom is "ParaChat" that allows webmasters to set up a free chat (see http://www.parachat.com/faq/webmasters.htm for more information). The public chat line that I use with my students originates in Mexico (see http://foros.planet.com.mx/chattiempolibre/ for more information).

My Home Page

In order to facilitate the use of technology for this project, I created a home page to provide the students direct links to a variety of Hispanic online newspapers and the two selected chat rooms (see http://www.unh.edu/spanish/lina/spanish631.html for more information). This home page also includes useful search engines to pursue additional resources.

Promise of the Internet:
Connecting to the National Standards

As the profession at large has come to agree, learning a foreign language includes being able to communicate, understanding the target culture, making connections with other disciplines through the foreign language, developing insights into one's own language and culture through comparisons of the target language and the native language, and participating in multilingual communities at home and abroad (Standards for Foreign Language Learning, 1996). The important five C's—Communication, Cultures, Connections, Comparisons and Communities— encourage teachers to create integrated instruction for both inside and outside of the classroom. The online activities created for this project connect easily to the five C's of the National Standards.

The Cultures Goal indicates that "students cannot truly master the language until they have also mastered the cultural contexts in which the language occurs" (p. 27). The wide range of content areas found in online newspapers encompasses the study of art, literature, music, history, and daily life. Online newspapers provide students with valuable, up-to-date information which facilitates their understanding of cultural phenomena including both products and perspectives of the target culture. Reading online newspapers helps students become familiar with Hispanic cultures so they feel free to discuss, express, and exchange their ideas with others via online chats.

According to the Connections Goal, students "reinforce and further their knowledge of other disciplines through the foreign language" (p. 50). Reading different subject areas of online newspapers broadens students' understanding of other fields and expands their knowledge of professional needs.

The Comparisons Goal states that students "demonstrate under-standing of the concept of culture through comparisons of the cultures studied and their own" (p. 56). Different sections of the newspaper such as "Sports," "Economics," "Arts," and "Entertainment" provide engaging opportunities for students to compare and contrast the native and target cultures. In addition, using the Spanish online chat originating in Mexico allows students to discuss and exchange ideas with native speakers.

> Unlike the asynchronous interaction among e-mail users, the online chat engages users in a real-time conversation in which they receive immediate responses and feedback.

Researchers have stressed the need for more opportunities to use the target language beyond classroom settings (e.g., Ellis, 1988; Swain & Lapkin, 1986; Swain & Wong Fillmore, 1984). In support of the Commu-nication Goal, online chats provide opportunities for students to discuss a variety of topics in a collaborative learning environment. Furthermore, students present and share information collected from online newspapers with their peers and instructor through oral presentations. The online chat room enables students to develop a sense of target language communities, together with a feeling of personal enjoyment and enrichment, as encour-aged by the Communities Goal.

Overall, both online newspapers and chats open innovative avenues for students to acquire a foreign language. Reading online newspapers creates valuable opportunities for students to read, interpret, and analyze authentic texts in order to gain insights into the target culture (Knight, 1994). Online chats promote communication and discussions among stu-dents in the target language. The combined and integrated use of online newspapers and chats allows learners to address all the goal areas of the Standards for Foreign Language Learning (1996).

Using the FACE Model

Over several semesters of working with the Internet in my Spanish classes, I have developed the FACE model to assist the process of using online technology. The FACE model consists of four phases: Facilitation,

Access, Collaboration, and Evaluation. The model promotes a learner-driven environment in which students are responsible for their own learning. It also encourages collaborative learning among students and incorporates holistic assessment to monitor students' progress and measure their learning outcomes. I will explain each phase of the FACE model and illustrate what I have done to implement it.

Facilitation

Unlike more traditional approaches in which the teacher plays a central role in classroom instruction, the Facilitation phase places the teacher in the role of facilitator. In this phase, the teacher guides and advises students rather than taking control and making decisions for them. The teacher encourages students to become independent, reflective, and responsible learners.

For instance, at the beginning of the semester, I explain to the students the purpose, content, and procedures for doing the online activities and define their responsibilities and mine. Students are required to:

- read online newspapers and chat online once a week outside class
- keep weekly journals in which they express their reactions to readings and online discussions as well as raise questions and voice concerns
- select and organize materials for the cultural project
- decide which material to include in the portfolio

My responsibilities are to:

- provide the guidelines and assessment criteria for the Internet project
- structure and monitor online activities, and participate in chats to keep students on task; when the students misinterpret the texts and/or wander off the target discussion, I lead them back to the original topic
- assist students outside of class with their online readings and final cultural project by asking and answering questions through online chats and e-mail interactions

The Facilitation phase clarifies the responsibilities of the teacher and the students and defines successful completion of the Internet activities.

Access

During the Access phase, teachers need to make sure students feel comfortable using the network. Most importantly, they need to consult with the computer center for scheduling training sessions. My students attend a three-hour workshop during the first week of classes in which they learn the following:

- how to locate my home page
- how to access, explore, download and upload information from Netscape Navigator
- strategies for using search engines to gather the information they need for their final research project

After the training, the schedule for the computer rooms on campus and the schedule for the chat room are provided to the students so they can reserve a computer station when needed. I create an e-mail distribution list for the class in order to post news and topics online. A list of the students' e-mail addresses is distributed so that they can also send messages to one another or ask for help when needed on an individual basis. E-mail, however, is not the main tool for online discussion. Rather, the primary instrument is the private chat room that is used once a week. The Access phase, like the Facilitation phase, encourages students to become independent, risk-taking language learners by gaining the technical skills to explore the target language and culture through the Internet.

Collaboration

Collaborative learning is essential to help students maximize their own zone of proximal development, as identified by Vygotsky (1978). Vygotsky defined the "actual development level as determined by independent problem solving and the level of potential development as determined through problem solving under adult guidance or in collaboration with more capable peers" (p. 86). He emphasized how important it is for learners to observe, participate, and interact with others in community.

Collaborative learning strategies have been shown to enhance motivation and foreign language achievement (Johnson & Johnson, 1985; Kramsch, 1987; Nunan, 1992). During the Collaboration phase, students work with their peers via online communication. The collaboration creates a supportive and non-threatening environment that helps students build self-confidence toward learning a foreign language. A variety of online activities can be employed during the Collaboration phase. The procedure for the online discussion is:

- I select the topics for weekly online discussion (current events and general topics such as sports, economics and politics) and send them via e-mail to the students the day before the discussion.
- To ensure collaboration, I assign each student to a small group, and each group takes turn being in charge of the weekly online discussion.
- After the students receive the topic via e-mail, the group in charge of the online discussion prepares questions for the class. Questions are sent via e-mail.
- Students join the chat room from 4 p.m. to 5 p.m. every Wednesday.
- All students then chat online using the guiding questions the group provided. They interact, negotiate, and debate among themselves while I observe, coach, and provide feedback when appropriate.
- As a follow-up in class, each group briefly reports on what they found interesting in the online discussions to reinforce their oral skills.

Online discussions are worth 10% of the final course grade. Students are allowed to miss a total of three online discussions without penalty. The grade is lowered incrementally for each absence beyond these three (for instance, from A- to B+ or from B+ to B). Brief oral reports in class that follow up on the online discussions count as class participation, worth 15% of the final course grade. Students are encouraged to ask or answer questions and make comments during these group oral reports. Oral participation is graded based on a total of questions or comments they make during each discussion. I use the scale of 5=A, 4=B, 3=C, 2=D, 1=F to keep track of students' participation.

In addition to the weekly online discussion, students are required to prepare a group presentation as part of the final project (see Appendix A for the culture project guidelines). The group presentation is worth 5% of the final grade. Each group, consisting of three or four students, selects a topic of interest and prepares an oral report using resources from online newspapers and other web sites identified by using search engines. Students share Internet sites with those who work on a similar topic. In addition to helping each other with their oral presentations, they also support each other on the final individual project through peer editing. The feedback and input students receive from their peers help them revise the content, organization, and grammatical structures for the final version. Students no longer work by themselves but rather within the group. Such a collaborative learning environment promotes a positive, effective learning experience for the students.

Evaluation

Evaluating students' work is crucial to ensure their learning outcomes. During the Evaluation phase, I incorporate holistic portfolio assessment into the project (see Lee, 1997a, for details). The portfolio assessment has three distinguishing characteristics: (1) student involvement, (2) evaluation and reflection of both the process and product of learning, and (3) work collected over time. During the semester, each student compiles a portfolio based on the following components:

- sample printouts from online chats
- weekly one-page journal entries about the news articles read online
- a final culture project (see Appendix A)
- monthly self-evaluations (see Appendix B)

Each component is graded separately based on five categories: content, organization, language, style, and appropriateness. In addition to the portfolio, I conduct a "Survey of Your Experience with Online Activities" at the end of the semester. The aim of the questionnaire is to ascertain students' reactions to the online activities (see Appendix C).

A final interview either individually or in a small group is also included for this project. Students who research similar topics are interviewed together while I observe their reactions and listen to their opinions about the project. Students are asked to explain the most valuable, interesting, and difficult aspects of the project and to describe their experiences with Internet activities (see Appendix D for sample interview questions). They are encouraged to express their reactions and concerns about using the Internet. To evaluate the integration of online technology in this course, in order to improve the course and to find more effective uses for technology in instruction, I collected data from students' monthly self-evaluations, surveys, and interviews.

I have implemented the FACE model in the current project for two semesters, and the project has become part of the required course work for students in fifth-semester Spanish courses. This project is also part of my ongoing classroom-based research on Internet technology.

Learner Perspectives on Using the Internet

The following summary of students' perspectives on using online technology is drawn from students' monthly self-evaluations, the results of "Survey of Your Experience with Online Activities," and the final interviews conducted in Fall 1997. A total of 31 students from two sections participated in this study.

Overall, students reacted positively to the inclusion of the Internet. When asked if online activities helped them improve their language skills in general, most students agreed that the online activities enhanced the development of their language skills (question 1) and their understanding of Hispanic culture and people (question 5). More than 60% of students agreed that online chats helped them improve their writing of Spanish (question 6) and that they would like to continue using the Internet in future Spanish courses (question 9). Interestingly, more than 70% of students reported that online newspapers helped them read better in Spanish (question 3) and increased their knowledge of Spanish vocabulary (question 4).

According to the self-evaluations, more than 75% of students indicated they gained confidence in using Internet tools and that they learned technological skills as well. One student commented:

> I have discovered many interesting things on the Internet. Through our home page I also learned the terminology of the Internet in both Spanish and English which I didn't know before. Now I feel much more comfortable using the computer. I strongly believe people should have some knowledge of the Internet; especially, it is a powerful tool for foreign language learners.

Another student also confirmed the value of the Internet and how its use changed his perspective on learning a foreign language:

> I had never thought about using the Internet until I took this course. ... cyberspace is a great place where you can read authentic materials in the target language and meet native speakers. Now I feel I can relate more with others what I've learned about Hispanic language and culture. To me, online activities provide meaningful contexts to master foreign language skills. I think every foreign language learner should take advantage of [the] endless resources on the Internet.

Networking, however, can be very frustrating and troublesome because of slow access and/or the lack of adequate numbers of computers at the times desired by the students. Because the limited number of computer stations had an impact on their free time, some students were unwilling to wait to use a computer. Of the thirty-one students in my classes this semester, eight students were not convinced about the value of using the Internet. One student said during the interview:

> It was difficult for me to find a time to talk with other students online. The extra half-hour required is *not* in the course catalog. When I made my schedule I was counting on three hours a week and then homework and studying on my own time. It can not be assumed that someone can just go to a computer lab and do work at any given time. There are often crowds, lines or network problems.

Other students pointed out the difficulty of obtaining Internet printouts due to the limited number of printers available and technical problems in the lab. A few students became discouraged. They said that they spent little time writing online and produced only short messages.

In their self-evaluations, four students who had never used the Internet before this project indicated that three hours of training were not enough, and they complained of frustration about the amount of time and energy they expended. Finally, they suggested that extra training time be provided for students who needed more guidance and assistance.

Reactions to Reading Online Newspapers

Based on the data drawn from the final interviews, most students agreed that newspapers had great potential for providing up-to-date knowledge of the world and enhancing cultural learning. These resources allowed them to explore and examine a variety of information as well as read authentic materials. In addition, students indicated that the cultural knowledge gained from online readings helped them reflect on their own culture and further compare the target culture with their own. For instance, one student began to look at his own culture from the perspective of the target culture through interacting with native speakers. This student remarked, "it was important for me to realize how lucky I am to be in the United States after knowing how much Mexicans have to struggle to survive, and some of them moved to this country to look for better opportunities."

Students also agreed that the topics proposed by the instructor via e-mail the day before the online discussion also helped them focus on specific readings in the newspapers. Students mentioned in their self-evaluations that they found most of the topics interesting and challenging (see Appendix E for a sampling of the topics). Some students reported that particular topics required them to learn specific vocabulary such as that related to natural phenomena like El Niño, the environment, and geography. A couple of students indicated that they preferred to read topics of their own choosing rather than the assigned topics, some of which they considered dull and boring, such as the latest news about taxes in Spain. One student admitted that she did not actively participate in some of the online chats because she was not interested in the topics and found it difficult to talk about things with which she was not familiar.

While some students claimed that they found it difficult to read and understand certain articles in the newspapers, they agreed that the use of online dictionaries, photos, and graphics helped them better comprehend and interpret the texts. Students further indicated that they learned a great deal of practical words and expressions from the newspapers, especially the terminology for professional needs such as in business and law. During the final interview, one student commented:

> I didn't really like to read newspapers online at first. But since it was part of the requirement of this course, I had no choice, but got myself accustomed to reading daily at most half an hour at the beginning. Then, I found myself not able to discuss topics online with my peers. I realized that I needed to pay more attention to the details when I read. I took notes for new words and expressions. Now I can read more and faster and I love it, especially CNN, my favorite site.

This student was able to articulate how his own strategies and his attitude changed over the course of the semester.

Reactions to Online Chats

Most students enjoyed using the chat room to interact and communicate with their peers and the instructor. According to their self-evaluations at the midpoint of the semester, students felt less anxious about using the target language and more comfortable expressing their ideas via online chats than at the beginning of the semester. Students appreciated the opportunities for using the target language outside the classroom. They liked the immediate feedback and collaborative responses online. One student who had used e-mail for his beginning Spanish class observed that, "it was much more fun to be able to receive the responses immediately via online chats than via e-mail. When I was online, I felt like I was communicating, negotiating, and exchanging information with others in a real-life situation. Chatting online is really a great way to reinforce one's language skills."

I found out that I had to come with better preparation to be able to be fully involved with the discussion.

Fifth-semester Spanish student

Final interviews with students showed that the students recognized the responsibility of making online conversation effective and productive. They understood how important it is to be well prepared and to get involved actively in the discussion. Students also acknowledged the value of working with their peers collaboratively. For example, during the final interview, several students commented on these realizations:

- I found out that I had to come with better preparation to be able to be fully involved with the discussion. I didn't think it was important for me to work with my peers until I realized that I also needed help from them to understand better their point of view.
- At first, I didn't like the idea of working in groups. Since I was in charge of printing the chat lines for my group, I had to remind myself to be on time and to ask for help when needed. The opportunity to use the chat room helped me build up a strong sense of responsibility and leadership.

The previous research shows that online communication encourages everyone, rather than some, to participate in the discussions. Kern (1995) and Warschauer (1996) demonstrate that students actually may benefit more from online chats than from conventional classroom discussion. One student commented on his self-evaluation, "I liked the idea of having an equal opportunity to participate in the online discussion, which is hard to find in a traditional classroom when the class is big and often dominated by some, but not all students." Later, when I asked this student to explain his point of view during the interview, he added:

I'm shy and I often don't like to speak in front of the class unless I'm called on. I also don't think the class time is enough for everyone to participate in everything. Online chats provided us with more opportunities to get ourselves involved in the discussion without feeling pressure. I think all the language courses should require students to use online chats. It was a very positive and rewarding personal learning experience for me.

When asked to compare the two chat rooms, one with their classmates and one with native speakers, some students preferred to interact with native speakers rather than with their own peers. One student who had strong linguistic skills commented:

> I disliked chatting with my classmates and I got frustrated with some of the basic questions my classmates asked during the online discussions. They should come better prepared to work together. I often felt that I had to repeatedly answer and clarify my point of view. [To] be honest, I preferred chatting with native speakers with whom I could communicate better and more.

This student continued:

> It sounded 'unnatural' to me when I communicated with my own peers because you don't really talk to your own people in another language. In my opinion, one acquires more 'real' language when talking with native speakers. For instance, I noticed that I have learned some useful Mexican idioms from online chats with native speakers.

On the other hand, some students indicated that they enjoyed interacting with their own peers more than with native speakers because they felt less anxious using the target language and asking questions. As students have varying levels of language proficiency and different learning styles, incorporating both kinds of online chats is a flexible way to appeal to a variety of learners.

The best thing about chatting online was that I learned to become actively involved in the discussions.

Fifth-semester Spanish student

The electronic tools allowed the students to monitor, reflect, and compose ideas at their own pace (Beauvois, 1997). During the interview, one of the students said:

> While using my linguistic skills as a means of communication with my peers via the online chat, I realized how important it is for me to understand others' ideas and to express myself effectively. At the beginning, I often felt frustrated at not being able to come up with what I wanted to say. I then had to slow down and found strategies for expressing my ideas coherently. The best thing about chatting online was that I learned to become actively involved in the discussions.

The process of composing messages also required students to use different learning strategies and styles for communication, an important factor in language competence (Oxford, 1990; Oxford & Ehrman, 1989). For instance, students reported that they often asked questions for clarification, a recognized communicative strategy (O'Malley & Chamot, 1990), when they had difficulty understanding messages from their peers. One student pointed out on the self-evaluation:

> I noticed how I had to change ways to make myself clear and understood when I answered the questions from my peers. Sometimes I realized that I misused Spanish words such as "realizar= to carry out" vs. "darse cuenta= to realize" or "atender= to assist" vs. "asistir= to attend" and I would correct my errors by repeating what I said in the right way. Self-correcting really worked out well for me. I'm now more aware of what I write.

In the interviews, students also reported that the use of synchronous online chats created a less stressful environment for foreign language learning than communicating in the classroom. As suggested by Beauvois (1993) and Horwitz and Young (1991), the lowering of learners' anxiety can have an impact on the quality of communication, as well as the degree of motivation. Students were more involved in the interactive activities. Students indicated that they expressed their ideas and opinions to others outside the classroom more willingly than when inside a traditional classroom. This is consistent with what other reserachers have reported in their studies (Coleman et al., 1992; Kelm, 1992; Pennington, 1996). For instance, one student commented in his self-evaluation:

> I usually don't like to participate in class because I often feel stupid when I make mistakes in Spanish. I had never used the chat room before, but I think the process of composing ideas and negotiating meanings via the chat room is a very effective way to reinforce language skills.

Students felt that online chats provided them with authentic written input and output, although some students who read slowly and poorly had difficulties understanding the words and expressions of others. Students reported that weekly online chats offered them a face-to-face-like interaction, and they felt that they were "virtually" in real-time communication with their peers. One student said with enthusiasm during the interview:

> I enjoyed so much chatting online and sometimes I didn't want to leave the room. It was as if I was talking to a group of people face-to-face. I could receive immediate responses and feedback from my peers even though I couldn't see them face-to-face.

This student added, "Online chats allowed me to freely express myself, to clarify ideas, and to ask and answer questions." Based on the printouts from the online chats, students' online writing showed that they used different strategies and discourse makers such as, "by the way," "anyway," "however," and "on the other hand," to express ideas and support opinions. Another interesting observation from the students was that they believed the process of composing online improved their thinking skills. They learned how to organize and analyze their ideas. Two students explained this as follows:

- When I wrote online, I learned how to make sense out of myself first, then I decided what I really wanted to say by using words like "first", "second", "finally" to organize my thoughts. I also observed how my peers expressed their ideas using different phrases such as "as if they were ..." and "by the way". I made myself use these expressions whenever I could.
- At first, I thought about English all the time before I wrote my ideas in Spanish. After writing online for a while, I noticed that I wouldn't have to go through English to write Spanish. My thinking skills have been improved from English to Spanish. It made me feel good about my Spanish.

Studies on computer-mediated communication have shown improvement of both oral and written communication of language learners (e.g., Beauvois, 1997; Kern, 1995, 1996; St. John & Cash, 1995). In order to measure students' overall oral skills, a taped Spanish oral test I developed based on the ACTFL Oral Proficiency Guidelines (American Council on the Teaching of Foreign Languages, 1986) was administered to the students at the beginning and the end of the semester. The test results indicated improvement in the students' speaking skills. This may suggest that successful written communication via online chats can lead to better oral communication as well.

Reactions to the Culture Portfolio

Portfolios provide the students with a meaningful way to reflect on their acquisition of the target language and culture. Most students reacted positively to the portfolio assessment. They enjoyed composing the portfolio and felt satisfied with the culture project. When asked about the experience of working on the portfolio, one student said:

> It was a lot of work, but it was worth it. The experience was very valuable to me because for the first time I learned how to set objectives, make plans, organize content, and self-assess my own work during the semester in order to produce good quality work.

Another student added:

Creating my own portfolio was a wonderful way to improve my critical thinking skills and made me take responsibility for my own learning. Besides it helped me monitor my learning progress. The monthly self-evaluation was also very helpful. It allowed me to track areas of strengths and weaknesses and fix problems before I handed in the work for the final grade.

The use of portfolio assessment to focus on the learning process, in conjunction with traditional testing focused on product, offers a balance in evaluating students' work. In addition, the portfolio is a means of offering students a significant language-learning experience that fosters their self-confidence and motivates them. For example, during the final interview, one student said:

What I liked the most about this course was the portfolio assessment. I believe it is the most effective way to evaluate students' performance. I not only learned specific areas of Hispanic culture using Internet resources, but also I learned to take control of my learning. At the beginning, I was overwhelmed by the amount of work I had to do for this project. Later, I was able to engage in the process by following the instructions and worked very hard to accomplish my goals. At the end of the project, I was really proud of myself when I handed in my final portfolio. I would like to have opportunities to work on other projects using the portfolio assessment.

Conclusion and Pedagogical Implications

Foreign language students need to have opportunities to use the target language and acquire the target culture outside the classroom. Online interactions promote more equality of participation, which is particularly beneficial for those students who are reluctant to speak out in the traditional classroom setting. The online activities described in this chapter not only provided students with a meaningful way to practice their language skills (Communication Goal) but also allowed them to explore Hispanic culture and to develop both target and native culture perspectives (Cultures and Comparisons Goals). Most importantly, online discussions via chat rooms helped students develop their critical thinking skills and their willingness to assume responsibility for their learning.

The process of using the four-phases of the FACE model—Facilitation, Access, Collaboration and Evaluation—for Internet activities allowed students to become independent and reflective language learners. With the instructor's assistance and guidance, students were held accountable in making decisions and in contributing time and effort to carry out Internet activities effectively and successfully. Using the FACE model as a framework also created a learner-driven and stimulating atmosphere where learners shared and exchanged ideas with each other to gain valuable language-learning experiences. The students showed the willingness to work together and establish classroom community where they put their language knowledge to use and to communicate with their classmates in the target language.

Additionally, this work with learners in an online environment has implications for the future of computer-assisted language learning. To achieve significant impact on foreign language education, accessibility to computer technology must be improved (Bush, 1997). This project stresses the necessity of making computers more accessible to students so that Internet resources may become an integral part of foreign language teaching and learning. Clearly, increasing the number of available computers and providing adequate training in using the Internet are prerequisites for integrating instructional technology into foreign language education. Students with advanced computer skills should be encouraged to produce their work online in order to share the information they have gathered with other foreign language learners who use the Internet. Foreign language teachers interested in integrating the Internet into their teaching are encouraged to explore and experiment with web-based instruction using the FACE model.

References

American Council on the Teaching of Foreign Languages. (1986). *ACTFL Proficiency Guidelines*. Hastings-on-Hudson, NY: ACTFL.

Barson, J., Frommer, J., & Schwartz, M. (1993). Foreign language learning using e-mail in a task-oriented perspective: Interuniversity experiments in communication and collaboration. *Journal of Science Education and Technology, 2*(4), 565–584.

Beauvois, M. H. (1992). Computer-assisted classroom discussion in the foreign language classroom: Conversation in slow motion. *Foreign Language Annals, 25*(5), 455–464.

Beauvois, M. H. (1993). E-talk: Empowering students through electronic discussion in the foreign language classroom. *The Ram's Horn VII*, 41–47.

Beauvois, M. H. (1994). E-talk: Attitudes and motivation in computer-assisted classroom discussion. *Computers and the Humanities 28*, 177–190.

Beauvois, M. H. (1997). Computer-mediated communication (CMC): Technology for improving speaking and writing. In M. D. Bush & R. M. Terry (Eds.), *Technology-enhanced language learning* (pp. 165–184). ACTFL Foreign Language Education Series. Lincolnwood, IL: National Textbook Company.

Beauvois, M. H. (1998). Write to speak: The effects of electronic communication on the oral achievement of fourth-semester French students. In J. A. Muyskens (Ed.), *New ways of learning and teaching: Focus on technology and foreign language education* (pp. 93–116). AAUSC Issues in Language Program Direction. Boston: Heinle & Heinle Publishers.

Bush, M. D. (1997). Implementing technology for language teaching. In M. D. Bush & R. M. Terry (Eds.), *Technology-enhanced language learning* (pp. 287–350). ACTFL Foreign Language Education Series. Lincolnwood, IL: National Textbook Company.

Canale, M., & Swain, M. (1980). Theoretical bases of communicative approaches to second language teaching and testing. *Applied Linguistics 1*, 1–47.

Chun, D. M. (1994). Using computer networking to facilitate the acquisition of interactive competence. *System, 22*, 17–31.

Coleman, D. W., Crookall, D., & Oxford, R. L. (1992). Computer-mediated language learning environments. *Computer-Assisted Language Learning, 5*, 93–120.

Cononelos, T., & Oliva, M. (1993). Using computer networks to enhance foreign language/culture education. *Foreign Language Annals, 26*(4), 527–533.

Ellis, R. (1988). *Classroom second language development.* London: Prentice Hall.

González-Bueno, M. (1998). The effect of electronic mail on Spanish L2 discourse. *Language Learning and Technology.* [Online serial], *1*(2), 55–70. Retrieved January 11, 1999, from the World Wide Web: http://polyglot.cal. msu.edu/llt.

Horwitz, E. K., & Young, D. J. (1991*). Language anxiety: From theory and research to classroom implications.* Englewood Cliffs, NJ: Prentice-Hall.

Johnson, D., & Johnson, R. (1985). Cooperative learning: One key to computer assisted learning. *The Computing Teacher, 13*(2), 11–15.

Kelm, O. R. (1992). The use of synchronous computer networks in second language instruction: A preliminary report. *Foreign Language Annals 25*(5), 441–454.

Kern, R. G. (1995). Restructuring classroom interaction with networked computers: Effects on quantity and characteristics of language production. *The Modern Language Journal, 79*, 457–76.

Kern, R. G. (1996). Computer-mediated communication: Using e-mail exchanges to explore personal histories in two cultures. In M. Warschauer (Ed.), *Telecollaboration in foreign language learning: Proceedings of the Hawaii symposium* (pp. 105–119). Honolulu, HI: University of Hawaii, Second Language Teaching and Curriculum Center.

Knight, S. (1994). Making authentic cultural and linguistic connections. *Hispania, 77*(2), 288–294.

Kramsch, C. J. (1987). Interactive discourse in small and large groups. In W. Rivers (Ed.), *Interactive language teaching* (pp. 17–30). New York: Cambridge University Press.

Kuttenberg, B. M., & Zeller, I. (1997). Transcontinental links via e-mail. *Northeast Conference Newsletter 42*, 42–50.

Lafford, P. T., & Lafford, B. A. (1997). Learning language and culture with internet technologies. In M. D. Bush & R. M. Terry (Eds*.), Technology-enhanced language learning* (pp. 215–262). Lincolnwood, IL: National Textbook Company.

Lee, L. (1997a). Using portfolios to develop L2 cultural knowledge and awareness of students in intermediate Spanish. *Hispania, 80*, 355–367.

Lee, L. (1997b). Using Internet tools as an enhancement of C2 teaching and learning. *Foreign Language Annals, 30*(3), 410–427.

Lunde, K. R. (1990). Using electronic mail as a medium for foreign languages study and instruction. *CALICO Journal, 7*, 68–78.

National Standards in Foreign Language Education Project. (1996). *Standards for foreign language learning: Preparing for the 21st century.* Yonkers, NY: Author.

Nunan, D. (1992). *Collaborative language learning and teaching.* New York: Cambridge University Press.

Oliva, M., & Pollastrini, Y. (1995). Internet resources and second language acquisition: An evaluation of virtual immersion. *Foreign Language Annals, 28*(4), 551–559.

O'Malley, J. M., & Chamot, A. U. (1990). *Learning strategies in second language acquisition.* New York: Cambridge University Press.

Oxford, R. (1990). *Language learning strategies: What every teacher should know.* New York: Newbury House/Harper & Row.

Oxford, R., & Ehrman, M. (1989). Psychological type and adult language learning strategies: A pilot study. *Journal of Psychological Type, 16*, 22–32.

Pennington, M. C. (1996). *The computer and the non-native writer: A natural partnership.* Cresskill, NJ: Hampton Press.

St. John, E., & Cash, D. (1995). Language learning via e-mail: Demonstrable success with German. In M. Warschauer (Ed.), *Virtual connections: Online activities and projects for networking language learners* (pp. 191–197). Honolulu, HI: University of Hawaii, Second Language Teaching & Curriculum Center.

Sanaoui, R., & Lapkin, S. (1992). A case study of an FSL senior secondary course integrating computer networking. *Canadian Modern Language Review, 48*, 525–553.

Savignon, S. J. (1983). *Communicative competence: Theory and classroom practice.* Reading, MA: Addison-Wesley.

Sutherland, R., Anderson, K., & Van Handle, D. (1995, June). Internet: The ultimate collaborative learning environment. Paper presented at CALICO '95 Annual Symposium, Middlebury, Vermont.

Swain, M., & Lapkin, S. (1986). Immersion French in secondary schools: The goods and the bads. *Contact, 5*, 2–9.

Swain, M., & Wong Fillmore, L. (1984, March). Child second language development: Views from the field on theory and research. Paper presented at TESOL Convention, Houston, Texas.

Vygotsky, L. S. (1978). *Mind in society: The development of higher psychological processes.* Cambridge, MA: Harvard University Press.

Warschauer, M. (1996). Motivational aspects of using computers for writing and communication. In M. Warschauer (Ed.), *Telecollaboration in foreign language learning: Proceedings of the Hawaii symposium* (pp. 64–81). Honolulu, HI: University of Hawaii, Second Language Teaching & Curriculum Center.

Appendix A. Guidelines for the Culture Project

I. Objectives

Increasing your knowledge of Hispanic culture is an extremely important part of your language-learning process. Therefore, the purpose of this project is for you to carry out some research on cultural aspects of Spain, Mexico, or another Latin American country. You should select one area of interest (see the handout for possible topics) and start reading materials on the Internet. You should incorporate some of the information you gather for this project in your writing assignments and oral presentations for this course. In addition, you are required to use the chat room and/or e-mail to communicate and discuss the cultural aspects of your research with your peers and/or instructor.

II. Procedures

1. Select the topic that interests you most.
2. List three major components/aspects you want to investigate about the topic.
3. See your instructor for advice or suggestions.
4. Start searching for sources via the Internet. Spanish magazines, newspapers, videotapes, and books are also good resources.
5. Write a 4–5 page final report in Spanish.

6. Share your project with your instructor at the end of the semester.

III. Criteria for evaluation
Your project will be evaluated based on the following:

1. Complete draft of your paper   30%
2. Final copy of your paper   40%
3. Supporting materials   10%
4. Oral interview   20%

Each item will be graded on its content, organization, language, style, and appropriateness.

Appendix B. Monthly Self-Evaluation

This worksheet is to help you evaluate your own progress in learning Spanish language and culture.

Checklist: Which of the following activities have you been participating in?
1. Have you been reading online newspapers?
2. Have you been writing weekly journals?
3. Have you been participating in "Hora de Café?
4. Have you been chatting online?
5. Have you been keeping printouts of online chats in your portfolio?

Reflective Questions
6. What other things have you been doing to improve your Spanish?
7. What specific areas of Spanish do you think you need to improve? Why?
8. What have you learned from the online activities?
9. Which of the Internet activities have you enjoyed the most? Please briefly explain.
10. What have you learned about yourself as a learner by doing this culture project?

Appendix C. Survey of Your Experience with Online Activities

Please fill out this questionnaire as honestly as possible. Your answers are absolutely confidential. Thank you very much for your time and effort.

	SA	A	N	D	SD
1. Online activities helped me improve my language skills in general.	5	4	3	2	1
2. I enjoyed reading online newspapers.	5	4	3	2	1

3. Online newspapers helped my reading skills in Spanish.	5	4	3	2	1
4. Reading online newspapers increased my knowledge of Spanish vocabulary.	5	4	3	2	1
5. Online newspapers helped me to better understand Hispanic people and culture.	5	4	3	2	1
6. Online chats helped me write better in Spanish.	5	4	3	2	1
7. I enjoyed using the chat room weekly.	5	4	3	2	1
8. I felt comfortable discussing topics via the online chat room.	5	4	3	2	1
9. I would like to use Internet technology for my other Spanish courses in the future.	5	4	3	2	1

SA=strongly agree (5), A=agree (4), N=no opinion (3), D=disagree (2), SD=strongly disagree (1)

10. What aspect(s) of the Internet activities did you find the most and the least useful/enjoyable in learning Spanish? (Be specific.)
11. What were the most difficult things you found in the online activities? (Be specific.)
12. What comments/suggestions do you have to improve the online activities?

Appendix D. End-of-Semester Oral Interview Questions

1. Briefly explain your experience in creating this project.
2. Describe your experience doing the online activities.
3. Share with me some of the cultural information in your portfolio.
4. Tell me what materials you used to support your culture project, including where and how you found the materials.
5. Explain the most valuable and interesting part of this project and why.
6. Describe the most difficult or least important part of this project and why.
7. Tell me if this project met your original goals for culture learning and why.
8. Overall, tell me how the experience of this project improved your language skills.

Appendix E. Sample Topics for Online Discussion

1. President Clinton's trip to Brazil, Argentina and Venezuela
2. Puerto Ricans and U.S. radar plan for drug traffic
3. Urgent action in Chiapas, Mexico
4. Princess Diana and the car accident
5. The debate about coded information on the Internet
6. Gabriel García Márquez and the Cervantes Award
7. Clara Janés, the winner of the National Translation Prize
8. Mother Teresa: India's saint
9. The wedding of Cristina to Iñaki in Barcelona
10. The Sahara and its people
11. El Niño news and resources
12. Current political situation in Chile
13. The President of China in Mexico
14. The Cuban writer Guillermo Cabrera Infante and the Cervantes Award in Literature
15. Soccer tournament (1997–1998) in Latin America

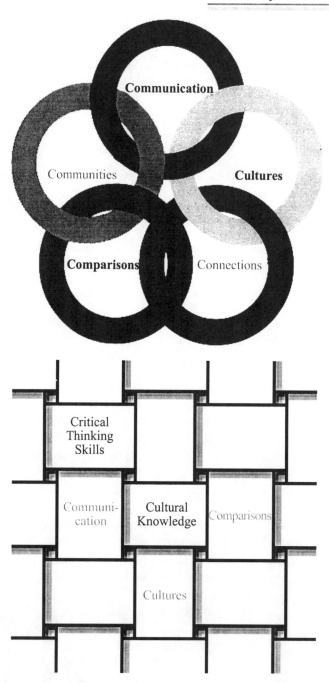

Bridges and Boundaries: Growing the Cross-Cultural Mind

Vicki Galloway

Georgia Institute of Technology

Yo soy yo y mi circunstancia.

José Ortega y Gasset

O n the Mexican side of the Bridge of the Americas that both joins and separates El Paso and Juárez, a giant Mexican flag was recently erected to "remind the Mexican citizens that live here about our history and our laws" (to quote President Ernesto Zedillo). But the installation of this enormous flag sparked a furor among some El Paso residents, who then clamored for the raising of an even more massive Stars-and-Stripes on the U.S. side of the bridge. While the Mexican government claimed that the flag served to symbolize solidarity, cultural pride, and historical conscience—a drawing in of border cities to the collective heart of a nation, outraged El Paso residents measured the flagpole and called their local officials in protest. From one side of the border, the flag was viewed as an adversarial defiance of border-guarding efforts, a territorial encroachment, a burlesque of U.S. grandeur, a challenge to duel. From the other side came a different perspective (translated here):

> Can't those El Paso residents see that the flag has nothing to do with them, nor with their city? As I see it, that gigantic Mexican flag only indicates

that, yes, Mexico is there, and isn't it beautiful? It's a matter of pride, folks. And when it comes to pride, Mexicans rank second to none. (Olvera, 1997)

Indignation was unleashed far from the border as well. A letter to the editor of an Atlanta newspaper responds to two questions posed in a previous issue of the newspaper: "Why are Americans so angry about this Mexican flag?" and "If we switched borders in this situation, would we find a Canadian flag so controversial?"

Concerning the flap over a 300-pound Mexican flag at the U.S. border, a letter writer ... says that if the flag were Canadian, there would be no controversy. The writer is comparing oranges and apples by comparing Canada, a country almost like ours, with a—let's face it—Third World country, from which so many of its citizens are flooding across our borders daily. (Lerch, 1997)

Lest one be tempted to characterize this controversy as a clash of cultural perspectives, it bears reminding that to experience such conflict one must be aware that another perspective exists. It is the assumption of sameness that triggers facile interpretation, immediate judgment, and turgid culture-ranking criteria. As Lévi-Strauss has stated, perhaps the true contribution of a culture consists precisely in its *difference* from others. He captures our mission as teachers of foreign languages and cultures:

The sense of gratitude and respect which each single member of a given culture can and should feel towards all others can only be based on the conviction that the other cultures differ from his own in countless ways, even if the ultimate essence of these differences eludes him or if, in spite of his best efforts, he can reach no more than an imperfect understanding of them. (1995, p. 7)

In the flag-raising story lie two metaphors to guide our classroom culture-teaching efforts: *bridges* and *boundaries.* Just as the Bridge of the Americas allows effortless movement of one's own cultural baggage across borders, in our classrooms, pre-fab culture bridges do not on their own expose or challenge pre-judgment of cultures, do not on their own lift the veil of ethnocentrism that impedes the perception of other values, perspectives, and patterns of thought. As they join the selected coordinates of two distinct realities, bridges blend and blur boundaries. We recognize these "bridges" in the foreign language classroom: our untiring efforts to summarize, describe, encapsulate, factualize, and sanitize a culture for boxed delivery to students. To tame and contain this tentacled creature, we present *highlights*; we deliver *impressions*: "The extended family is very important to Hispanics;" "the French have five weeks of vacation per year," "Germans value order and structure." But while such generalizations may ring "true" from *our perspective,* they will never be wholly accurate, since their real meaning simply cannot be accommodated by an *outsider's* frame of reference. Moreover, having no other sense-making system for the intake of these data, learners simply superimpose their own culture's template (Galloway, 1992, 1997).

Bridges of culture facts produce only fiction: not the *real* culture, but a hybrid warped in reference to our own; not its *internal* sense, but the sense we have given it; not its inner dynamic, but only the blips it displays on our own culture's radar screen. As Kramsch notes, "What we should seek in cross-cultural education are less bridges than a deep understanding of the boundaries. We can teach the boundary, we cannot teach the bridge" (1993, p. 228). It is precisely the boundaries, the defining edges of *separate realities* that we must have learners discover and negotiate as we guide them not only to enter the other culture *on its own terms*, but also to re-enter their own. And surely there is nothing easy, quick, efficient, or neat about this process.

In this chapter, "teaching" culture in the foreign language classroom will be viewed as growing the cross-cultural mind. Implicit in this view is a distinction between assessing the *products* of discrete performance and fostering the *process* of inquiry; between the rigidity of measurable *knowledge* and the flexibility of measurement-resistant ways of thinking; between delivering to the unquestioning student and eliciting from the reflective learner; and between classrooms directed toward the avoidance of conflict and those engaged in its recognition and negotiation. In their essay, "Maturing Outcomes," Costa and Garmston posit an authentic vision for continuous lifelong learning as one that reaches beyond the presentation of disparate facts or the performance of discrete activities to connect to broader transcendent meanings and processes, to tap the wellsprings or energy sources that create wonderment and fuel human thinking (1998). Indeed, our commitment to nurturing the cross-cultural mind may require reinvigorating energies and redirecting our focus from that of lower-level *instructional* mechanics to that of the "mature" *educational* outcomes, deep learning processes, and complex thinking traits that serve lifelong learning.

A true commitment to cross-cultural communication requires nothing less than an honest "paradigm shift" in our classroom construct of teaching culture. Rosado defines a paradigm shift as a movement away from taken-for-granted boundaries and old explanations that no longer capture reality to accommodate the emergence of a new way of thinking, valuing, and perceiving the world (1997). The publication of the *National Stand-*

ards for Foreign Language Learning (1996), a cluster of "broadly conceived purposes and objectives for language study" (Phillips, 1997,
p. xii), claims to capture this paradigm shift and is perceived by some as
the course that is "set" for foreign language educators (Jeffries, 1996).
Indeed, one need only peruse the assorted "standards-based" curriculum
guides and workshop announcements via the Internet to appreciate their
enthusiastic reception in the foreign language teaching community. Yet,
confusion persists in defining the place of culture in our language-teach-
ing perspectives and practices: A standards-based workshop an-
nouncement, for example, bears the title "Culture as the Core," but describes the aim of the workshop as *"integrating* culture *into an established*
language curriculum."

National standards cannot be magic bridges to transport us beyond our
own tired boundaries; they cannot guide our investment in the "mature"
outcomes that are needed to grow cross-cultural minds. If standards
merely entice us to tweak established curricula, if we respond to them by
simply sandwiching in a new "culture unit around standard 2.2" or by
dressing up old practices in the fashion of the moment, we will not have
altered the cross-cultural landscape of foreign language education. As
Rosado (1997) cautions, we cannot become what we need to be by remaining what we are.

This chapter will use the broad goal areas of the National Standards as
vantage points from which to derive a new vision of cross-cultural education in the belief that "whether the goal is Communication, Connections, Comparisons, or Communities, Cultures are the recurring subtext"
(Schwartz & Kavanaugh, 1997, p. 99). Along the way we will hear the
voices of emerging cross-cultural minds as classroom learners negotiate
the boundaries of other realities and construct their own bridges of understanding. These learner voices reveal the very personal and individual
process of cross-cultural learning. These voices tell us what is authentic
and real about cross-cultural conflict, and they *teach us* how to be, first
and foremost, teachers of culture.

A true commitment to cross-cultural communication requires nothing less than an honest
"paradigm shift" in our classroom construct of
teaching culture.

Culture as "Products, Practices, and Perspectives"

"Culture is not one thing. I'm starting to believe it's everything."

"Mac," second-year Spanish student

A sign in the elevator of a (presumably reputable) Paris hotel, reads "Please leave your values at the front desk." By its somewhat jarring error, the sign reminds us that meaning is not in words but in minds. To share a language—a culture—is to share assumptions of meaning. A most difficult lesson for foreign language learners is precisely that of assumption and expectation: Because they are parts of different sense-making systems, words from one language do not have facile or entirely reliable counterparts in another; indeed, they may codify meanings or clusters of meanings in one culture that are entirely alien to another. Foreign words that appear conceptually straightforward or even formally similar to those of another language and culture may bundle entirely different ranges and fields of significance. While within one's own frame of reference, one's own language seems sensible and cohesive, it will likely appear arbitrary and chaotic to the outsider who lives a different reality. For this reason, as *language* teachers, we guide learners to make sense of the new language by discovering its own internal patterns; we guide them to *construct* a system of communication separate and unblended with their own.

But language is only part of the communication system called culture. Language thrives only through the lifeblood of culturally shared meanings, perceptions, and values. This same process of construction, then, is required in our approach to teaching culture for, just as in language, one culture's "logic" is not accessible through another culture's values. Indeed, perhaps the Paris hotel sign should be hung in our own classrooms for, in a culture-learning context, its unintentional message takes on new significance: "This is an other-culture construction site. Please leave your values at the front desk."

The *National Standards for Foreign Language Learning* include two broad goal statements that represent culture learning as the development of an understanding of the practices and products of a culture in terms of the perspectives of the culture that creates and maintains them. These products, practices, and perspectives roughly correspond to Wells's categorization of the "resources" (1994) and Even-Zohar's "repertoire" of a

culture (1997). While at the literal level, the *Standards* invoke relationships between practices and perspectives and between products and perspectives, the undercurrent of these statements is that of meaningful interdependence. Indeed, to limit classroom culture teaching to the display
or presentation of a culture's products, such as a food item or a musical
piece; or to isolate practices, such as greetings or dining customs; or to
focus solely on perspectives through impressions and generalizations, is
to remove threads from a fabric—once loosened and separated they become insignificant or, worse, connect unnaturally in learners' minds to
form grotesque patterns. As one teacher remarked:

> ... my students do not seem to be impacted by the cultural information being
> presented. They are not able to identify with the cultural information be-
> cause although it may be interesting, it is not relevant to them, and what
> cultural information they do learn seems to come off as trivial knowledge
> that has little effect on them or their lives. (Schwartz and Kavanaugh, 1997,
> p. 105)

Perhaps our mission itself requires a context shift: from "I teach language (and culture if there's time)" to "I teach *culture*, through the tools
of its language." Indeed, if we take as our primary mission the development of cross-cultural communication, the language will lend its adapt-
ability, versatility, and malleability to every learning context. A language
agenda where culture never fits will be exchanged for a culture agenda
where language is the currency. And just as we would never think of
teaching language by simply handing students a dictionary, we cannot
think of teaching culture as "presenting" students discrete products or
practices. Cross-cultural minds are grown from the inside. If our aim is
to develop the traits of reflection, introspection, and critical analysis, our
efforts will focus on nurturing self-direction in the individual (see also
Wenden, this volume). Thus, the repertoire of product, practice, and perspective is not limited to teacher lesson plans but should be shared with
learners as their *own* resource for cross-cultural observation, inquiry, reflection, and discovery.

For learners to observe a culture critically, they must be given the tools
from the beginning (see Galloway, 1992, for activities that foster cross-
cultural discovery and connection in the foreign language classroom).
During the second week of a first-year, first-quarter Spanish class, for
example, students were taught the words *producto, práctica, perspectiva*
as tools for observing their own culture and others. In their first assignment with these tools, they were to write the title "Mi cultura" at the top
of the page and, under the heading "Productos," to choose from their

textbook vocabulary the words for at least four things they would consider "products" (television, quiz, notes, free time, etc.*)*. They then listed words related to these products under the category of either "Prácticas" (e.g., listening, learning, watching, writing, studying) or "Perspectivas" (e.g., easy, difficult, work, rest), as in Figure 1. When they had completed their lists, they were to draw as many connecting lines as possible to capture their own associations of products to practices, practices to perspectives, perspectives to products, and so on. As anticipated, a task the students initially thought would be easy, ultimately produced frustration, with lines crossing over, superimposing, circling so many other lines that many students remarked apologetically, "You won't be able to read this. Can I copy it over?"

Figure 1. *Mi cultura*
Productos
televisión
prueba
apuntes
ratos libres

Prácticas	*Perspectivas*
mirar	trabajo
escuchar	fácil
aprender	difícil
escribir	descanso
estudiar	

Indeed, these students had just learned their first lesson about the "messiness" of culture. They were reminded that these three aspects are a way of looking at a culture and that they had just looked at their own. In a paired task, they were then to take two of the "products" and devise statements to explain their connecting lines, with the sole requirement that each statement begin either with *Aquí...* ("Here ...") or *En mi cultura*.... While their linguistic tools were very limited at this earliest stage of learning, their personal messages came through clearly: "Aquí, mirar televisión y estudiar es difícil (fácil)." "Aquí, televisión es descanso y necesito aprender." "Aquí, necesito estudiar con (sin) televisión." "Aquí, no hay televisión, hay trabajo." "Aquí, en clase, televisión es aprender, no descanso." "No mirar televisión es fácil (difícil)." Their statements illustrated not only the wealth of variations of products in practice and the changing nature of products in use, but the changing nature of all components according to the constellation. Aspects of their own "U.S. student culture" surfaced as well: The linkage of the product *television* with the practice of *studying*, either as an aid or an intrusion; the conflict of *rest* or *leisure* with the obligation to *work*; the distinction between *learning* and *free time*. Their final task was to convert their statements into questions for interviewing five classmates. And from classmates' responses, they summarized the variety of individual preferences that exist among the options generated by a people. These learner-generated data allowed the formation of some conclusions, recorded in simple Spanish on the board and copied in students' "culture-learning notebooks":

- *En una cultura, un producto≠ una práctica ≠ una perspectiva.*
- *Una cultura = gente y personas* ("the group and the individual")

One additional, critical, cross-cultural observation surfaced in this particular lesson with beginning students: the difficulty of expressing the meanings of one culture through the code of another. A student observed: *"¿Trabajo es una perspectiva? ¿Es un producto? ¿Es una práctica?* ("Is 'work' a perspective, a product, or a practice?"). Indeed, the word "work," saturated with the sense of U.S. culture, evokes all of these: a product, a practice, a moral principle, a "doing" way of seeing the world. Students were asked to brainstorm the ways we use the word "work" in English: A machine, an idea *works*; one *works* out to exercise but also *works out* a plan, *works up* a sweat, *works off* the pounds, *works* it all *into* his schedule; he can *work* something loose, *work* someone hard, *work on* someone to change his mind, *work up* to a confession, even order a hamburger with *the works*. Yet, as students would discover in subsequent lessons, the words *trabajo* and *trabajar*, while dictionary translations of "work," neither extend the same ranges or fields of meaning nor codify the same constructs. Words are products of their cultures. And cultures are different. On the board was written a third statement:

- *Un idioma es el producto de su cultura. Una cultura≠otra cultura ∴ un idioma ≠ otro idioma*

As students then "entered" the Hispanic world through authentic texts that carried its voices, their culture-processing tools were applied, sharpened, conceptually refined. Moreover, learners began to *own* these tools;

as one student expressed in her course evaluation, they became the "curse" of their cultural complacency.

Products and Goods

Products are all that a culture conceives, creates, or uses to mediate activity; they may be material (clothing, shelter, transportation, food, tools, literature, etc.) or abstract (ideas, rules, norms, laws, organizational structures, modes of thought and expression, and so on). Without doubt, the most powerful and versatile of a culture's products, the "master product" that mediates all others, is language. But, like language, all products are codified, symbolic in some sense, as they arise from and are embedded in their culture's own distinctive "web of significance" (Geertz, 1973, p. 4). Products, or artifacts, in their constant social processes of construction, consumption, and negotiation, connect humans to each other within the loosely shared associational framework that is their culture's reality. Indeed, even though we may casually remark that a person is a "product" of his or her culture, we recognize that persons are not merely products of a culture, but also its constructive participants, "actively creating a world that is always in the process of creating them" (Gover & Conway, 1997).

At even the earliest levels of foreign language learning we may guide students' entrance into another culture using the notion of "product" to plant the seeds of cross-cultural inquiry and the strategic habits that encourage complex thought and reflection. Artifact-study techniques, for example, use a common cultural product to elicit an exhaustive list of questions and then share speculations: What is it made of? What is it similar to? Where, how is it used? Who is its user? Where is it found (*not* found)? What is its value, significance? and so on. Such techniques, aside from developing good habits of inquiry, hypothesis formation, and divergent thinking, encourage learners to see products not as mere objects, but as meaning-and context-driven tools that function in systems where everything is connected. A simple styrofoam coffee cup, for example, can be used to generate thinking not only about the connectedness of one's own U.S. culture, but about the perspectives that drive and align this system of connections. In a first-year Spanish class, the styrofoam cup was used to help students capture the U.S. thought-and-action network that embeds the notion of "disposability" as pre-reading for a series of authentic Hispanic texts that exposed a different perspective on the notion of "worn goods"— one reflected in the practices of repair, renovation, conversion, recycling. In a second-year Spanish class discussing cities, environment, and public welfare, it was used to capture U.S. "lifestyle" in terms of the perspectives that power it and the products and practices that support it and ensure its perpetuation: Following up a Hispanic newspaper article on "garbageology," students were instructed to analyze one aspect of U.S. culture through the styrofoam coffee cup. A glance at some essay titles reveals, via just one artifact, the intricate connections between U.S. issues of time, health, mobility, environment, and consumption habits.

> *Conducir con mi taza de poliestireno* ["Driving with my Styrofoam Cup"];
> *Rápido. Tengo prisa* ["Make it Fast! I'm in a Hurry"]; *Así comemos y así
> moriremos* ["As We Eat, So We Die"]; *Lecciones de salud en una pequeña
> taza* ["Health Lessons in a Little Cup"]; *¿Botar o reciclar?* ["To Toss or
> Recycle?"]; *En el año 2050 se ve la misma taza* ["In 2050 the Same Cup Is
> Seen"]; *Mi basura y yo* ["My Trash and I"]

In an intermediate-level Business Spanish class, students played the roles of market analysts for a styrofoam cup manufacturer that wished to sell the product in Latin America. Their task was to explain in detail, citing specific evidence, why it would or would not "sell" within these cultures, with each student presenting a different aspect of the argument. In each of these cases, a product was used to help learners define what it means *to be* within their boundaries, to see systemic aspects of their own culture and claim its ownership, to reach into their culture to pull out something whose roots resist separation. In each of these cases, the notion of "product" was not as simple as it seemed.

Among those things that a culture considers its products, Even-Zohar distinguishes those that are "tools" from those that are perceived as "goods" by the culture (1997). Goods are a culture's properties, both tangible and intangible, that are valued as indicators of status or prestige. While one culture's concrete "good" may be a private swimming pool, another's may be running water. While one culture's abstract good may be durable friendship, another's may be self-sufficiency. The potential for *acquiring* goods is likewise defined by the culture that proclaims their value: While one culture may reference the acquisition potential of these goods *outside* the realm of individual control, in decree of fate or birthright, another may reference it *outside* the individual but *inside* the force of the collective, and still another may reference it *entirely inside* the individual and thus conclude that these goods lie within reach of all those who are willing to exert the *effort.* So powerful are these notions that, indeed, those whose views differ will not "speak the same language." As

Even-Zohar notes, one culture's notion of valued products is not only non-exportable, it is intrinsically judgmental:

> Goods which cannot be evaluated by an established market cannot have value and therefore are not marked as "culture." Therefore, social entities may be labeled as "having no culture" by other social entities, if diagnosed as not being in possession of the required and acknowledged set of goods. (1997, p. 20)

In the attempt to avoid such judgment, classroom teachers may shy away from all but bland, U.S.-conforming images of other cultures; in response to teachers, textbook publishers may use non-controversial stock photos that depict not "middle-class" in context, but what middle class *looks like* to U.S. students. Yet, we cannot guide learners to examine their own "product-goods" mind-set, much less achieve mature understanding of another, if we present only illusions in fear of the "conflict" or judgment that may arise from authentic images. A class of second-year Spanish students was shown two photos of a Salvadoran family at home: one of the family gathered around the dinner table, the other of a mother and daughter hanging laundry on a line in back of their house. Students were given 30 seconds to look at the photos and then write down *one impression*, supported by the particular observations or evidence that fed the impression. The following typical response (translated here) captures the students'-observers' perception of "poverty" as the *absence of expected* products.

Impression: It's a poor family.

Evidence: There is no refrigerator, no washing machine. The stove is very small. There are lots of calendars on the wall. There are no rooms, only curtains to separate. Water for washing clothes and dishes is in "bowls" outside. The light is small [there is little light?]. The bathroom is outdoors.

For the majority of these students, "looking for" had replaced "seeing." In follow-up to this first observation task, they were asked to discuss what *they* would feel like being there: Would they be uncomfortable? Why or why not? Those who answered "yes," invariably cited the outdoor toilet. Many commented on how much work would be involved in maintaining a household without plumbing. Students were then asked to observe the photos again, now describing what was *there* instead of what was "missing." This time they were able to see the products (material and abstract) valued by the family itself: the carefully tended flowers that blossomed in pots in the back yard; the pictures on the calendars tacked to the walls (a mother reading to her child, the Last Supper, a family at dinner, angels, a nature scene); the snapshots of a young girl in a white dress, two small children smiling; the tidy array of water basins and the immaculateness of the home; the family sharing in dinner conversation, the mother and daughter helping each other at work. Then they were shown the note handwritten on the back of one of the photos. It was from the *señora* of this Salvadoran family and read in Spanish: "This is my mansion." As a homework assignment, students were given the following writing task: "Write a letter to this Salvadoran family describing *your* "mansion." Before writing, think about what you learned from class discussion and your own observations of the family in the photo: What will you focus on in your description?"

Practices and Perspectives

Viewing a culture solely in terms of observable products presents a dangerous perception trap, for the invention and implementation of all forms of product reside in *practice* or activity. In a very real sense, products have no meaning out of the context of activity. But just as the notion of "product" is not confined to tangible objects, the notion of "practice" is not confined to physical or observable action. *Practice* refers to the human activity that simultaneously codifies and decodes the products. In isolation, neither products nor practices can inform. By the same token, no observation of products in practice will inform *solely* about one aspect of the culture, for as there is no simple, one-to-one relationship between *product* and meaning, there is no such simple relationship between *practice* and meaning or between *product* and *practice*—all are intricately and intimately connected.

It is often the seemingly so familiar that most perplexes, for perceived familiarity tempts the observer to infuse his own culture's associational framework. In Hispanic cultures, the cluster of practices embedded in the familiar context of job application is a typical example: U.S. Spanish students studying hiring practices in the Hispanic world are often quick to judge Hispanic job advertising as "discriminatory" in its obvious specification of sex, age, marital status, or physical appearance; likewise with résumé requirements of photo, birth date, and professions of the applicant's parents. In job-interview simulations where, as in the Hispanic world, questions are not confined to an applicant's educational and professional credentials but may probe any aspect of the applicant's "total person," students are invariably startled to receive a question regarding their "personal" lives ("You can't ask that!") and often become uncomfortable when pushed to respond. Into these Hispanic hiring and job-seeking contexts, learners typically infuse their own culture's notions of "public" and "private," assume their own culture's "invisible doors" and, not finding them, judge Hispanic practices as unfair, exclusionary, indiscreet, invasive.

In the first weeks of a first-year Spanish class, this theme of "invisible doors" was explored in preparation for a unit on self description, careers, and job-seeking based on authentic Hispanic documents. To first examine the meanings associated with closed vs. open doors, students surveyed each other in groups of four and summarized to the class their group's responses to the following questions: *When is your door closed? When is it open? What does a closed/open door mean?* Responses indicated that students closed doors for concentration, contemplation, private conversation, and modesty—in other words, to *separate* themselves from others; they opened them to invite, meet, display—in other words, to *involve* themselves with others. Yet, when asked the *meaning* of a closed or open door, students confronted their own conflict of needs: While opening or closing a door is a neutral action, seeing an open or closed door evokes judgment. The need for privacy thus conflicts with the need not to be judged by others as antisocial, timid, standoffish.

¿Cuándo está cerrada la puerta de tu dormitorio?

> Necesito (Tengo que) estudiar/ leer/trabajar; Voy a practicar español; Tengo una prueba; No quiero ser sociable; No quiero conversar; No puedo escuchar/pensar; Soy desordenada; Necesito descansar; Tengo que pensar; Necesito dormir; No tengo ropa; Necesito hablar por teléfono; etc.

¿Cuándo está abierta la puerta de tu dormitorio?

> Quiero conversar; Me gusta tocar la guitarra y cantar con la puerta abierta; Quiero ser sociable; Quiero amigos; Hay una fiesta; Quiero conocer gente; No tengo que estudiar/leer/hacer tarea; en mis ratos libres; Quiero jugar; Quiero escuchar música, etc.

¿Qué significa una puerta abierta?

> Amistoso, sociable, extrovertido, alegre, divertido; fiesta, descanso; jugar; entrar; etc.

¿Qué significa una puerta cerrada?

> Reservado, tímido, introvertido, antipático; estudioso, serio, trabajador; desordenado, responsable; no entrar; trabajo; etc.

These U.S. notions of "private" vs. "public" were expanded from the concrete to the intangible as students brainstormed on the existence of "invisible doors" in their culture. As anticipated, students produced "doors" between student life and career, private and social life (*yo y otros*), personal and professional life. Students even insisted there is not *one* door between a person and his or her professional life, but a series—private *to* personal *to* social *to* professional. As students then approached the voices of the Hispanic workplace through its own job-application documents, they noticed in this world not only the absence of their own privacy-and-separation "doors" but also the presence of other, unexpected ones. They were reminded that our doors are our culture's products, constructed to satisfy values and perceived needs. Not only will these needs and values differ from one culture to another but, as students had noted in this activity, even within a culture itself, they are likely to be in constant tension.

> ... to cross [our boundaries] we must define them. We must know where we are "coming from" in order to discover a "new" place.

A people's own ways of viewing the world, its *perspectives,* propel the creation of products and practices and align them as a cohesive sense-making system. A culture's perspectives express how what is done or believed functions in the whole of life. Yet, within this sense-making system, among its creators and consumers, the meeting of minds will never be total or exact. Its internal diversity (age, gender, geographical region, socio-economic strata, ethnicity, national origin, language, religion, etc.), as well as its internal groupings of sub-cultures or co-cultures prohibit its capture through a single scenario or static snapshot. As vibrant systems in constant flux, in constant surprise at their own internal diversity and in constant negotiation of their own self-produced tensions and internally generated conflicts, cultures do not run smoothly. "Conflict" is culture's pressure valve and growth mechanism. It is through conflict that all change and learning take place—in the collision of points of view that unsettles complacency, in the encounter of the new that requires re-framing of the old, in the clash between one practice that can only be forwarded at the expense of another.

Our culture's perspectives offer ranges of options; they are our generative capacity. Yet, because they also bind our vision and limit our understanding, they are the boundaries we must cross to enter another culture. To cross them, we must define them. We must know where we are "coming from" in order to discover a "new" place.

Culture Learning as Comparisons and Connections

"Cross-cultural learning means ... learning in a class where there are people of different backgrounds and cultures, [and] learning about a subject and ... how it relates differently to different cultures."

Matt, third-year student

For language teachers committed to cross-cultural communication it is perhaps fostering the believability of otherness that represents the ultimate challenge, for people tend to see what they believe rather than believe what they see (Joy, 1990). Words and deeds of another people, if not experienced and interpreted within the cultural context that assigns their meaning, may merely attach themselves to the outside observer's own sense-making system, neither touching his notion of self, nor inviting understanding of "other." Thus, while one's own culture has texture, is supremely complex and basically indescribable, the other culture remains a static collection of quirky little life forms, simple and without definition. Indeed, a culture can become believable only if we are able to capture a notion of what it is *to be* from the other perspective.

In this endeavor, the two words "connection" and "comparison" may be our touchstones. The *National Standards* characterize these two goal areas as connection with other disciplines and development of insight into the nature of language and culture. However, here we will push them a bit farther, pull them a bit deeper, to view them as the very heart of the process of cross-cultural understanding, where *comparison* is the application of cognitive and affective strategies to generate experiential analogues or metaphors, and where *connection* is the learning process of feeding known into new, and of expanding and broadening through multiple perspectives.

The Assumption of Difference

The question "Is there such a thing as U.S. culture?" commonly evokes a "yes but no" response from students. The "yes" is invariably supported by the recitation of beliefs embodied in U.S. historical documents and in the tenets of capitalism. The "no" arises as students conclude: "We're not really one culture, but many" or "There are cultures within cultures." Being the insider thus affords a special perspective and cautions us that perhaps the age-old culture-teaching debate of *similarity vs. difference* may not be productive. As human meets the world there are similarities in basic need; yet, the perception and weight of these needs are culturally formed. Aspects of systems designed to meet these needs may seem similar; yet, their particular realizations and coordinates will offer a *unique* reality in delicate and dramatic ways. With this understanding we may flesh out a "meaning" of *comparison* for use in the cross-cultural laboratory of our classrooms. *Webster's Unabridged Dictionary* provides the important distinction that we compare things of the same class *with* each other but compare things of unlike classes *to* each other. Because assumption of likeness permits one culture to leech into another in the interpretation of observations, it is the assumption of difference that needs to be our point of departure. The challenge of neutralizing this notion of difference, of defusing the potential explosion of judgment, may perhaps be met through the word "unique."

Owning a Cultural Identity

In a third-year literature class devoted to the theme of "identity," the word *yo* ("I") was written on the board and students were given one minute to create a list of all the things that composed their identity. To expand their personal lists and thus create a more culture-representative sampling, items were shared and merged into a class composite, with tallies representing the number of times each was mentioned (the time limit was imposed to capture a sense of individual priorities). The class list was then analyzed for frequency of response.

1. *education* (major, courses, school, academic organizations)
2. *goals* (goals, plans, dreams)
3. *work and work related aspects* (job, profession, position, etc.)
4. *abilities and preferred activities* (with sports most frequent)
5. *material goods* (car, house, clothing, salary, etc.)
6. *genetic factors* (race, sex, age, appearance)
7. *personality traits* (honesty, humor, etc.)
8. *friends, fraternities, and sororities*
9. *family* (parents, siblings, pets)
10. *religion*

This list would be used throughout the course to help learners claim ownership of their own culture's notion of "identity" as they entered the world of Hispanic voices. For now, it allowed the class to make some interesting observations: (1) their notion of "identity" as beginning with independent Self (self-development through education) and *future orientation* in personal goals and aspirations; (2) the status of work as a definer of Self, and the emphasis on *doing* in abilities and activities; (3) the relatively high ranking of material goods as rewards and signifiers of personal achievement. Students noted that the first seven categories were related to individual attributes, with friends, family (defined as parents, siblings, and pets) as less immediate identifiers. Nationality, culture, ancestry, language, politics were not mentioned by the U.S. students; however, they ranked as primary components on the lists of the four *foreign* students in the class (two from France, two from India), all of whom had been in the U.S. at least three years. One of these students explained that being a *foreigner* in the U.S. took a prominent place in her identity, marking her difference: *"Aquí, mi cultura y mi lengua son una gran parte de mi identidad porque aquí, soy diferente."* Indeed, it was this very comment and the discussion that ensued that prompted an on-the-spot re-ordering of the original syllabus in order to explore the notion of *bicultural* identity.

Separating "Mine" from "Yours"

In the autobiographical poem, "Convocación de palabras," the Chicano writer Tino Villanueva chronicles his search for "freedom" in the creation and expression of his own identity and that of his people: Because he is not of one culture, but of two, he "means" not in one language, but in two, and his voice must be that of both. Beginning with the line *"Yo no era mío todavía"* (I wasn't mine yet) the poet recounts his self-evolution as he labors to control the "writer's" words in English in order to express the duality of his identity. He feels his own Self forming through the power of each word and, in the final verse, spells his freedom:

> Tenaz oficio/ el de crearme en mi propia imagen/ cada vez con cada una al pronunciarla:
> *postprandial*
> *subsequently*
> y de escribir por fin con voluntad/las catorce letras de mi nombre/y por encima/la palabra
> *libertad.*[1]

The poem was read in class and students were simply asked to write their own personal reaction as homework. While ordinarily a pre-reading task would have been used to elicit some analogical experience that would orient learners to the message and guide cross-cultural entry, this time students were given only a simple question: "What is 'identity' to this

U.S. writer of Mexican origin?" The omission of the pre-reading task was purposeful: Previous class experience had shown that learners typically "misread" this poem; however, it was precisely the misreadings that always produced the learners' deepest self-reflections on their own approaches to Otherness—awareness of the infusion of their own values, prominence of their own stereotypes, quickness of their own judgment. Indeed, in reacting to this poem, many students, viewing the writer as a foreigner, interpreted his examples of English-learning as the typical struggles of the immigrant; they interpreted his insertions of word lists either as signs of the difficulty of English or as indicators of the high standards that prevail in U.S. schools (although few students could define all these English words and confessed that they had never even seen some of them). They then skipped to the final word, *libertad*, and saw this, the word that captured for them the essence of their own culture, as meaning that the poet wanted to be "one of us." One student comment, translated here, reflects some of these misreadings:

> The poem is about a Mexican who, on coming to the U.S., struggles with the English language. He finds schools much harder here and has a difficult time coping with the higher standards he encounters. He thinks that by learning big words he will be more like us and fit in and that becoming a part of U.S. culture will spell his "liberty."

Students' reactions to the poem revealed that many were viewing the Mexican-American identity issues almost entirely in terms of "U.S. culture assimilation," of a battle between wanting to fit into mainstream U.S. culture—of "wanting what we have"—and feeling rejected. In follow-up discussion, they confessed to not understand the identity issues confronted by those who negotiate membership in two cultures. One of the French students in the class offered her assessment of what it is like to live in another culture—to be the same yet different, to have essentially " two lives" that shift back and forth in consciousness, according to the situation, to be the same person but also "different."

Students were asked to reflect on personal situations in which they had felt "different" or out of place (How did they feel? Why?) and, using Villanueva's poem as a framework, compose their own poem to reflect this very personal experience. Our formal approach to the personal, social, and political identity of the "Chicano" then began with Rosaura Sánchez' short story "Se arremangó las mangas," in which a Mexican American professor, initially taken for a waiter at a cocktail party, "sells out" his identity and people in order to fit into the mainstream. In follow-up, students were asked to consider the extent to which we in the U.S. give an identity to Mexican Americans, and by association, to Hispanics in general, that is not their own. To what extent are observed "differences" interpreted and judged as reversed images of ourselves, the negatives to our own positives? Students brainstormed stereotyped images of Mexicans in the U.S.—images that have spilled over to mold caricatures of Hispanics in general: poor, always late, too many children, immature, poorly dressed, uneducated, etc. They then turned to their "U.S. identity" lists to see if these judgments could be coming from their own values system. In a task that required them to link these stereotypes to their own associations in one sentence (with each clause joined by *lo que* ["which"]), they experienced the chain reaction of their own culture's meaning system, the freight of their own values:

> "No puntual" significa que no es responsable, *lo que* significa que no tiene motivación, *lo que* significa que no tiene metas, *lo que* significa que no tiene interés en el futuro, *lo que* significa que es inmaduro.

> "Pobre" significa que no tiene dinero, *lo que* significa que no tiene muchas cosas, *lo que* significa que no tiene educación, *lo que* significa que trabaja con las manos, *lo que* significa que nunca va a tener éxito.[2]

Another poem by Villanueva was then read and discussed in class in light of this judgment trap. "Que hay otra voz" depicts the struggles of the Mexican migrant worker and, through the use of code-switching (insertion of English words), invokes the presence of one culture living in the midst of another. Class discussion teased out contrastive notions between two cultures: time, man and nature, "home" and work, material and non-material "goods," as well as the condition of being of one culture (*ser*) and living in another (*estar*). Students were then asked to prepare a dramatic presentation of the poem to attach a living experience to the idea conveyed by the title ("There *is* another voice"). Their task was first to collaborate in teasing from the poem those voices that originated from the Anglo culture and those that originated from the Mexican immigrant. (For a discussion of the "voices" of authentic texts, see Galloway, 1997.) This task required students to separate the conditions and circumstances of the immigrant's U.S. residence (as well as the outsider's perception of him in this residence) from the Mexican and his culture. Once they had separated the voices, they presented their dramatic reading, with the U.S. voice uttered in unison by the full force of the thirteen "Anglo-culture" students; the immigrant voices uttered separately by the five other students, as depicted in the following excerpt (lines should be read horizontally from Anglo to Chicano voice).

U.S. *"Anglo" voice, in unison*	*Chicano voice, solo*
Horarios inalterables ...	... la madrugada
mecánicamente despierta el reloj de	
timbre ...	... (¿de qué tamaño es el tiempo?)
	...
Tú, cómotellamas, ...	... mexicano, latino,
Meskin, skin, Mex-guy, Mex-Am, Latin-	
American, Mexican American, ...	... Chicano,
tú, de los ojos tibios ...	... como el color de la tierra,
	...
tú, de los *blue-jeans* nuevos pareces	
retornar cada año ...	... como fuerza elemental,
temporal–	... arraigado entre el ser y el estar de ...
... un itinerario	Eres ganapán, ...
... estás aquí de paso.	
	...
	... pesas
tu saco de algodón — cien libras	
que en los sábados ...	... se convierten en pesos miserables.[3]

These immigrant voices had depicted a different being from the one captured by Anglo-culture judgment: one living in a cyclical time frame; one united with the earth and Nature's forces; one warmed by the company of his own, his family, his music; one whose bowed and soiled body planted and harvested the crops of another's land; one viewed by the "other" as a commodity but viewed by himself through the "elemental force" of his Mexican roots, his Chicano brotherhood.

Many of the issues of Chicano identity illustrate the pitfalls of the decontextualized comparison of one culture with another. Members of one culture living in another, Mexican migrant workers were observed by those of the dominant culture in terms of contrasts of appearance and surface-level behaviors. Their situations having placed them outside the sense-making context of their own culture, they appeared not as the norm, but as the anomaly; their valued products and practices, observed outside the internal logic of the culture that created them, were subject to an outsider-imposed meaning. Indeed, as Castañeda notes, it is the *etic* perspective (that of the outsider looking in) that causes Mexico itself to seem so opaque to the beholder from abroad, that renders the foreign regard "so distorted, so blind, so mistaken":

The advent of a "modern" Mexico—business-oriented, outward-looking, sympathetic to most things American—blurred the contours of a different Mexico: one that, despite the convergence of ideas among the elites of both nations, remained profoundly different from the United States, and capable of generating the very surprises that have cropped up in the past couple of years. (1995, p. 24)

It was this Mexico, "profoundly different from the United States," that we sought to explore on its own terms. While debating the themes of U.S.–Mexico relations helps learners clarify their own perspectives, such debates often stay behind U.S. boundaries, divorced from the Mexican reality. To reach beyond present explanations and conjectures, the students in this class required more information—contemporary data to expand the literary voices of writers we would study in class: Octavio Paz, Carlos Fuentes, Rosario Castellanos, and others. Using the theme of the Mexican migrant as an investigative axis, students divided themselves into groups according to their area of interest or specialty and chose their own research perspectives: One group chose the economic perspective, one chose the political perspective, and another chose the socio-historical perspective. Others chose to work individually, researching such issues as family, health, and urbanization. Each group was to teach an audience-friendly lesson (in Spanish) of no more than 15 minutes. Their presentation was to offer some insights to the group that would help explain Mexican migration from the Mexican perspective and end with a provocative question for the group. Because only authentic Mexican texts (readily available via the Internet) were used as sources, the results of their research revealed the complex interconnectedness of all the issues raised. Indeed, because all aspects of a culture are inherently connected, any one theme—in this case, the Mexican migrant—can be the wedge that raises cultural roots for observation. In their exploration of Mexican identity, students had encountered not one identity, but many. And their journey into *México profundo* had barely begun.

The study of Mexican identity in this literature course occupied a full four weeks, with the learners themselves setting course direction through their own interaction. Their questions and comments in one task exposed threads of thought requiring connection. Their interests and fields of expertise propelled their interdisciplinary research as well. Indeed, the time taken to explore the web of one culture provided a deeper understanding of its internal logic while encouraging the development and refinement of durable and transferable strategies of cross-cultural examination. The opportunity to enter a culture more fully through literary and journalistic sources, interdisciplinary perspectives, and constant dialogue afforded perhaps a more unique portrait than could be obtained by a "representative" sampling of Hispanic literary works. And for students carrying the deceptive notion of "Hispanic" as one people, it was a powerful lesson in the distinctiveness of each Hispanic culture. Indeed, for language teachers committed to teaching culture, a constant multi-disciplinary and multi-genre perspective is required, for the real picture of a culture does not emerge solely through its language and literature.

What insights had learners gained from this experience? One student commented:

> Mexico seems to be not one culture, but many.... I suppose you could say there's no real mass society in the U.S. either, but there is in a way, because there is a concept of middle class by which we characterize our values, but it's hardly the same concept at all in Mexico and this explains a lot ... [I'm] beginning to see pieces fit together like a puzzle and make sense ("from the inside," as you say)—issues of "class," health, urbanization, ethnicity, politics, women and family, language (!)... Then again, everything we read just seems to make the picture more complex... Now, we're really getting into the idea of Mexican identity, or Mexican *search* for identity, and I can really see the enormous weight of history in this. In the U.S. we ignore our history. It's like, "well it's over, time to move on." Mexicans live their history every day.

Connecting and Comparing: The Kluckhohn Model

The final week of this third-year literature class focusing on "Hispanic identity" was devoted to helping students tie the patterns they had discovered through authentic Hispanic voices into a more cohesive system of values. In this regard, the schematic model developed by the anthropologists Florence Kluckhohn and Frederick Strodtbeck (1976), presented in Figure 2, allowed connected observations and broad system comparison. In the Kluckhohn taxonomy, a culture's dominant values and accepted ranges of variation may be seen as its system of options and preferred responses to five basic problems presumed to be shared across cultures: (1) perception of human nature, (2) perception of man in nature, (3) temporal orientation, (4) mode of activity, and (5) relational orientation. Rather than categorize cultures in static caricature, the model is fluid and dynamic, allowing the visualization not only of a culture's dominant preferences (A *over* B *over* C, A+B over C, etc.) at a given point in its story, but of its variant tensions and its reordered preferences over time. For each of the five basic problems (listed vertically), there are ranges of preference (listed horizontally). Ortuño notes that all alternatives are present in all societies at all times, but are differentially preferred (1991).

Figure 2. The Kluckhohn Model of Value
Orientations and Ranges of Variation

Human nature	Evil	Neutral	Good and evil	Good
Man and nature	Subjugation to nature	Harmony with nature	Mastery over nature
Temporal	Past	Present	Future
Activity	Being	Being-in-Becoming	Doing
Relational	Lineality	Collaterality	Laterality
	(Authoritarian)	(Collectivist)	(Egalitarian)

By connecting their own observations through the Kluckhohn model, learners were able to see the vast systemic differences between "white middle-class
U.S. culture" and the Hispanic cultures whose voices they had analyzed
through the class readings. Indeed, summarizing the alignment of the U.S.
values system nearly straight down the right side of the taxonomy, Ortuño notes
that the composite of the U.S. values orientation puts it in the minority of the
world's cultures and serves as a good predictor of where potential conflicts
might lie as students cross their own cultural boundaries (1991). The orientation
of Hispanic cultures tending toward the left and middle of the taxonomy displays vast differences between the two preferred-values systems.

Mainstream U.S. culture, for example, with its emphasis on change and
innovation, experience and experiment, autonomy, self-control, and constant
striving, caused students to orient U.S.-culture views of *Human nature* toward the "man is basically good" belief system. Recognizing that "Hispanic"
covers many cultures, students tentatively noted a Hispanic tendency toward
human nature as a mixture of *Good and evil*, where a belief in the goodness
of humanity is tempered by preferences for correct thinking, respect for
authority, and learning by principles. Indeed, Ortuño contends that Hispanics
tend to view humanity as good and evil, depending on circumstances, and
use a very "person-centered" set of criteria that takes into account not only
the inner dignity and uniqueness of individuals, but also their social status
and social interaction. (1991, p. 453). Students had no difficulty orienting
U.S. culture toward the *Mastery over nature* values system, where Nature
is perceived as external and subordinate to man. In sharp contrast to the
"control" outlook of U.S. culture, an "accepting" outlook was seen as
permeating many Hispanic cultures, particularly the animistic indigenous
cultures, where man, as part of nature, is thus both in harmony with it and
at the mercy of its mysterious powers. Fatalism or the so-called "lottery
mentality," so prominent in much of Hispanic literature, reflects a world
view that does not award man a dominant, let alone omnipotent, position
over the forces of nature. Students noted, for example, that this view per-

vades the poem "Que hay otra voz" discussed previously—the Mexican worker's skin and eyes are the color of the earth, he wears the soil of his labor, he bears the pain inflicted by the harsh elements of nature, he accepts his lot in life.

Castañeda contends that time-consciousness divides U.S. and Hispanic cultures as much as any other single factor (1995). Indeed, students did not hesitate to capture U.S. mainstream culture's monochronic view of time and a *Future + Present over Past* values orientation that focuses on the present as prelude to the immediate future. While a future orientation implies such things as goal-setting, diagnosis, risk evaluation, and planning, combined with a present orientation, it poses conflict in the need for instant gratification and the assessment of progress-by-the-moment. On the other hand, using this model, students tended to orient Hispanic polychronic views of time as present-dominated or a mixture of *Present + Past over Future* as they had perceived Mexicans'profound sense of history, of past as living spirit from which the present draws its vital energy. Indeed, if the future colors the present in the U.S. perspective, the past does lend a different texture to present time in Mexican society. However, the notion of time in Hispanic cultures is not quite so easily captured by the past-present-future framework; it rather defies the Kluckhohn linear representation. The notion of time as circular echoes through much of Hispanic literature, for example, confounding U.S.-student readers, for whom time must always "march on" and produce change. In terms of principal *Activity orientation*, students described the U.S. mainstream as a *Doing* culture that focuses on products, accomplishments, achievements, and material success. Words such as *(un)productive, input/output, competition*, so difficult to translate from English to Spanish, reveal a values framework that is self-focused and work-centered, concerned with utility and pragmatism. In contrast, students oriented Hispanic cultures toward the *Being* values— living and enjoying life as it comes, focusing on friendships and the development of social relations. They noted a similar contrast regarding *Relational* preferences. In U.S. mainstream culture, for example, the Self, identified with the individual and sharply separated from the Other (by invisible doors), is the basic unit of social organization. Students thus construed U.S. mainstream culture as a *Lateral + Collateral* combination in which group membership does not define Self, but rather promotes the individual goals or interests of members; social obligations are not necessarily binding; kinship and friendship ties exist but are external to the individual and are not of the extended, intricate, and self-defining nature that characterizes the dominant *Collateral* orientation of Hispanic cultures. To the Hispanic's *Collateral* orientation of Self in contract with Group, of nurturing connections and favor-exchanges and the obligatory cultivation of reciprocity (which U.S. learners often interpret as "personal invasion"), students added *Lineal* values to express the existence of status hierarchies within collective relationships. (For excellent classroom exploration of this topic, see Álvarez Evans & González, 1993.)

Use of the Kluckhohn model must be accompanied by a few caveats. First, the model is itself the product of a "cultural mind" and necessarily constrained by what that mind's eye could perceive. Second, the coincidence of two cultures appearing to correspond to the same preference-orientation range for a given variable on this model should not necessarily imply similarity of these two cultures. Two cultures may appear to have a dominant present-time orientation, for example, and yet their notions of present time may be quite distinct. Third, as Mestenhauser notes, although there is a "fit" among a culture's choices, the variables are independent of each other, without any implied or inherent hierarchical order (1998). Moreover, no culture is "captured" at any given point in its story merely by its dominant preferences, for these are always in constant interplay with its accepted variants, with the belief clusters of groups within the group. While Ortuño suggests that this taxonomy can be used with language learners at all levels to analyze everything from a specific textbook culture note to a specific literary piece (1991), it has been discussed here as a summative connection-and-aligning device, to help students ultimately coalesce their learning into a view of a system. Indeed, if this model is used with learners (with the caveats mentioned), questions of how and when to use it are important. If we impose an automatic sense-making scheme before learners have had the opportunity to fight their own battles and develop their own strategies, we may depict the cross-cultural-understanding process as a simple map-plotting act. Further, while the Kluckhohn model is extremely flexible, it is only a tool and depends on the quality of observation, quantity of knowledge, and authenticity and variety of sources. Textbook notes, already compromised by the outsider's voice, will undoubtedly produce the impression that cultures are flat, static, and homogeneous and can be compartmentalized and classified neatly. Moreover, since the model is built on the notion of options and preferences, each option having many preference permutations, only the actual experience of many authentic Hispanic voices can capture the internal dynamism of a living culture.

Culture as Communication and Community

*"[T]he underlying goal of language learning is communication. But ...
for what purpose? ... To communicate effectively..., I must learn about a person's background, values, where he's coming from."*

Keshav, third-year Spanish student

Edward Hall's message in *The Silent Language* is one foreign language
teachers recite almost as a mantra: Culture is communication, communication is culture (1959). Yet, foreign language classrooms may be the only
place in the world where the two are so unnaturally separated. While all
indications are that communication has taken hold as the direction in foreign language classrooms across the country, culture is still considered
the "expendable fifth skill" (Kramsch, 1993, p. 1). The comment of a
college freshman, Tim, on the first day of his second-year Spanish class
reflects much the same view of language and culture as divorceable enti-
ties:

> I would say that culture is interesting, but I'm really here to learn the lan-
> guage. I know that it's important to know culture too, but I'm not sure it's
> going to help me speak the language.

While the foreign language classroom is the optimum site for other-
culture entry through the language, cross-cultural knowledge and understanding do not simply and effortlessly accrue from language learning,
arise automatically from contextualized language practice and communicative activities, or lie in a finite number of language-use contexts. The
process of communication has no mastery end point. And cultural contexts, not stable sets of predictable circumstances but fluid social con-
structions, are created and shaped by people in dialogue and thus are of
infinite constellations of place + situation + participants + roles + statuses
+ backgrounds + purposes + interactive sequences + time + mode + genre
+ language code, and so on. Kramsch notes that language teachers and
learners often overlook the fact that language in use both reflects and
creates context:

> ...conventional pedagogic practice tends to view context as a given, pre-
> existing reality that serves to disambiguate the meaning of language
> forms... Both teacher and learners tend to ignore the degree to which their
> use of language constructs the very context in which they are learning it
> (1993, p. 105).

Thus, the answers to teaching culture will not likely be found in exportable "culture" materials and product-measurement devices but in our own reflection on Hall's two statements: Communication is culture. Culture is communication. Language is a product of culture; it mediates communication, but it is not itself communication. Within every spoken exchange and between every written line beats the pulsating dialogue that is culture. As teachers of communication, therefore, our real aim, to be shared with students from day one, is to help students construct another cultural reality. And this is only done through the culture's own language tools. The *National Standards* summarize the development of "Communication" as "knowing how, when, and why to say what to whom." And in a separate goal area, called "Communities," the *Standards* speak to the notion of lifelong learning in the use of the language for personal enjoyment and enrichment. This section will focus on *communication* as culture and on growth of the cross-cultural mind in the "culture" of *community.*

In *The Great Good Place*, Ray Oldenburg mourns the sacrifice to suburbia of the comfortable and connective "third places" of America's past —those places apart from home and work where people used to gather easily, inexpensively, regularly, and pleasurably just to talk (1989). These *learning* places connect and unify people through the tonic of friendship, creating support networks, fostering counsel and debate. In essence, third places are those environments where community happens. Not a place but an experience, community is made from conversation. And conversation, both public and within each of us, is "our essential cultural inheritance into whose skill and partnership education initiates us" (Oakeshott, 1962, p. 198).

To initiate our foreign language learners into the skill and partnership of this cultural conversation, perhaps our first step might be to recognize a distinction between conversation and talk. Although talk is required for conversation, much talk is only that—of and on the surface of life. And much talk in our classrooms, where the air is achievement and the measure of success is quantitative, is display talk, whose sole purpose is to demonstrate the degree of lexical and structural utterance-control a learner possesses at a given point in time. Conversation, on the other hand, is not always convertible to the hard currency of measurement devices, for it is the shared experience of engagement, connection, relationship, revelation of uniqueness. While talk may be memorable to learners in terms of a linguistic feat, conversation is substantively and emotionally memorable. Indeed, Kramsch suggests that much of classroom discourse, constrained to superficial linguistic exchanges, simply doesn't go far enough, does not begin to adequately exploit the range of contextual possibilities (1993, p. 91).

The What, When, and to Whom of the Cultural Conversation

In spite of their other-language insecurities, foreign language learners find talk easier than conversation. As pure linguistic exchange, talk is non-threatening; it does not require personal investment of the conversation caliber. It does not involve the same quality of substantive decisions regarding *what* to say or *when* to say it, nor does it require the constant *"to whom"* relational attention to the interlocutor that characterizes the nurturing give-and-take aspects of natural conversation. The following incident may demonstrate that the decision of *what* to say is not merely one of vocabulary and that the decisions of *when* and *to whom* have tangled cultural roots and broad cultural consequences.

A class of second-year Spanish students attended a dinner at my home with four Hispanic students of different nationalities, including one recent arrival to the U.S. Students grouped randomly at three tables for dinner, although I asked the Hispanic students to sit at various tables to foster conversation in Spanish. From the sounds of the voices, dinner conversations appeared lively, the topics varied. However, at the end of dinner I realized that all conversation throughout the evening had basically been maintained by the same handful of students; one table, at which two Hispanics and two U.S. students were seated, had been relatively silent. In casual exchange at the start of the next class, these two students, Jennifer and Kristen, described their dinner "conversation" something like this (reconstructed here from memory, in abbreviated form, in English):

> **Jennifer**: I was sitting at a table with Kristen and the two Colombians.
> **Teacher**: Oh, great! So you got to know Roberto and his sister Patricia.
> **Kristen:** Yes, they were nice.
> **Teacher:** What did you talk about?
> **Jennifer:** Nothing really. *They didn't really ask me anything.*
> **Kristen:** We all gave our names and Roberto talked a bit. He speaks English, too. *Patricia didn't talk much.*
> **Teacher:** Why? Why do you think she didn't talk much?
> **Jennifer:** I don't know. *She was new. Maybe she was scared.*
> **Teacher:** You said they didn't ask you anything. What did you expect them to ask you?

Kristen: *About life in the United States?* I don't know.
Teacher: Were you uncomfortable speaking Spanish?
Jennifer: No, I wanted to practice Spanish *but I didn't know what to talk about.*
Kristen: *We didn't really know them. It was a little uncomfortable.*

As the italicized statements reveal, for some students, the act of "just plain conversation" as social activity can be uncomfortable, not for the linguistic challenges, but for the demands of constructing a relationship. For these women, it was the *what, when,* and *to whom* decisions that resulted in silence. Regarding the *what* to say, their comments reflect a stimulus-response view of conversation—they had awaited their stimulus from the Other, which didn't occur. Bellah et al., in fact, observe that the particularly American notion of the relationship between Self and society, combined with the gradual shift from a producer-based to consumer-based economy, has grown a U.S. culture in which people's sense of themselves comes to be centered around the "taking in" of objects, ideas, and images which are provided for them, rather than the construction of these ideas and images from only their own experiences (1985, pp. 38–39). This consumer-oriented mindstate often permeates classrooms as well, where students await to take in the instructor's planned activities, await their question and turn to speak, and talk for the approval of teachers rather than converse to build community. In terms of *to whom*, the girls noticed that Patricia did not speak much during the conversation, and they offered in explanation that she was "new," possibly scared; yet, they had not felt responsible for bringing her into a group, had not desired to know her and, instead of perceiving a cross-cultural learning opportunity, had limited the context to "what does this new arrival want to know about us?"

Perhaps the *when* of the young womens' silence is a cross-cultural study in itself. In U.S. culture, the consumption of food tends to dominate the concept of dining; thus, once the food is consumed, the dining event is over. In Hispanic cultures, however, dining is a premier social event imbued with interactional *obligation*. The custom of the *sobremesa*, an after-dinner chat that may last hours, reflects a relational orientation and perception of Self that is Other-centered rather than One-centered. Food is enjoyed in large part for the pleasure derived from the company of those with whom it is shared. And it is in conversation that the company of others is experienced in *being*. Indeed, if the culture we are teaching is one rooted in the value of friendship systems and social relationships, such as are Hispanic cultures, attention to the art of conversation may result in the most profound of all cross-cultural learning experiences.

The How and Why of the Cultural Conversation

An example illustrates that the issues of *how* and *why* are also not as simple as they may seem. In a third-year Business Spanish class in which debate is a standard component, students had chosen to treat the topic "Affirmative Action" in a unit on Human Resources. The topic itself had prompted a great deal of pre-debate discussion—how to express the U.S. meaning in Spanish, whether the U.S. meaning was transferable to the Hispanic world, and, finally, whether any current movements or legislation in the Hispanic world were directed toward similar aims or derived from comparable conditions to those of the U.S. To find answers to their questions, students consulted Hispanic newspapers, magazines, and official documents via the Internet. They found that the advocacy of "legalized preferential treatment" was an issue being debated in many Hispanic countries, particularly in documents from Chile, Colombia, Mexico, Peru, and Spain, and that its meaning appeared more (though not exclusively) embedded in discussion of the rights of women and handicapped than in issues of race, ethnicity, or cultural group. Their reaction to the *language* of these authentic texts, however, produced its own culture lesson. Some supporters of affirmative action expressed outright anger at the Spanish term used throughout the documents, *discriminación positiva*, and objected to the constant use of words such as *preferencial*, whose direct translation to English evoked quite negative connotations for them. After much (at times, tense) discussion among students, one African American, Henry, captured the dilemma: It was not the Spanish word he rejected; rather, it was having to use this Spanish word to describe the *unique U.S. condition*. He loudly proclaimed to the class (translated here):

> I'm not going to use the term "discriminación positiva." It's not the same. The only term I can use to debate affirmative action in the U.S. is "affirmative action." Here, the situation is different. I can't translate the situation here into another language where the situation is different.

Henry had made a significant cross-cultural observation: the difficulty and deceptiveness of trying to express one society's history and cultural perspective through the language created by *another* society to express its own, different, perspective and condition. Indeed, this pre-debate discussion had afforded the class some insight into communication: The real *how* of communication is not ripe for picking at the surface level of words and grammatical structures. It resides in the cultural mind.

This same debate also produced cross-cultural observations regarding the *why* of communication. Structured to provide opportunities for both rehearsed and spontaneous speech, the actual debate had presentational and interactive phases. In the presentational phase, each side had the opportunity to present rehearsed arguments. Students were told they would receive a baseline grade on this component that considered quality of both content and expression—in other words, use of vocabulary and grammatical accuracy would be evaluated in this rehearsed segment (a reading of notes would incur an automatic 20-point deduction). When both sides had given their arguments, the interactive (or what students have termed the "*ataque*") phase began. Students received one point added to their baseline scores for each substantive and comprehensible contribution to the argument, regardless of the grammatical and lexical accuracy of their expression. However, each contribution had to be either (1) in response to a particular member of the opponent team and prefaced by a summary of what she or he had said (for example, "John, you said that ..." or "When you said that ... did you mean...?") or (2) connected to the topic of a previous speaker, with such gambits as: "speaking of ..." or "regarding the aspect of...." This protocol was to encourage good listening and confirmation of student–student comprehension, foster conversational connection, and discourage student delivery of pre-planned decontextualized statements. Further, students were informed that I would neither mediate the conversation for them nor provide words for them unless deemed essential. In most cases, students had to find a way to rephrase what they wanted to say without depending on the instructor as "dictionary." This debate format has proved motivating to students who not only invest in careful pre-debate preparation and research but become fully engaged in spirited discussion that does not close simply because a class session ends. Although some students participate more than others in the interactive phase, in the debate of "Affirmative Action" in this Business Spanish class, I had noticed that one ordinarily outspoken student, Robert, who had delivered a very cogent and persuasive argument in the presentational phase had become suddenly silent during the interactive phase, in spite of subtle attempts to coax him into the conversation. Afterwards, I praised his presentation and inquired as to his silence during the discussion. He replied (summarized here in English.):

What's the use? Here, everyone was arguing from their emotions, and sometimes they were even repeating themselves. After about 10 minutes I decided I wasn't going to participate anymore. It was obvious I wasn't going
to *change anyone's mind.* And if I wasn't going to be able to change anyone's mind, why should I even bother discussing the topic? I don't understand the purpose of expressing my ideas if nothing is *gained by it.*

Robert's comment reveals the *why* of conversation from his U.S. perspective and thus exposes some vast cultural differences: the U.S. view
of *doing* motivated by purpose and resulting in ends, products, accomplishments *vs.* the Hispanic view of *being* that revels in the experience
itself; the U.S. view of Self as One-defined vs. the Hispanic view of Self
as Other-joined. Indeed, Hispanic students debate issues freely and constantly and are often very surprised at U.S. students' reluctance to involve
themselves in such conversations, at their lack of expressed opinion or
preference (often interpreted as being uninformed), or at their frequent
bland rejoinder "*¡qué interesante!*" Kramsch makes a similar observation
of U.S. learners of German—that U.S. students are generally much less
seriously committed to defending their opinion than German students
would be in a German academic context, where opinions are more likely
to be personal stands that are worth justifying and defending. However,
she connects this causally to the classroom, where she concludes that
"foreign language teachers generally shy away from too conflictual a
clash of opinions, especially if they pertain to sex education, religion, or
politics" (1991, p. 85). Robert's comments reveal a different, deeper explanation for his reticence—a cultural explanation that had been exposed
through dialogue. Indeed, culture learning is all about dialogue.

Robert had vowed at that moment that he could not change. No one
would ask him to. Cross-cultural understanding does not involve aban-
donment of one's own cultural psyche, the substitution of another system
of values, or even necessarily the adoption of other behaviors. Yet, in the
intimate confrontation of this cultural conflict, Robert did change. He
became more conscious of his own culture as *his*; and by seeing it as
separate and identified, he was able to tuck it back a bit as safe and un-
threatened in order to "risk" more comfortably trying out a different role
for himself. He had also apparently begun a cross-cultural dialogue with
himself: Reflecting on a second debate, in which he was able to do something he had previously found nonsensical, he created his own sense of
"wonderment." In his final course evaluation, he commented:

The second debate was more fun, maybe because I talked more. I tried to
imagine myself in a Hispanic context throughout and, even though the topic
was one I felt very strongly about, I didn't think in terms of changing peo-

ple's minds. I focused instead on how I clarified my own thoughts and expressed my own ideas and it felt good. I'm not sure I'm able to achieve another's outlook because I still was not that interested in the unconvincing arguments of those on the opposing side, but I think I did show respect for their ideas (and for the debate itself) by participating and responding. OK, so there is some fun in "conversation." I admit it. But I wonder if it's just my own ego gratification???

If our aim is to help students understand what it means *to be* in those cultures where third places are active in the mind, we will need to create this culture in our classrooms. And if we view growth of the cross-cultural mind as a lifelong process, we will want to use dialogue to dig into the big issues of communication. Certainly, our mission is too important to define the communication–culture connection solely in terms of the teaching of discrete sociolinguistic protocols, too complex to view culture as simply the content of discussion, and too urgent to treat culture merely as a set of stock "contexts." Cross-cultural situations are everywhere in the foreign language classroom. While at every moment, in every exchange, our culture's assumptions speak our minds, it is only constant dialogue that truly opens them.

Dialogic Communities

Dialogue as whole-class reflective discussion, according to Wells, not only fosters the development of the collaborative ethos of a community of inquiry, it also provides the setting in which knowledge is co-constructed, as students and teacher together make meaning on the basis of each other's experiences (1994, p. 19). But can there also be dialogue places outside the classroom? Can the Internet's "electropolis," for example, serve as a third place for building community in exchange, a safe haven for reflection and conversation? (See Lee, this volume.) As an adaptation of the dialogue journal, students at all levels of language study may participate in cross-cultural reflection via a cyber-journal, once a week sharing their cross-cultural reflections via e-mail or chat room formats with a group of classmates. In such cyber-interaction, students can explore different cultural topics with each other, share impressions, reactions, interpretations of literary works or journalistic readings, discuss research data, even correct each other's Spanish. Yet, while "cyber-conversing" in written form allows learners the opportunity to attend to the linguistic aspects of their messages, it should not be confused with the self-investment process of writing; and while the e-mail format allows the transfer of messages swiftly from one party to another, it should not be confused with the spontaneous, participatory, turn-taking process of face-to-face conversation. The written dialogue of the Internet, a series of message-retrieving and -packaging acts, builds its own type of community. Students feel they are talking to each other, yet in a mode that allows them unpressured time to think about their ideas. As one first-year student remarked (translated here):

> I like to communicate via e-mail because I can talk about a lot of things, and I'm not scared. I can use the dictionary if needed. And I can think about my ideas and those of others.

In the dialogue of the cross-cultural classroom, it will be the experience of interacting with authentic texts that will provide the richest source of input for learners' cross-cultural discovery. Indeed, if there is one word that captures the essence of our mission in growing the cross-cultural mind, it is "authenticity," for no amount of knowledge or pedagogical expertise can capture on the bridge of anecdote the dynamism, inner diversity, and internal logic that lies behind the boundary of another reality, as the voices of those who *live* behind that boundary. As they approach authentic texts, learners will require support and guidance not only to separate their own culture's voices from the voices of the target culture, but to sort the voices within the target culture—groups from groups, group from individual—to experience the complexity and uniqueness of each culture, and of their own. Through authentic voices from a variety of disciplines, the language and culture are experienced as one. Through the continuous connection of these voices, knowledge is broadened, deepened, refined, reconfigured for application to new problems.

And in the cacophony of voices there is yet another type of dialogue to be nurtured: introspective dialogue with oneself. While the dialogic exchange of meaning characteristic of oral speech is ideally suited to collaboration, it is writing that enables the self-dialogue of reflection and imagination. Reflective writing, as the ultimate thinking device, allows learners the opportunity to explore their own perceptions, reinterpret experiences, envision alternatives, create new self awareness. The constant interaction of all these dialogue modes, each one contextualizing the other, each one challenging assumptions, each one consolidating, stretching and connecting to the other, grows the cross-cultural mind.

Conclusion

This chapter has suggested a new concept of mission in the classroom that derives from viewing ourselves first and foremost as teachers of culture. As learners enter new places with their own culture's baggage, it will be our task to help them identify it, claim ownership of it, turn back to deposit it, and enter anew. This is, indeed, a never-ending process—one whose value lies less in the completeness of the knowledge gained than in the strategic thought exercised, the imagination and resourcefulness cultivated. Each visit will be an awakening, producing new knowledge and connecting it to the known; each will bring learners closer to pulling from the internal logic of another culture; each will expose new conflicts and ambiguities, provoke new wonderment; and each will afford learners a sharper vision of themselves. In the knowledge of our boundaries lies the recognition that we are all different. In our cross-cultural minds lie our bridge to understanding.

Notes

[1] The text translates roughly as follows:

An unyielding job/ that of creating myself in my own image/ each time with each word pronounced:

postprandial

subsequently

And to write finally with will/ the fourteen letters of my name/ and above/ the word

freedom

[2] Text translates roughly as: "Not punctual" means not responsible, which means unmotivated, which means without goals, which means lack of interest in the future, which means immaturity.

"Poor" means he has no money, which means he has few things, which means he has no education, which means he works with his hands, which means he's never going to be successful.

[3] Text translates roughly as:

U.S. "Anglo" voice, in unison	Chicano voice, in solo
Inalterable schedules	... the crack of dawn
the alarm clock mechanically awakens	...(what size is time?)

...

You, what's your name, ...	... mexicano, latino,
Meskin, skin, Mex-guy, Mex-Am,	
Latin-American, Mexican American, ...	... Chicano,
you, of tepid eyes ...	... like the color of the earth,

...

you, with the new blue-jeans,
  seem to return every year ...   ... like an elemental force,
transitory—   ... rooted between the *ser* and *estar* of ...
... an itinerary   You're a drudge,...
... you're just passing through.

...

                                                   ... you weigh
your sack of cotton—a hundred pounds
that on Saturdays ...   ... are changed into your pittance.

References

Alvarez Evans, G., & González, O. (1993). Reading "inside" the lines: An adventure in developing cultural understanding. *Foreign Language Annals, 26*, 41–48.

Bellah, R.N., Madsen, R., et al. (1985). *Habits of the heart*. Berkeley: University of California Press.

Castañeda, J. (1995). Ferocious differences. *The Atlantic Monthly, 7*, 68–76.

Costa, A.L., & Garmston, R.J. (1998). Maturing outcomes. In *Restructuring education*. Seattle, WA: New Horizons for Learning. Retrieved Jan. 11, 1999, from the World Wide Web: http://www.newhorizons.org.

Even-Zohar, I. (1997). Factors and dependencies in culture: A revised draft for polysystem culture research. *Canadian Review of Comparative Literature, 24(1)*, 15–34.

Galloway, V. (1992). Toward a cultural reading of authentic texts. In H. Byrnes (Ed.), *Languages for a multicultural world in transition* (pp. 87–121). Northeast Conference Reports. Lincolnwood, IL: National Textbook Co.

Galloway, V. (1997). Constructing cultural realities: "Facts" and frameworks of association. In J.Harper, M. Lively, & M. Williams (Eds.), *The coming of age of the profession* (pp. 129–140). Boston: Heinle and Heinle Publishers.

Geertz, C. (1973). *The interpretation of cultures*. New York: Basic Books.

Gover, M., & Conway, P. (1997, November). To borrow and bestow: Identification as the acquisition of value. Paper presented at the Association of Moral Education Conference, Atlanta, GA.

Hall, E. T. (1959). *The silent language*. Garden City, NY: Doubleday and Company, Inc.

Jeffries, S. (1996). National foreign language standards: Can we get there from here? In Z. Moore (Ed.), *Foreign language teacher education* (pp. 2–35). Lanham, MD: University Press of America, Inc.

Joy, C. (1990). *Believing is seeing: Attitudes and assumptions that affect learning about development*. New York: National Clearinghouse on Development Education.

Kluckhohn, F. R., & Strodtbeck, F.L. (1976). *Variations in value orientations*. Westport, CT: Greenwood.

Kramsch, C. (1993). *Context and culture in language teaching*. NY: Oxford University Press.

Lerch, B. (1997, October 20). It's a matter of respect. [Letter to the editor.] *The Atlanta Journal and Constitution*.

Lévi-Strauss, C. (1995). Culture and development, In *Our creative diversity: Report of the world commission on culture and development*. Paris: Culture and Development Coordination Office.

Mestenhauser, J.A. (1998). International education on the verge: In search of a new paradigm. *International Educator, 8* (23). Retrieved Jan. 11, 1999, from the World Wide Web: http://www.nafsa.org/publications/ie.html.

National Standards in Foreign Language Education Project. (1996). *Standards for foreign language learning: Preparing for the 21ˢᵗ century.* Yonkers, NY: Author.

Oakeshott, M. (1962). The Voice of poetry in the conversation of mankind. In *Rationalism in politics and other essays* (pp. 197–247). London: Metheun.

Oldenburg, R. (1989). *The great good place.* New York: Paragon House.

Olvera, J. (1997). Una solución para la conmoción de la bandera en la frontera entre Texas y México. *Hispanic Link News Service,* October 26. Retrieved Jan. 11, 1999, from the World Wide Web: http://www.latinolink.com/opinion/opinion97/1026HI2E.htm.

Ortega y Gasset, J. (1983). Meditaciones del Quijote. *Obras completas,* Vol. I. Madrid: Revista de Occidente.

Ortuño, M. (1991). Cross-cultural awareness in the foreign language class: The Kluckhohn model. *Modern Language Journal,* 75 (4), 449–59.

Phillips, J.K. (1997). Collaborations: Meeting new goals, new realities. In J.K. Phillips (Ed.), *Collaborations: Meeting new goals, new realities* (pp. xi–xviii). Lincolnwood IL: National Textbook Co.

Rosado, C. (1997). *The concept of cultural relativism in a multicultural world.* McKinleyville, CA: Rosado Consulting for Change in Human Systems.

Sánchez, R. (1990). Se arremangó las mangas. In Z. Sacks DaSilva & N. de Marval-McNair (Eds.), *Experiencias: Lectura y cultura* (pp. 188–90). New York: Harper & Row.

Schwartz, A. M., & Kavanaugh, M.S. Addressing the culture goal with authentic video. In J.K. Phillips (Ed.), *Collaborations: Meeting new goals, new realities* (pp. 96–139). Northeast Conference Reports. Lincolnwood, IL: National Textbook Co.

Villanueva, T. (1991). Convocación de palabras. In A. Labarca & R. Halty Pfaff, *Convocación de palabras.* Boston: Heinle and Heinle.

Wells, G. (1994). Text, talk and inquiry: Schooling as semiotic apprenticeship. In N. Bird (Ed.), *Language and learning.* Hong Kong: Institute for Language in Learning.

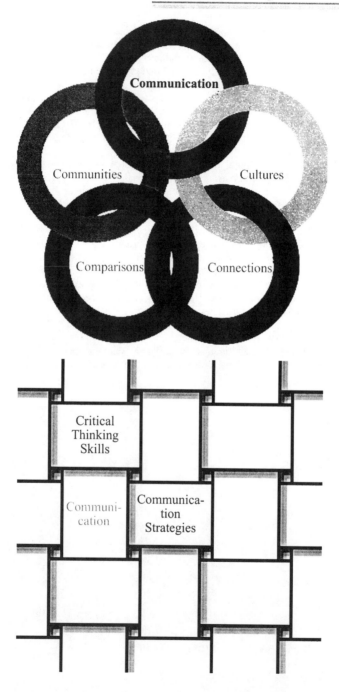

Performance Assessment for Language Students

Ghislaine Tulou and Frances Pettigrew
Fairfax County (VA) Public Schools

Educators have long been aware of the fundamental link between teaching and assessment. For many years, the goal of testing was to produce a grade on which to compare one student to another. In recent years, however, educational experts have questioned the reasons for grading and assessing and have proposed a paradigm shift in the focus of testing, from "sorting and selecting" to "teaching and learning" (Canady, 1993; Guskey & Johnson, 1996). This shift has resulted in increased attention to the impact of assessment on the learner. As Wiggins (1994) states, "Assessment should be designed and conducted to improve performance, not just audit it" (p. 70).

In the foreign language field, concerns about "testing what you teach" were heightened in the 1980s as the focus of instruction shifted to proficiency and communicative competence. In today's communicative classroom, students are encouraged to use their language skills in authentic and meaningful situations (Omaggio, 1993). Hancock (1994) asks how language tests could better reflect the actual language use that this instructional approach demands, especially given the practical considerations of large numbers of diverse students and limited resources. Teachers have begun to search out alternative assessments that go beyond the traditional focus on achievement, including such innovations as Simulated Oral Proficiency Interviews (Stansfield & Kenyon, 1992), portfolios (Amado et al., 1996; National Capital Language Resource Center, 1997; Speiller &

Yetman, 1996), learning logs or journals (Valette, 1994), and the focus of this chapter, performance assessment (Fairfax County Public Schools, 1997; Jackson et al., 1996; Valette, 1994). The National Standards for Foreign Language Learning (1996) set additional benchmarks to guide teachers and learners. (For an overview of the link between content standards and authentic assessment, see Liskin-Gasparro, 1996).

These changes in the education and foreign language communities find support as well in the broader public arena that is increasingly focused on outcomes and accountability and concerned about preparing the students of today for the perceived demands of the 21st century. It is in the nexus of these social and educational movements that the Performance Assessment for Language Students (PALS) project was conceived. This chapter describes an ongoing project in Fairfax County (VA) Public Schools to design and implement performance tasks and evaluate the ability of language learners.[1] As members of the project team, we will trace the history of the project, discuss the development and use of performance tasks for on-going assessment and instruction as well as for year-end assessment, and explore the reactions of learners. The PALS project continues to be refined by and to benefit from the many teacher and student voices that inform it.

The PALS Project

In the summer of 1995 we joined a task force of Fairfax County foreign language teachers that was formed to study and begin the implementation of alternative assessment in the classroom. These teachers began their work by reflecting on their own teaching practices and asking themselves the following questions taken from the Fairfax County Public Schools document: "Middle School Grading and Reporting: Rationale for Change" (1996).

- Do assessment results represent what students have learned and are able to do with the acquired knowledge?
- Do these results give students clear feedback with respect to their progress in language proficiency?
- Do we establish a classroom climate which encourages students to take risks with the language, allows them to make mistakes and helps them learn from their mistakes?

- Do current grading practices focus on what students DO know rather than on what they do *not* know?
- Do we clearly communicate to parents and students exactly what a student should know and be able to do by the end of the school year?
- Do we average grades for the entire year to determine a final grade, or do we actually assess progress and mastery by the end of the year?
- Do we have high expectations for all students?

These questions helped the group look beyond traditional achievement tests, which evaluate students on specific learned material and which place more value on form than function. In order to create assessments that focus on what the students know and can do in the language, the group designed a variety of performance tasks that place the students in real-life situations where they need to use the foreign language. The group also developed scoring criteria, or rubrics, by which to rate the student performances. These tasks and rubrics focused on students enrolled in the first year of high school language study, level 1. Over the course of the next three summers, the PALS team designed tasks and developed rubrics for levels 2 and 3 (students in their second and third year of high school language study). During each successive school year, the tasks and rubrics were piloted by the foreign language department at McLean High School in levels 1, 2, and 3 in the French, German, and Spanish classes. In 1997–98, Langley High School and West Springfield High School piloted the tasks and rubrics in their level-1 French, German, and Spanish classes. In 1998–99, level-1 teachers in all Fairfax County intermediate and high schools implemented the PALS program with their students. In the summer of 1998, Latin, Japanese, and Russian teachers in Fairfax County joined the project, adapted the rubrics to meet the needs of their languages, and created tasks.

Designing Performance Tasks

Performance tasks ask learners to perform, create, or produce something that requires them to show what they have learned and can do. The PALS project decided to use performance tasks for both formative (ongoing) and summative (end-of-year) assesssment. Based on recommendations from Herman, Aschbacher, and Winters (1992) and Jackson et al. (1996), the PALS group designed performance tasks that:

- Engage the students in simulated real-world tasks
- Have more than one right answer
- Reward skill development, creativity, and linguistic accuracy

- Promote problem-solving skills and tap higher-level thinking skills (especially in upper levels)
- Let the students know how their performance will be evaluated before they perform the task.

Because the productive skills lend themselves to open-ended responses more readily than the interpretive skills of listening and reading, the PALS group decided to begin by focusing on speaking and writing. Specifically, the project designed one-way presentational tasks, which, as stated in Standard 1.3 of the Communications goal of the National Standards, allow students to "present information, concepts, and ideas to an audience of listeners or readers on a variety of topics" (1996, p. 41). The presentational mode was selected because it offers each student the opportunity to perform to the best of his or her ability without relying on a peer's performance or expertise. In order to reduce the possible subconscious assistance from sympathetic teachers, it was agreed that all speaking tasks would be recorded and evaluated as the teacher listened to the tape.

Using PALS for Formative Assessment

"Performance assessments tasks give you a chance to be creative and show how much you know. [They are] especially helpful if you don't do well on normal tests."

Level-3 student

Performance tasks for formative assessment are tied to individual units of study and are therefore given at regular intervals of six to eight weeks. Students produce written or spoken samples, or both, at the end of each unit. These formative assessments provide valuable feedback to the students and teacher on the quality of their communicative skills and help students recognize strengths and weaknesses and design a plan for improvement.

Task Templates

As the teachers developed performance tasks, they established a common format or template so that all tasks would include the same basic elements:
- theme and topic (as determined by the school curriculum)
- a statement of the task objective

- the task description
- the minimal requirements for completing the task
- suggestions
- directions

Figures 1, 2, and 3 present three sample writing tasks for level 1, one each for French, German, and Spanish. The tasks described here are the prompts used to elicit the student texts presented and analyzed in the next section.

Figure 1. PALS Writing Task 1
Level 1: French/German/Spanish

Theme: Student Life
Topic: School, Leisure Time
Task Objective: To write about your busiest day
Task Description: Your school is planning to create a web page on the Internet. On that page, the designers would like to let students of other countries know about the life of teenage students at your school. *Choose your busiest day and write a paragraph about what you do in the morning, afternoon, and evening.*

Minimum requirements:
Write about:
a. one activity you do in the morning
b. two activities you do in the afternoon
c. two activities you do in the evening
Write 12 sentences (100 words or $^1/_2$ page).

Suggestions: You may use a graphic organizer such as a day planner, as given below; choose your busiest day and jot down your activities.

Directions: You may not use a dictionary.

Scoring Criteria: Level-1 writing rubric
Write as much as you can. Show what you can do.

✳ ✳ ✳

Choose your busiest day ...

day of the week: _____

morning	
afternoon	
evening	

Figure 2. PALS Writing Task 2
Level 1: French/German/Spanish

Theme: Home Life
Topic: Home and Family
Task Objective: To describe your house.
Task Description: Your home is for sale. The real estate agent has some clients who speak French/German/ Spanish and are very interested in your home. Unfortunately, your real estate agent doesn't speak any foreign languages and needs you to write a description and fax it to him immediately. *Write a description of your home on the fax form.*

Minimum Requirements to Meet Expectations:
Include:
a. the number of floors
b. the rooms and their size, color, and location
Write 12 sentences (100 words or $^1/_2$ page).

Suggestions: You might want to include information about schools, stores, parks, libraries, restaurants, and modes of transportation that are close to your home.

Directions: You may not use a dictionary for this task.

Scoring Criteria: Level-1 writing rubric

Write as much as you can! Show off what you can do!

Teacher Note: Provide a fax form for the students.

Figure 3. PALS Writing Task 3
Level 1: French/German/Spanish

Theme: Socializing
Topic: Greeting and Introducing, Physical Description
Task Objective: To write about yourself, your family, your free time activities
Task Description: You are going to host an exchange student from Austria/Senegal/Venezuela. Write him/her a letter about yourself, your family, and your free time activities.

Minimum Requirements to Meet Expectations:

- Introduce yourself
- Describe yourself, your free time activities and your family
- Use letter format
- Write at least $^1/_2$ page

Suggestions: You may want to mention friends, your likes and dislikes.

Directions: You have 15 minutes to write. You may not use a dictionary.

Scoring Criteria: Level-1 writing rubric

Write as much as you can! Show off what you can do!

Use of Tasks in Formative Assessment

Because performance assessment is ongoing, it provides learners continuous, meaningful feedback throughout the year. The PALS project developed analytic rubrics for evaluating student progress.

Applying Analytic Rubrics for Formative Assessment

Scoring rubrics make public what is to be judged and how it is to be judged. Analytic rubrics break down the task being evaluated into its component parts or domains, such as comprehensibility, fluency, and grammar. Since specific components of the task are evaluated separately, students receive clear feedback with regard to their strengths and weaknesses. As a result, analytic rubrics are a valuable instructional tool.

The PALS group has written analytic speaking and writing rubrics for levels 1 (see Figures 4 and 5), 2, and 3.[2] The rubrics for speaking and writing are similar in that they both include the domains of task completion, comprehensibility, vocabulary, and grammar. In addition, the speaking rubric measures fluency and pronunciation, while the one developed for writing measures mechanics and level of discourse. The rubrics were written in terms that are general enough to be applicable to all speaking and writing tasks throughout the year. They incorporate terminology and concepts from the ACTFL Revised Proficiency Guidelines (1986) and the International Baccalaureate rubrics (International Baccalaureate Organisation, 1996).

The PALS rubrics are based on a range of four levels of performance with each assigned a corresponding point value: Does Not Meet Expectations (one point), Almost Meets Expectations (two points), Meets Expectations (three points), and Exceeds Expectations (four points).

The rubrics and the differences between the levels are clear—it is easy to see what you need to do to improve your writing and speaking skills.

Level-2 student

Scoring and Grading Formative Tasks

The PALS group discussed how to equate the "Meets Expectations" level of performance to a grade. The members of the group readily agreed that it should not merit an A because we wanted to encourage the students to go beyond the requirements of the task. Consideration was given to equating a "Meets Expectations" to a C. However, experience in the classroom indicated that students attempted to reach so far beyond their skill level that communication broke down. Consequently, the PALS group agreed that "Meets Expectations" would be treated as equivalent to a B level of performance on the Fairfax County Public Schools grading scale. Thus, the other equivalencies were established: A, for "Exceeds Expectations," C for "Almost Meets Expectations," and D or F for "Does Not Meet Expectations."

Each domain of the rubric is scored individually, and these ratings are then totaled to calculate the final grade. However, since analytic rubrics use a 4-point scale for each domain, it is essential that these points be converted appropriately to the standard grading scale of the school system or institution and that they accurately reflect the level of performance. For example, when a student scores a 3 on each domain of the level-1 speaking rubric, the total score is 18 out of 24 points. If placed directly into a percentage, the grade would be 75, which is a low C on the grading scale. However, a 3, or "Meets Expectations," in each category should produce a B. Because of that discrepancy, points cannot be converted directly to percentage grades, and must, instead, be adjusted mathematically to convert rubric scores to grades (see the scoring chart in Figure 4 for the conversions from raw scores to percentages).

Figure 4. Analytic Rubric for Speaking Tasks — Level 1

Task Completion
1 Minimal attempt to complete the task and/or responses frequently inappropriate.
2 Partial completion of the task, responses mostly appropriate yet undeveloped.
3 Completion of the task, responses appropriate and adequately developed.
4 Superior completion of the task, responses appropriate and with elaboration.

Comprehensibility
1 Responses barely comprehensible.
2 Responses mostly comprehensible, requiring interpretation on the part of the listener.
3 Responses comprehensible, requiring minimal interpretation on the part of the listener.
4 Responses readily comprehensible, requiring no interpretation on the part of the listener.

Fluency
1 Speech halting and uneven with long pauses and/or incomplete thoughts.

2 Speech choppy and/or slow with frequent pauses; few or no incomplete thoughts.
3 Some hesitation but manages to continue and complete thoughts.
4 Speech continuous with few pauses or stumbling.

Pronunciation
1 Frequently interferes with communication.
2 Occasionally interferes with communication.
3 Does not interfere with communication.
4 Enhances communication.

Vocabulary
1 Inadequate and/or inaccurate use of vocabulary.
2 Somewhat inadequate and/or inaccurate use of vocabulary.
3 Adequate and accurate use of vocabulary.
4 Rich use of vocabulary with frequent attempts at elaboration.

Grammar
1 Inadequate and/or inaccurate use of basic language structures.
2 Emerging use of basic language structures.
3 Emerging control of basic language structures.
4 Control of basic language structures.

Scoring Chart								
Task Completion	$^1/_2$	1	$^1/_2$	2	$^1/_2$	3	$^1/_2$	4
Comprehensibility	$^1/_2$	1	$^1/_2$	2	$^1/_2$	3	$^1/_2$	4
Fluency	$^1/_2$	1	$^1/_2$	2	$^1/_2$	3	$^1/_2$	4
Pronunciation	$^1/_2$	1	$^1/_2$	2	$^1/_2$	3	$^1/_2$	4
Vocabulary	$^1/_2$	1	$^1/_2$	2	$^1/_2$	3	$^1/_2$	4
Grammar	$^1/_2$	1	$^1/_2$	2	$^1/_2$	3	$^1/_2$	4
Raw Score:								

	Score	%	Score	%	Score	%	Score	%	
	24	100	18	87.0	12	74.0	6	61.0	
	23	97.8	17	84.8	11	71.8	5	58.8	
Conversion Table	22	95.7	16	82.7	10	69.7	4	56.7	
	21	93.5	15	80.5	9	67.5	3	54.5	
	20	91.3	14	78.3	8	65.3	2	52.3	
	19	89.2	13	76.2	7	63.2	1	50.2	
Converted Score:[a]								%	

[a]If you use a point system in your gradebook instead of percentages, take the student percentage score, divide it by 100, and multiply this result by the maximum number of allotted points. The product yields the number of student points.

Figure 5. Analytic Rubric for Writing Tasks — Level 1

Task Completion
1 Minimal attempt to complete the task, and/or content frequently inappropriate.
2 Partial completion of the task, content mostly appropriate, ideas are undeveloped.
3 Completion of the task, content appropriate, ideas adequately developed.
4 Superior completion of the task, content appropriate, ideas well developed and well-organized .

Comprehensibility
1 Text barely comprehensible.
2 Text mostly comprehensible, requiring interpretation on the part of the reader.
3 Text comprehensible, requiring minimal interpretation on the part of the reader.

4   Text readily comprehensible, requiring no interpretation on the part of the reader.

Vocabulary
1   Inadequate and/or inaccurate use of vocabulary.
2   Somewhat inadequate and/or inaccurate use of vocabulary.
3   Adequate and accurate use of vocabulary.
4   Rich use of vocabulary with frequent attempts at elaboration.

Grammar
1   Inadequate and/or inaccurate use of basic language structures.
2   Emerging use of basic language structures.
3   Emerging control of basic language structures.
4   Control of basic language structures.

Mechanics
1   Inaccurate spelling, use of accents, punctuation and/or capitalization.
2   Somewhat inaccurate spelling, use of accents, punctuation and/or capitalization.
3   Mostly accurate spelling, use of accents, punctuation and/or capitalization.
4   Few or no errors in spelling, use of accents, punctuation and/or capitalization.

Level of Discourse
1   Attempted use of complete sentences, no or almost no cohesive devices.
2   Predominant use of complete yet repetitive sentences, no or almost no cohesive devices.
3   Emerging variety of complete sentences and some cohesive devices.
4   Variety of complete sentences and of cohesive devices.

For scoring chart and conversion table, see Figure 4.

Student Models

Models of student performance on the French, German, and Spanish tasks from Figures 1, 2, and 3 illustrate the application of the rubrics. The samples are presented as the student authors wrote them. English versions are provided, but most errors cannot be readily translated. An explanation of the rating follows each text.

French Sample 1. Rating Exceeds Expectations

Vendredi va être un jour occupée. Je vais aller au lycée, à pied, le matin. Mes leçons sont très facilles, et j'aime mes leçons. Je vais faire le math (je n'aime pas), une classe avec les ordinateurs (c'est bof), historie (j'adore, c'est fantastique), et biologie. Biologie est ma clase preferé, c'est très facille pour moi et très interessant.

Le matin, je vais aller au lycée à sept heures. Je vais travailler jusqu'à deux heures et quart. Après le lycée, je vais aller au mall pour une heure. Je vais rentrer à chez moi et je mange un banane, ou une pomme (j'adore les fruits).

Le soir, mes parents vont aller en boum (ne pour pas les jeunes). Je vais rester à la maison avec mes sœurs. Mes sœurs s'appellent Jennifer (elle à douze ans) et Sophie (elle à cinq ans). Sophie est sympa (et très drôle), mais Jennifer est très désagréable. Alors vendredi va être un jour très occupée.

Friday is going to be a busy day. I am going to go to high school, on foot, in the morning. My classes are very easy, and I like my classes. I am going to do Math (I don't like), a class with computers (it's OK), history (I adore it, it's fantastic), and biology. Biology is my favorite class, it is very easy for me and very interesting.

In the morning I am going to go to school at seven o'clock. I am going to work until a quarter past two. After school, I am going to go to the mall for an hour. I am going to return home and I eat a banana, or an apple (I adore fruit).

In the evening, my parents are going to go to a party (not for young people). I am going to stay home with my sisters. My sisters are called Jennifer (she is twelve) and Sophie (she is five). Sophie is very nice (and very funny), but Jennifer is very disagreable. So Friday is going to be a very busy day.

Justification of Rating using the Analytic Rubrics

Task Completion	4 pts.	The student completes the task with elaboration discussing morning, afternoon, and evening activities
Comprehensibility	3 pts.	The text is comprehensible but does require minimal interpretation *(e.g., ne pas pour les jeunes, mall, je vais rentrer et je mange.)*
Vocabulary	4 pts.	There is rich use of vocabulary for this level. The writer uses a variety of verbs and adjectives *(e.g., je vais aller, sont, aime, adore, travailler, rentrer, manger, rester, facile, fantastique, intéressant, sympa, drôle, désagréable).* She also mentions a variety of classes and activities.

Grammar	3 pts.	There is emerging control of basic language structures, in spite of some errors in adjective agreement *(e.g., occupée, facile, préférée)* and some missing articles *(e.g., historie, biologie, en boum).*
Mechanics	3.5 pts.	The mechanics are mostly accurate with relatively few errors in accents and spelling *(e.g., facille, historie, à douze ans).*
Level of Discourse	4 pts.	There is a variety of complete sentences and cohesive devices *(e.g., jusqu'à, alors, le matin, mais, après le lycée).*

This sample produces a raw score of 21.5 out of 24 points. Using the scoring chart (see Figure 4) the percentage grade is 94.5%, an A, which therefore falls in the range of "Exceeds Expectations."

French Sample 2. Meets Expectations

Samedi est ma journée plus occupée. Ma jour commencet à six heures le matin. Je vais a parc et travercer au pont. Aprés, je parle avec l'agent de police. Beacoup belle filles est voici, c'est trés bon parce-que j'aime beaucop regarder elles. Aprés, je vais chez moi et rest jusqu à dix heures. Prochain mes aimis vont chez moi, et nous allons au parc et jouer au basket. Midi, je vais au resteraunt et manger. Je mange l'hamburger, l'eau minéral, du poulet et du pain. Mon ami Chris manget du poisson et pain avec fromage. L'apres midi je vais au cinema et regarder un film. Toujours nous mangent chocolât au cinéma. Apres, nous allons chez Michelle, elle est la petit fille de Chris. Elle a besoin travailler à la banque. Aprés ça, Chris et moi allons au restieraunt "Cool Hands" et jouer au billiards. Je joue bon que Chris. Le soir je reste chez moi et finir mes devoirs pour lundi et mardi. A neuf heures Chris et Michelle vont chez moi encore. Nous allons au resteraunt "Amphora" et mangent. Quand nous finissons dinner nous allons nous maisons et regarder la télé. Je ne faire pas du ski et je n'faire pas du bateau mais samedi est ma journée plus occupée.

Saturday is my busiest day. My day starts at six o'clock the morning. I go to park and cross at the bridge. After, I speak to the policeman. Many pretty girls is here, it is very good because I really like to look at them. After, I go home and stay until ten o'clock. Next my friends come to my house, and we go to the park and to play basketball. Noon, I go to the restaurant and to eat. I eat the hamburger, the mineral water, some chicken and some bread. My friend Chris eats fish and bread with cheese. In the afternoon, I go to the movies and to watch a film. Always we eat chocolate at the movies. After, we go to Michelle's, she is Chris's little girl. She needs to work at the bank. After that, Chris and I go to the restaurant "Cool Hands" and to play pool. I play good than Chris. In the evening I stay home and to finish my homework for Monday and Tuesday. At nine o'clock Chris and Michelle go to my house again. We go to the restaurant Amphora and eat. When we finish dinner we go we houses and to watch TV. I don't to go skiing and I don't to go boating but Saturday is my busiest day.

Justification of Rating using the Analytic Rubrics

Task Completion	3.5 pts.	The student discusses morning, afternoon, and evening activities and adds interesting details; however, the last sentence is a little jarring to the reader because it does not follow the logical sequence of activities described earlier in the passage.
Comprehensibility	2.5 pts.	The text is mostly comprehensible requiring some interpretation (e.g., *prochain* instead of *alors* or *après*, *nous maisons*, *est voici*, and the reader questions the lunch consisting of a hamburger and chicken at a restaurant.)
Vocabulary	3 pts.	There is a wealth of lower-frequency vocabulary used (e.g., *traverser un pont, jouer aux billiards, rester chez moi, beaucoup belle filles*) but there are also some inaccuracies (e.g., *est voici, petite fille, prochain.*)
Grammar	2 pts.	There is emerging use of basic language structures. Some verbs are conjugated correctly (e.g., *est, vais, aime, vont, allons, mange, joue*) but half the verbs do not show control of the present tense, particularly when they follow the conjunction "et" (e.g., *nous mangent, allons et jouer).* There are also frequent errors of articles (e.g., *l'hamburger, __chocolat*) and gender (e.g., *beaucoup belle filles, eau minéral*)
Mechanics	3 pts.	The spelling and accents are mostly accurate, although there are some errors (e.g., *aimis, resteraunt, beacoup*)
Level of Discourse	4 pts.	There is a variety of complete sentences and cohesive devices (e.g., *après, parce que, toujours, encore, mais, le soir*)
This sample produces a raw score of 18 out of 24 points, 87 %, B, and falls in the range of "Meets Expectations."		

French Sample 3. Almost Meets Expectations

Lundi est ma jour occupé. Dans le matin ma méré prépre le céral. Mon péré va allons ou buréau à huit heure. Ma méré va allons ou buréau à sept heure. Je vais ou lyceé à sept heure et demie. Je plus tard. Je vais ou biologie. Biologie est mon cours premire. Le cour fisit à neuf heure et huit. Le midi je mange un sandwich et je parle avec mes copains. Aprés le ecôle, je rentre à la maison. Je à pied avec mon chain. Je péprer le diner pour le nuit. Je fais mes devoirs. Je mange le diner avec ma famille. Je dormir à dix heure.

Monday is my busy day. Inside the morning, my mother prepares cereal. My father is going go or office at eight o'clock. My mother is going go or office at seven o'clock. I go or high school at half past seven. I later. I go or biology. Biology is my class first. The class finishes at 9:08. Noon I eat a sandwich and I talk to my friends. After school I go home. I on foot with my chain [dog]. I prepare the dinner for the night. I do my homework. I eat dinner with my family. I to sleep at ten o'clock.

Justification of Rating using the Analytic Rubrics

Task Completion	2.5 pts.	The student completes the task by mentioning morning, afternoon, and evening activities, but the sentences about the mother and father are marginally appropriate and the ideas are undeveloped.
Comprehensibility	2 pts.	The text is mostly comprehensible but does require interpretation on the part of the reader (e.g., *vais allons, je plus tard, je à pied, avec mon chain*).
Vocabulary	2 pts.	The vocabulary is somewhat inadequate and inaccurate. Only one class is mentioned; the choice of vocabulary is limited and some words cause the reader to guess (e.g., *je plus tard, fisit, mon chain*).
Grammar	2 pts.	The writer is mostly accurate when using the subject and verb with *je* but the near future is incorrect (*va allons*), there are verbs omitted (*je plus tard*) and agreement problems (*le nuit, le école*) . There is insufficient evidence of correct grammar other than subject-verb agreement to demonstrate emerging control, thus the rating of emerging use.

Mechanics	2.5 pts.	The spelling is somewhat inaccurate (e.g., *prépre, céral, premire, fisit)* as are many accents (e.g., *péré, buréau, ecôle).* There are no errors in punctuation and capitalization.
Level of Discourse	2.5 pts.	The writer is starting to use a variety of subjects and verbs although many of them still follow the pattern "Je + verb + object" with some cohesive devices (e.g., *le matin, à huit heures, après l'école).*

This sample produces a raw score of 13.5 out of 24 points, a grade of 77%, a C, and falls in the range of "Almost Meets Expectations."

German Sample 1. Exceeds Expectations

Hallo!
   Ich heiße Michelle, aber meine Freunde kennen mich wie Mickey. Ich gehe in die Schule und hab'ich viel Freunde. Ich bin groß und brunette. In meine Freizeit, mache ich die Sports. Ich spiele Basketball, Volleyball, und Tennis. Auch, sammle ich die Briefmarken. Ich gehe in das cinema mit meine Freunde in den Wochenende. Hier in Amerika, haben wir viele Sehenszeigkarten. In D.C., haben wir das Washington Monument. Mi familia ist sehr groß. Ich habe vier Schwestern und drei Bruders. Auch, hab'ich zwei Großmuttern und zwei Großvattern. So, hab'ich vier Großeltern. Das Wetter hier ist sehr toll! Es ist sonnig und hell. Du sollst hier in den Sommer kommen.
   Aufiedersehen.
Mickey

Hi!
   My name is Michelle, but my friends know me as Mickey. I go to school and have I many friends. I am tall and brunette. In my free time, I play sports. I play basketball, volleyball, and tennis. Also, I collect stamps. I go to the movies with my friends on the weekend. Here in America, we have a lot of sights. In DC, we have the Washington Monument. My family is very large. I have four sisters and three brothers. Also I have two grandmothers and two grandfathers. So I have four grandparents. The weather here is very nice. It is sunny and bright. You should come here in the summer.
   Goodbye.
Mickey

206 Ghislaine Tulou and Frances Pettigrew

Justification of Rating using the Analytic Rubrics

Task Completion	4 pts.	This sample demonstrates superior completion of the task. The content is appropriate and well organized with elaboration about free time activities, the family, and the climate (e.g., *Das Wetter hier ist sehr toll! Es ist sonnig und hell. Du sollst hier in den Sommer kommen.*).
Comprehensibility	2.5 pts.	The text is comprehensible, but it does require some interpretation (e.g., *in das cinema, sehenszeigkarten, Mi familia*).
Vocabulary	3 pts.	This sample demonstrates an adequate and accurate use of vocabulary, but it also exhibits creative applications such as *meine Freunde kennen mich...* and prepositional phrases (e.g., *in D.C., mit meine Freunde*).
Grammar	3 pts.	Even though there is control of basic language structures, there are some grammatical errors (e.g., *viel Freunde, in meine Freizeit, in den Wochenende*).
Mechanics	4 pts.,	There are very few errors in spelling (e.g., *Freizeit, Aufiedersehen*) and punctuation (*Auch, habe ich.*).
Level of Discourse	4 pts.,	This sample demonstrates a solid use of varied sentence structures: *Hier in Amerika haben wir...; Du sollst hier en den Sommer kommen.* It also includes several cohesive devices (e.g., *aber, auch, und*).

This sample produces a raw score of 20.5 out of 24 points, a grade of 92.5% (see Figure 4), a B+, and falls in the range of "Exceeds Expectations."

German Sample 2. Meets Expectations

Hallo Heidi!
   Ich heiße Katja. Ich bin fünfzehn jahr alt. Ich sehe schlank aus. Meinen Haar ist blond. Leute sagen mich hubsch. In meine Freizeit hore ich Musikkassetten. Ich mache Poster für mein Zimmer. Mein Vater ist groß une dunkel. Meine Mutter ist hubsch und hell. Sie sind sehn nett. Ict hab drei

schwester und vier Bruder. Sie heissen Margit, Gretchen, Sarah, Stephan, Jon, Bob, und Mike. Meine Lieblingschwister ist Margit. Wir gehen am Ferien meh. Es ist Spaß! Ich liebe Sie.
Hertzliche Grüße

Hello Heidi!
My name is Katja. I am fifteen years old. I am slim. My hair is blond. People call me pretty. In my free time I listen to cassettes. I make posters for my room. My father is tall and dark. My mother is pretty and light. They are very nice. I have three sisters and four brothers. They are called Margit, Gretchen, Sarah, Stephan, Bob, and Mike. My favorite sister is Margit. During our vacation, we go to [the sea]. It is fun. I love them.
Fondest greetings.

Justification of Rating using the Analytic Rubrics

Task Completion	3.5 pts.	The content is appropriate and adequately developed with some elaboration: *Leute sagen mich hubsch; es ist Spaß; ich liebe sie.*
Comprehensibility	3 pts.	The sympathetic reader has no trouble comprehending the information in the letter except for *Wir gehen am Ferien meh.*
Vocabulary	3 pts.	This sample demonstrates adequate and accurate use of vocabulary, except *es ist Spaß.* The student used a variety of verbs (e.g., *heissen, sagen, aussehen, lieben*).
Grammar	3.5 pts.	There is control of the basic language structures: subject-verb agreement, possessive adjectives, and word order. However, there are several grammatical errors: *fünfzehn Jahr, Leute sagen mich, in meine Freizeit, meinen Haar.*
Mechanics	3 pts.	The mechanics are adequate in spite of a few errors: Umlaut (e.g., *hubsch, hore, Grüße*); capitalization (e.g., *jahr*) and punctuation (e.g., *hab*).
Level of Discourse	2.5 pts.	There is a variety of complete sentences, but they include only one cohesive devise: *in meine Freizeit.*

This sample produces a raw score of 18.5 out of 24 points, 88%, a B, and falls in the range of "Meets Expectations."

German Sample 3. Almost Meets Expectations

Liebe student,
   Ich heisse Jonathan. Ich bin 15 jahre alt. Ich bin aus Jacksonville, Florida.
Wie heisst du? Wie alt bist du? Ich spiele lacrosse une Ich schwimme. Was
machst du in deiner freizeit? Ich live in das einfamilien haus. Es hat 3 toiletten,
1 Wohnung, und 1 Kuche. Es ist gross. Es hat 11 zimmer. Was ist du haus wie?
Tschus!
Jonathan

Dear student,
   My name is Jonathan. I am fifteen years old. I am from Jacksonville, Florida.
What is your name? How old are you? I play lacrosse and I swim. What do
you do in your spare time? I live in a single family house. It has three bathrooms,
an apartment and a kitchen. It is large. It has eleven rooms. What is your house
like? Bye!
Jonathan

Justification of Rating using the Analytic Rubrics

Task Completion	2.5 pts.	This sample is short and undeveloped although appropriate. The student does not describe himself nor tell about his family.
Comprehensibility	2 pts.	The task is mostly comprehensible but requires interpretation even by a sympathetic reader: *Was ist du Haus wie? Ich live.*
Vocabulary	2 pts.	Vocabulary is somewhat inadequate and lacks sufficient variety to attain the adequate level: *ich heisse... Wie heisst du? Ich schwimme.* The only nouns used are *Lacrosse, Toiletten, Wohnung, Kuche, Zimmer,* and *Haus.*
Grammar	2.5 pts.	This sample shows emerging use of basic language structures. Although these structures are used correctly in memorized utterances, when the student creates with the language, the level of accuracy drops, and there are very few examples of basic language structures (for example, the student uses no inverted word order, few subject pronouns)

Mechanics	2 pts.	This sample demonstrates some inaccurate spelling (e.g., *einfamilien haus, Kuche, Tschus*). There are also many capitalization errors: *jahre, lacrosse, Ich, freizeit, einfamilien haus, toiletten, zimmer, haus.*
Level of Discourse	2 pts.	There is a predominant use of complete but very simple sentences with no cohesive devices.

This sample produces a raw score of 13 out of 24 points, a grade of 76%, a C, and falls in the range of "Almost Meets Expectations."

Spanish Sample 1. Exceeds Expectations

Mi casa tiene tres pisos. En mi casa hay tres dormitorios y tres baños. Hay un baño en la planta bája al lado de la sala y la cocina. La cocina es grande, y tiene un refrigerador blanco y una estufa. En el primer piso hay un dormitorio y un baño y una sala. En el sala hay dos sofas y una mesa pequeña y una television. En el segundo piso hay dos dormitorios y un baño. El dormitorios son blancos. Cada dormitorio tiene dos ventanas. Mi casa está cerca del autobus. Está lejos de la escuela. Está cerca de la iglesia. Compra mi casa, por favor.

My house has three floors. In my house there are three bedrooms and three bathrooms. There is a bath downstairs next to the living room and kitchen. The kitchen is big, and has a white refrigerator and stove. On the second floor there is a bedroom and a bath and a den. In the den there are two sofas and a little table and a TV. On the third floor, there are two bedrooms and a bath. The bedrooms are white. Each bedroom has two windows. My house is near the bus stop. It is far from the school. It is near the church. Buy my house, please.

Justification of Rating using the Analytic Rubrics

Task Completion	4 pts.	This sample demonstrates superior completion of the task because the student gives a detailed and organized description of the home. The writing flows and the student really tries to help the real estate agent sell the house. The final sentence is a nice conclusion.
Comprehensibility	3 pts.	The text is comprehensible; only one sentence requires interpretation (e.g., *el dormitorio son blancos*) because the reader is uncertain of the number of white bedrooms.

Vocabulary	4 pts.	The sample demonstrates a rich use of learned vocabulary: names of rooms, color, size, and additional information about each room.
Grammar	4 pts.	This sample demonstrates control of basic language structures. Verbs are conjugated correctly, adjectives agree with nouns and are placed correctly, definite and indefinite articles are appropriately selected.
Mechanics	3.5 pts.	The text contains no errors in spelling, punctuation, or capitalization, although there are a few errors in the use of accents (e.g., *bája, sofas, television, autobus*).
Level of Discourse	3 pts.	There is an emerging variety of complete sentences with some cohesive devices (e.g., *en mi casa, en el primer piso, en el segundo*). Although repetitive, these cohesive devices do advance the flow of the text.

This sample produces a raw score of 21.5 out of 24 points, a grade of 94% (see Figure 4), an A, and falls in the range of "Exceeds Expectations."

Spanish Sample 2. Meets Expectations

Mi Casa
  Mi casa es muy limpio y grande. Mi casa es blanca. Hay dos pisos en mi casa. Mi casa tiene solo una cocina, dos baños, cinco dormitorios, una sala, un comedor, y un garaje. Mi cocina es blanca. Está en el piso. Mi cocina tiene la estufa, y el refrigerador. Mi cocina está a la derecha del comedor. Mi comedor tiene seis sillas y una televisión. Mi madre limpian la casa todos los días. Me gusta mi casa mucho.

  My house is very clean and big. My house is white. There are two floors in my house. My house has only one kitchen, two bathrooms, five bedrooms, one living room, one dining room and a garage. My kitchen is white. It is on the floor. My kitchen has a stove, and a refrigerator. My kitchen is to the right of the dining room. My dining room has 6 chairs and a TV. My mother clean the house every day. I like my house a lot.

Justification of Rating using the Analytic Rubrics

Task Completion	3 pts.	The task is complete. The student writes an appropriate description of the home, and the ideas are adequately developed.
Comprehensibility	3 pts.	The text is comprehensible but does require minimal interpretation from the reader in one instance: *Está en el piso.*
Vocabulary	3 pts.	The vocabulary in this sample is adequate and accurate. The word choices are appropriate but there is no evidence of a rich variety of vocabulary.
Grammar	4 pts.	The text demonstrates control of basic language structures. (e.g., articles, *ser* and *estar, gusta*; although there is an error with *mi madre limpian*).
Mechanics	4 pts.	There are no errors in spelling, punctuation, capitalization, or use of accents.
Level of Discourse	2 pts.	There is a predominant use of complete yet repetitive sentences with no cohesive devices.
This sample produces a raw score of 19 out of 24 points, or a grade of 89 %, a B, and therefore falls in the range of "Meets Expectations."		

Spanish Sample 3. Almost Meets Expectations

Mi casa es muy grande. Son tres pisos en mi casa. Hay cuatro baños, cuatro dormitorios, dos comedores, dos salas, y garaje grande. Los baños tienen duchas. La concina tiene el refrigerador y la estufa. Los Dormitorios están en primo piso, y so muy grandes. Hay dos baños en primo piso. La concina está derecha de la sala grande. El comedor es a lado de la sala pequeña. Son muy ventanas en mi casa. Hay diecisiete ventanas en la planta baja y cuatorce ventanas en el primo piso. Mi casa es barata tambien.

My house is very big. They are three floors in my house. There are four bathrooms, four bedrooms, two dining rooms, two living rooms, and big garage. The bathrooms have showers. The kitchen has the refrigerator and the stove. The Bedrooms are on cousin [first] floor, and are very big. There are two bathrooms on cousin [first] floor. The kitchen is right of the big living room. The dining room is next to the small living room. They are very windows in my house. There are 17 windows on the main floor and fourteen windows on the cousin [first] floor. My house is inexpensive also.

Justification of Rating using the Analytic Rubrics

Task Completion	3 pts.	This sample completes the task. Its content is appropriate, and the ideas are adequately developed. It describes the number of floors, names several rooms and their size, and tells where they are located.
Comprehensibility	2.5 pts.	The text is mostly comprehensible, requiring some interpretation on the part of the reader. The reader has to pause to comprehend (e.g., *en primo piso* and *so muy grandes*) The reading of the text is slowed due to other frequent but minor errors such as *a concina* and *son tres pisos*
Vocabulary	2.5 pts.	The vocabulary of the text is adequate for the task and level because it uses a variety of newly-learned vocabulary related to the topic. However, it is somewhat inaccurate due to such errors as *primo piso* and *muy ventanas*.
Grammar	2.5 pts.	There is evidence of emerging control of some basic language structures. (e.g., word order, noun-adjective agreement and *tiene*). However, there is less control of other basic language structures such as the use of articles, and there is cohfusion about the uses of *ser, estar,* and *hay*.
Mechanics	2.5 pts.	Punctuation, capitalization, and use of accents are mostly accurate, but there are some errors in spelling (e.g., *concina, so,* and *cuatorce*).
Level of Discourse	2 pts.	There is predominant use of complete yet repetitive sentences. These sentences make repeated use of only four different verbs *ser, hay, tener* and *estar* . There is only one cohesive device (e.g., *tambien*).

This sample produces a raw score of 15 out of 24 points, a grade of 80.5 %, a C+, and falls in the range of "Almost Meets Expectations."

Using Rubrics as Instructional Tools

While PALS assesses student performance, one of its key goals is more student-oriented. Unlike traditional tests, the PALS process involves students in evaluating their learning and teaches them techniques and strategies to build their language skills. When students know what is expected of them, where they are, and where they are going, they can take better control of their own learning.

We recommend that students receive the speaking and writing rubrics early in the school year and learn to apply them using models of student performance the teachers provide. After working with the models and receiving feedback from the teacher on the accuracy of their scoring, the students continue to practice applying the rubrics by scoring each others' samples and, once again, comparing their scores with those of the teacher. Soon, they are able to apply the rubrics to their own samples with surprising accuracy. This in-depth and ongoing practice with the rubrics gives the students a clear understanding of the characteristics of each level of performance within each domain and enables them to see their own strengths and weaknesses. As a result of reflecting on their own performances, the students learn how to develop their language skills, and they are able to take more responsibility for their learning. Consequently, the use of rubrics throughout the school year and the process of peer and self-assessment combined with feedback from the teacher enable students to use the rubrics as instructional tools.

The PALS group has found the following six steps very effective in engaging students in the learning process and helping them improve their performance.

Step 1: Introduce the Domains of the Rubrics

To begin, the teacher explains to the students that they are going to produce an oral or written performance and shows models of typical performance tasks. The teacher then asks students to get into groups of three and write down what characteristics, or domains, they think describe the best performances. After three minutes of brainstorming, the students share their ideas. The teacher records these suggestions on an overhead transparency and links them to the domains of the rubrics. In this manner, the students and teacher develop a common understanding of the six domains.

Step 2: Teach Students How to Apply the Criteria

The teacher explains the four different levels of performance to the students. We have found it helpful to start with the "Meets Expectations" level. Students will immediately want to know how these four performance levels relate to grades, so the teacher explains that "Meets Expectations" is a B, "Exceeds Expectations" is an A, "Almost Meets Expectations" is a C, and "Does Not Meet Expectations" is a D or an F.

Next, the teacher presents the levels of performance for each domain. For example, in the domain of "Fluency," the class reads each descriptor and the teacher clarifies it. Once again, it is helpful to start with the "Meets Expectations" level of performance. In order to further ensure a good understanding of these levels, the teacher presents models or examples for each level of performance. The students then practice scoring two or three sample performances using the models and the rubrics.

Step 3: Give the Students a New Task to Perform

Once the students understand how their performance will be evaluated and have analyzed models of performance, they are ready to perform their own task. The teacher will state the objective of the task, give clear directions, and later, evaluate the performance but withhold the scoring results.

Step 4: Teach Students to Evaluate the Performances of Peers

The teacher will place students in groups of four or five. Each student has his or her sample performance, a copy of the rubric, and five peer-evaluation forms (see Figure 6). Each student will evaluate one domain of each sample performance from each of the four or five in his or her group. The teacher assigns a different domain to each student. For example, for a writing task, student A evaluates task completion, student B concentrates on comprehensibility, student C assesses vocabulary, student D verifies subject-verb agreement or other basic language structures. The peer-evaluation form guides students to provide specific evidence to support their assessments. When the peer-evaluation forms are completed, they are given to the student whose sample was evaluated. With this information, the student completes the scoring chart included on the rubric.

Figure 6. Peer Evaluation Form for Speaking Tasks, Level 1

Student Being Evaluated: _____

Task: _____ *Date:* _____

Peer Evaluator: _____

Domain Evaluated: _____ *Rating:* ____ /4

Comments: Wow!!(evidence)   Oops!! (evidence)

_____   _____

_____   _____

_____   _____

_____   _____

Step 4: Alternate

Have students evaluate their own performance. As students become more experienced with the process and familiar with the rubrics, peer assessment can be replaced by self-assessment. In order to self-assess the quality of their performance, students will need their sample of perform- ance, a copy of the rubric, and a student scoring sheet. The teacher will ask students to determine at which level they have performed for each domain of the rubric. They may use the scoring chart on the rubric. When appropriate, students should also provide evidence in their work that sub- stantiates their assessment.

Step 5: Give Students Feedback on Their Self-Evaluation

When the students have completed their student scoring sheets, they compare their evaluation with that of the teacher (from Step 3). If neces- sary, students recalibrate their understanding of the rubric with that of the teacher.

Step 6: Help Students Develop Plans for Improvement

When the evaluation process has been completed and the teacher and the student agree on the rating, the students complete the Performance Improvement Plan (PIP) (see Figure 7). The PIP encourages students to reflect on their work and take responsibility for assessing themselves. This process helps lay the groundwork for continuous improvement. The teacher then collects the PIP from each student and provides written feedback.

Figure 7: Performance Improvement Plan for Speaking Tasks, Level 1

Student: _____

Task: _____ *Date:* _____

My Score in each Domain:

Scoring Chart

Task Completion	$^1/_2$	1	$^1/_2$	2	$^1/_2$	3	$^1/_2$	4
Comprehensibility	$^1/_2$	1	$^1/_2$	2	$^1/_2$	3	$^1/_2$	4
Fluency	$^1/_2$	1	$^1/_2$	2	$^1/_2$	3	$^1/_2$	4
Pronunciation	$^1/_2$	1	$^1/_2$	2	$^1/_2$	3	$^1/_2$	4
Vocabulary	$^1/_2$	1	$^1/_2$	2	$^1/_2$	3	$^1/_2$	4
Grammar	$^1/_2$	1	$^1/_2$	2	$^1/_2$	3	$^1/_2$	4

Raw Score: _____

My strengths: _____

I need to work on: _____

In the beginning of the year, the teacher leads the students through the six steps in order to acquaint them with the PALS process. After the initial familiarization, it is important to review the rubrics regularly and to have the students use them to evaluate their own work and that of their peers. The students should have the opportunity to evaluate at least one speaking and one writing assessment per quarter.

Using PALS for Summative Assessment

*"Performance Assessment gives you a clear idea
of where you stand as a student."*

Level-2 student

In addition to using formative assessments at the end of a unit of study, similar speaking and writing performance tasks may be used for mid-year and year-end assessments. As used by the teachers piloting PALS, the purpose of the summative assessments is to chart the progress of each student on a proficiency continuum based on the ACTFL K–12 Performance Guidelines. By year-end, we anticipate that 85% of level-1 students should perform at a Novice High level or above, 85% of level-2 students should perform an Intermediate Low level or above, and 85 % of level-3 students should perform at an Intermediate Mid level or above. In our school system, teachers will submit a range of student performances, both in speaking and writing, to the Foreign Language Office. These samples will be rated by a committee of teachers over the summer in order to verify the ratings and adjust the target of 85%, if necessary.

Tasks for Summative Assessments

Because the mid-year and end-of-year tasks are not tied to a single unit of study and are used to establish a proficiency level, they need to be very open-ended and unrehearsed. Students also need to have several tasks to perform in order to assure a more reliable rating (Karen Breiner-Sanders, personal communication, February 20, 1998). In addition, the tasks should give level-1 and level-2 students the opportunity to perform at the novice and intermediate levels, and level-3 students the opportunity to perform at the intermediate levels. Consequently, PALS decided to develop three speaking and three writing tasks for each level of study to be used in French, German, and Spanish. In order to contextualize and link the tasks, each set of three was incorporated into one scenario, as the sample for level 3 illustrates (Figure 8); comparable tasks were created for levels 1 and 2.

The speaking test, which consists of three short oral prompts based on real-life tasks, is audiotaped. Students are expected to respond spontaneously (without prior preparation) to each prompt. They have only 60 seconds in which to read each prompt and organize each response (they may jot down notes within that time limit). Each oral response must be completed in 60 seconds. These procedures are similar to those developed for use with the Simulated Oral Proficiency Interview (SOPI) (Stansfield & Kenyon, 1992).

For the written test (see Figure 9), the three short written prompts are again based on real-life tasks. Students write in class without aid of a dictionary or prior preparation. The test should have a reasonable time limit (or be untimed), and students should write a minimum of 10–15 sentences (or $^1/_2$ page, approximately 100 words) for each prompt.

Figure 8. End-of-Year Speaking Tasks, Level 3

Scenario: As part of a program to promote global understanding, you have entered a contest to win a free trip to France/Germany/Spain. For the application you must submit three speaking samples on tape to share some of your ideas and show your linguistic ability.

Prompt #1 (60 seconds to prepare, 60 seconds to speak)
Describe the person you most admire and explain why. You may want to include a description of him/her and his/her influence on you.

Prompt #2 (60 seconds to prepare, 60 seconds to speak)
Describe your plans for the future. You may want to include summer, college, or career plans.

Prompt #3 (60 seconds to prepare, 60 seconds to speak)
Describe the best class you ever remember taking and tell why it was the best. You may want to include what you learned and how and why it affected you.

Figure 9. End-of-Year Writing Tasks, Level 3

Scenario: You are a reporter-at-large for your school newspaper and have been assigned to write three different articles on topics of interest to the students at your school.

Prompt #1 (10–15 sentences, or $^1/_2$ page, or 100 words)
Write a short article about holistic health for adolescents with suggestions for being a well-rounded, successful, healthy young adult. You may want to include diet, exercise, study habits, activities, and social life.

Prompt #2 (10–15 sentences, or $^1/_2$ page, or 100 words)
You have polled many of the student leaders at your school, asking their opinions on the advantages and disadvantages of living in this community. Now write a short article detailing life in your community from a teenage perspective. You may want to include activities, people, government, and suggested improvements.

Prompt #3 (10–15 sentences, or $^1/_2$ page, or 100 words)
As part of the last edition of the school newspaper, you are asked to write "The Year in Review" with highlights from this past school year. You may want to include events that took place, special memories, and an overall evaluation of the year.

Using the ACTFL K–12 Performance Guidelines in the Classroom

"The best thing about performance assessment is that it allows us as students to see where we fall on a big continuum against set standards."

Level-3 student

Summative assessment uses the ACTFL K–12 Performance Guidelines to place the student's performance on a proficiency continuum. Summative assessment may also use a holistic rating such as "Meets Expectations" or "Exceeds Expectations" to determine a general level of performance. Just as students need to learn to use rubrics as an instructional tool, it is important for them to understand that performance in a foreign language can be placed on a continuum, and the goal of the learner is to progress along that continuum. The ACTFL K–12 Performance Guidelines enable students and teachers to place a speaking sample on a continuum that ranges from novice to pre-advanced and merges afterward with the ACTFL Proficiency Guidelines (1986). The McLean High School Foreign Language Department created a visual to illustrate the progress of a typical foreign language student on the continuum (see Figure 10). As in Omaggio Hadley's (1993) illustration of ACTFL's Inverted Pyramid, the novice sections of the fan chart are relatively small. The intermediate sections are much larger because secondary students spend most of their years of foreign language study at the intermediate level. Furthermore, the advanced section is small because only students with substantial outside experience and education attain this level.

Figure 10. The Language Learning Continuum, Speaking
Fairfax County Public Schools

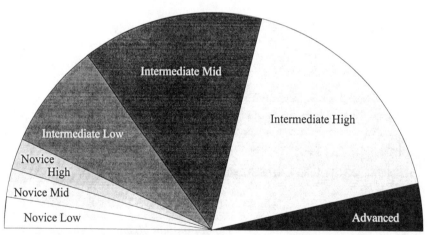

The teacher can use the visual in Figure 10 to explain the ACTFL K–12 Performance Guidelines, and the students can use it to chart their progress on the continuum and enhance their awareness of their proficiency. To further enhance their understanding of proficiency, the students receive a written summary of the characteristics of each level, based on the descriptors of the ACTFL Proficiency Guidelines (1986):

Novice Low
- Uses isolated words and a few high-frequency phrases to talk about very specific subjects, such as numbers, colors, and the names of common objects.

Novice Mid
- Uses isolated words, phrases and occasional memorized utterances, formulaic and stock phrases to talk about certain specific learned topics, such as weather, food, and names of family members.
- May contain long hesitations, silences, and/or repetitions and/or reversion to L1.
- May have poor pronunciation.

Novice High
- Shows emerging ability to create with language by expanding on learned material.
- Relies on personalized recombinations of words, phrases, and stock phrases.
- Shows sporadic and inconsistent creation of sentences.
- Uses simple vocabulary to talk about personal and limited topics.
- May have long hesitations and/or repetition and/or reversion to L1.
- May appear surprisingly fluent and accurate due to reliance on memorized utterances.
- May have poor pronunciation.

Intermediate Low
- Shows ability to create with the language using basic novel sentences marked by frequent errors of word choice and verb formation.
- Uses limited, simple, basic vocabulary to talk about topics related to self, family, friends, and everyday life.
- Produces little variety of information.
- Shows emerging control of the present tense and near future.
- Response may be halting with frequent groping for words and occasional reversion to L1.
- May have poor pronunciation.

Intermediate Mid
- Shows ability to create with the language using a variety of disconnected, discrete sentences with some errors in word choice and verb formation.
- May use a few cohesive devices.
- Shows control of present tense and near future.

- Shows control of basic vocabulary and the ability to talk about topics related to self, family, home, school, daily activities, leisure activities, personal preferences, and interests.
- Produces some variety of information.
- Shows good fluency but speech still may contain frequent pauses, repetitions, and frequent groping for words.
- May show inaccurate pronunciation of words and a strong non-native accent.

Intermediate High
- Shows evidence of connected discourse and emergence of organizational features.
- Produces longer sentences showing partial control of cohesive and subordinate devices.
- Shows control of present tense but uses the past tenses and the future inconsistently.
- Talks with ease about personal activities and immediate surroundings.
- Talks with limited ability about some areas of general interest.
- Has only occasional pauses or groping for words.
- Is usually understood by native speakers unaccustomed to dealing with non-native speakers.

Impact and Effect on Students

The teachers who have piloted PALS in their classrooms have observed positive effects on the attitudes of the students. As important as the teachers' observations, however, are the students' own views. In June 1998, we asked five level-3 classes to respond to the following: "Imagine that a new student came to your foreign language class last week as you were preparing for your final performance assessment. What would you tell him/her is the best thing about performance assessment in your foreign language class?" These responses are particularly meaningful because they express the students' insights in their own words. Examination of these responses revealed that they fell into several categories: expectations, teacher and peer feedback, fairness, keys to success, and self-awareness.

Expectations:

The performance assessment really helps you realize what's expected of you. It also helps you set goals for yourself and helps you understand the areas in which you need help.

It is very clear and tells exactly what needs to be achieved to reach the expectations for your level of study.

You get an idea of what is expected of you.

Teacher and Peer Feedback:

You get other people's opinions and most of the time that will help you become a better Spanish writer and speaker.

Good feedback.

I would tell him/her that the best thing about performance assessment is having your piece, whether oral or written, analyzed for different aspects of a piece and being told where you stand on those characteristics.

Fairness:

It is an accurate representation of your skill as a Spanish language speaker and writer.

It is a fair way to show actual ability to use French in a realistic situation.

Clear basis for grades, comprehensible grading scale, good idea of what grade is and why it's at the level it's at.

It is fair and by the grade you get you can see what you need to work on and what your strengths are.

Even though you make mistakes, it won't sink your grade!

The best thing about performance assessment is it is always fair to every student. You won't get a bad grade because the teacher dislikes you, and teacher's pets don't necessarily get a good grade.

Keys to Success:

Just try your best and don't be afraid to take risks on what you want to say.

Don't get nervous and just keep on talking no matter what — don't worry about any mistakes you make.

I would tell him/her to show off with everything you know.

It's easy to do well if you participate in class and do your homework.

The best thing is that you get a chance to start from scratch and show what you know.

Self-Awareness:

> It gives us suggestions on how to improve on our writing and speaking. It encourages us to learn more vocabulary and doesn't focus too much on grammar.

> I would say the best thing was that even if you do badly you can see what areas you are struggling in and try to work on that for the next assessment.

> Performance assessment allows you to see what you need to work on.

> It helps you strengthen your language or at least practice and it shows how much you know and it lets you know where you need help. The tapes are fun!

> It kind of lets people go at their own pace.

These responses confirm what we had hoped: that PALS provides clear expectations for student performance and facilitates feedback from peers and teachers. It encourages students to show what they know and can do in the language and helps them develop critical thinking skills to be more aware of their learning. Students believe that PALS is a fair and effective tool to involve them in their own learning, leading them to take ownership in the acquisition of skills and to become more responsible learners.

Responses to Student Survey

The question that prompted the student responses above was part of a survey investigating student understanding of the PALS process and their evaluation of its effectiveness.[3] The level-3 survey, administered to five classes with a total of 103 students, is included in the Appendix along with the survey results.

Most of the survey (questions 1–15) focuses on the students' understanding of the PALS speaking and writing rubrics and performance expectations and their perceptions of the usefulness of them. Over 80% of the students agreed that using the PALS rubrics provided them with a clear picture of their strengths and the areas where they needed to improve their foreign language skills. In addition, over 80% of the students reported that they understood the domains of the speaking and writing rubrics well enough to explain them, if asked to do so, except in the areas of grammar and level of discourse. The responses to the grammar questions approach the 80% level (78.2% for speaking and 79% for writing). The level-of-discourse percentage (67.6%) suggests that the students needed clearer explanations and better models for this domain.

Three questions (16, 17, and 18) ask about the effectiveness of peer assessment. Although there is a drop in the percentage of positive responses to these questions (62.1%, 66%, 52.4%), it should be noted that over half the students agreed that the peer-feedback process was beneficial. The survey did not request student explanations for their ratings, so it is not possible to speculate on the source of student dissatisfaction. However, additional comments on peer feedback were gathered in the five level-3 classes. In support of the peer assessment procedure, one student wrote, "I liked it because you got to listen to people who got higher grades and you could see what they did better. And you can see what you did wrong. Listening to myself and others helped me to realize my speaking ability. So I know what to do next time." Similarly, another student responded, "I thought it was helpful to listen to my tape so I could see where I needed to improve and where I was good. It helps overcome nervousness by listening to everyone's tape and honestly critiquing. Comparing your tape to others gives you an idea of where you stand." These students seem to be aware that analyzing the samples of other students' work exposes them to a variety of performances from which they can learn.

Two questions (19 and 20) elicit student views of self-assessment through the use of the Performance Improvement Plan (PIP). Despite the limited opportunity students had to work with this component (only one year), 63.7% of the students stated that the PIP was helpful to them as learners. Only 10.8% disagreed. Examination of some sample PIP self-analyses reveals the students' insights into their performance:

My strengths: I know what I want to say. I just need to say it.
I need to work on: Transition words, vocabulary, making sense in general, not pausing, knowing what I want to say, make sure I complete task and then elaborate.

My strengths: Grammar, fairly good vocabulary, speaking is comprehensible. I used the conditional and other expressions like "à votre place."
I need to work on: Fluency, transition words, elaboration/details. I hesitated several times, and more transition words would help. Further details would also fill in pauses.

My strengths: For the most part, easy to understand. Completion of most sentences. No tense problems. Not switching back and forth from present/past/etc.
I need to work on: Level of discourse and elaboration. There weren't many linking words in either sample—and more detail could have been given about the surroundings.

The self-awareness and reflection evident in these analyses are just what teachers and educators encourage. Considering the support of educators, it is interesting that 10.8% of the students did not find the PIP useful. Perhaps, as suggested by Wenden and Chamot elsewhere in this volume, teachers need to teach learners explicitly the value of developing the metacognitive skills of planning, monitoring, problem solving, and evaluating.

Question 21 asks students to comment about the fairness of the grade produced using the PALS rubric. It is encouraging that 69.6% of the students agreed that the use of rubrics produces a fair grade. However, 16.7% stated that they were uncertain, and 13.7% disagreed. Based on anecdotal evidence, the teachers in the PALS program suggest that analytic learners may benefit from the use of rubrics more than global learners. In an effort to accommodate these intuitive learners, the teachers have agreed to provide more models to the students in the future.

Six questions (22–27, 32) check the students' comprehension of the ACTFL proficiency continuum. Although 60.8% of the students stated that they understood the proficiency continuum based on the ACTFL Guidelines, a much higher percentage (approximately 80%) had a clear picture of novice, intermediate, and advanced performance. Most of the students (76.5%) disagreed with the statement, "My friends and I all perform at the advanced level," thus confirming their ability to identify their skill level on the ACTFL continuum.

Three questions (28–30) probe the comfort level of students and their willingness to take risks as they develop their skills in the language. The positive responses to these questions are close to 50% or slightly above. Testing, and oral performance in particular, are stressful experiences (Horwitz & Young, 1991), and the PALS teachers are committed to working with the students to help them view learning as a process and assessment as a step in that process. As students are given multiple opportunities to perform and some control over the selection of samples to submit for a grade, we expect that the students' comfort level and their willingness to take risks will increase.

Question 31 asks if the discussions of performance assessment and the explanation of the rubrics in English were worthwhile even though they took time away from speaking the target language. Nearly 80% of the students surveyed agreed that the discussions in English were beneficial. Though no data were kept regarding the amount of English used in the classes to explain the PALS procedures, after initial explanations, most teachers in the project transitioned into target language appropriate to their classes. The PALS project is considering developing rubrics in the target languages taught in our schools.

In general, the student responses overwhelmingly indicate a high level of understanding and confidence in PALS. Preliminary analysis of surveys of students at levels 1 and 2 corroborates these findings. It is clear that students value performance assessment and its role in language learning. One student remarked, "Performance assessment is good in our school for it shows you where you stand in the language and tells you exactly what you need to do to reach your level of expectations."

Why The PALS Acronym Fits

As PALS enters its fourth year, both students and teachers see the benefits clearly. Students appreciate the fact that they are evaluated on what they *can* do, not on what they can't do. Before they start work on a task they know the expectations for each level of performance. In addition, they are able to follow their progress on a continuum based on national guidelines. Because performance assessment focuses on what students can do and need to do in the language, some low-frequency structures lose their importance, and teachers collaborate as they identify the essential elements to be taught at each level of instruction. Furthermore, articulation is improved as teachers discuss students' levels of performance and establish inter-rater reliability. Students also learn to recognize the importance of the essential elements to be learned and are involved in identifying and improving their own level of performance. As a result, this active involvement on the part of the students creates a classroom environment in which students and teachers work as a team to build language skills.

Notes

[1]We would like to give special thanks to Martha Abbott, Coordinator of Foreign Language Instruction in Fairfax County Public Schools, who had the vision to begin this project in 1995 and whose support has been essential to its continuation. We would also like to thank Lori Bland, Research and Program Evaluation Specialist for Fairfax County Public Schools, for assisting with the rubrics and score-conversion charts. We are particularly grateful to our colleagues and our students at McLean High School and throughout Fairfax County for their input and support and for the invaluable role they play in the success of PALS.

[2]Speaking and writing rubrics for levels 1 and 2, along with other PALS information, are available on the World Wide Web at http://www.fcps.k12.va.us/DIS/OHSICS/forlang. Level-3 rubrics will be posted when they have been revised.

[3]The survey, adjusted slightly by level, was also given to 38 students in level 1 and 63 students in level 2. Only the level-3 results are summarized here. The results of the other surveys are available from the authors.

References

Amado, P. M., Aninao, J. C., & Sung, H. (1996). Development and implementation of student portfolios in foreign language programs. *Foreign Language Annals, 29*(3), 429–438.

American Council on the Teaching of Foreign Languages. (1986). *ACTFL proficiency guidelines.* New York, NY: Author.

American Council on the Teaching of Foreign Languages. (1998). *ACTFL K–12 performance guidelines.* New York, NY: Author.

Canady, L. (1993, December). *Grading practices which decrease the odds of student success.* Presentation given at the Virginia Association of Supervision and Curriculum Development Annual Conference, Williamsburg, VA.

Fairfax County Public Schools. (1996). *Middle school grading and reporting: Rationale for change.* Fairfax, VA: Author.

Fairfax County Public Schools. (1997, August). Building assessments that serve learning and instruction. Summer assessment seminar initiative.

Guskey, T., & Johnson, D. (1996, October). Reporting student learning. Presentation at the Association for Supervision and Curriculum Development (ASCD) Conference on Teaching, Learning, and Assessment, Dallas, TX.

Hancock, C. (Ed.). (1994). *Teaching, testing, and assessment: Making the connection.* Northeast Conference Reports. Lincolnwood, IL: National Textbook Co.

Herman, J., Aschbacher, P., & Winters, L. (1992). *A practical guide to alternative assessment.* Alexandria, VA: ASCD.

Horwitz, E. K., & Young, D. J. (1991). *Language anxiety: From theory and research to classroom implications.* Englewood Cliffs, NJ: Prentice-Hall.

International Baccalaureate Organisation. (1996). *Language B curriculum framework.* Wales, UK: Author.

Jackson, C., Masters-Wicks, K., Phillips, J., Reutershan, D. (1996). *Articulation & achievement: Connecting standards, performance, and assessment in foreign language.* New York: The College Board.

Liskin-Gasparro, J. (1996). Assessment: From content standards to student performance. In R. C. Lafayette (Ed.), *National standards: A catalyst for reform* (pp. 169–196.) ACTFL Foreign Language Education Series. Lincolnwood, IL: National Textbook Co.

National Capital Language Resource Center. (1997). Portfolio assessment in the foreign language classroom. [Workshop presentation].

National Standards in Foreign Language Education Project. (1996). *Standards for foreign language learning: Preparing for the 21st century.* Yonkers, NY: Author.

Omaggio Hadley, A. (1993). *Teaching language in context* (2nd Ed.). Boston, MA: Heinle & Heinle.

Speiller, J., & Yetman, B. M. (1996, November). Portfolio assessment: The Edison, NJ, project. Paper presented at the ACTFL Conference, Nashville.

Stansfield, C. W., & Kenyon, D. M. (1992). The development and validation of a simulated oral proficiency interview. *The Modern Language Journal 76*(2), 129–141.

Valette, R. M. (1994). Teaching, testing, and assessment: Conceptualizing the relationship. In C. Hancock (Ed.), *Teaching, testing, and assessment: Making the connection* (pp. 1–42). Northeast Conference Reports. Lincolnwood, IL: National Textbook Co.
Wiggins, G. (1994). Toward more authentic assessment of language performances. In C. R. Hancock (Ed.), *Teaching, testing, and assessment: Making the connection* (pp. 69–85). Northeast Conference Reports. Lincolnwood, IL: National Textbook Co.

Appendix. PALS Survey — Level 3

Please complete the following survey. Your honest responses and comments will be appreciated. Please read the following statements and rate them from A to E:

A= agree completely   B= agree somewhat   C = uncertain
D= disagree somewhat   E = disagree completely

Question	% A & B	% C	% D & E
1. The use of rubrics helps me understand my teacher's expectations.	89.4	2.9	7.7
2. The use of rubrics helps me see my strengths as a foreign language speaker and writer.	81.7	9.6	8.7
3. The use of rubrics helps me see where I need to improve my speaking and writing skills.	84.6	9.6	5.8
4. The use of models gives me a clear picture of how to meet or exceed expectations.	80.4	12.7	6.9
5–10. If asked, I can explain the levels of performance of the following domains of the speaking rubrics:			
5. Task Completion	88.9	6.1	5.1
6. Comprehensibility	84.0	7.0	9.0
7. Fluency	82.2	12.9	5.0
8. Pronunciation	85.1	9.9	5.0
9. Vocabulary	84.2	11.9	4.0
10. Grammar	78.2	15.8	5.9

11–15. If asked, I can explain the levels of performance of the following domains of the writing rubrics:			
11. Task Completion	89.1	5.9	5.0
12. Comprehensibility	81.2	9.9	8.9
13. Level of Discourse	67.6	20.6	11.8
14. Vocabulary	88.8	8.2	3.1
15. Grammar	79.0	12.0	9.0
16. Using the rubrics to assess other students' performances in small groups helps me see my own strengths.	62.1	17.5	20.4
17. Using the rubrics to assess other students' performances in small groups helps me see how I can improve.	66.0	13.6	20.4
18. The evaluations I received from my peers were helpful to me.	52.4	17.5	30.1
19. Using the Performance Improvement Plan is helpful to me as a learner.	63.7	25.5	10.8
20. Completing the Performance Improvement Plan focuses my attention on what I need to do to improve.	59.8	29.4	10.8
21. Using the rubrics produces a fair grade.	69.6	16.7	13.7
22. I understand the proficiency continuum based on the ACTFL Guidelines.	60.8	27.5	11.8
23. I have a clear picture of a Novice High performance.	82.4	9.8	7.8
24. I have a clear picture of an Intermediate Low performance.	82.5	11.7	5.8
25. I have a clear picture of an Intermediate Mid performance.	82.5	11.7	5.8
26. I have a clear picture of an Intermediate High performance.	79.6	11.7	8.7

27. I have a clear picture of an Advanced performance.	79.6	11.7	8.7
28. The use of rubrics and the ACTFL Guidelines encourages me to take risks as a foreign language speaker.	48.1	26.9	25.0
29. The use of rubrics and the ACTFL Guidelines encourages me to take risks as a foreign language writer.	51.9	23.1	25.0
30. The use of rubrics and the ACTFL Guidelines helps me feel more comfortable as a language learner.	58.3	19.4	22.3
31. Discussion of Performance Assessment and explaining the rubrics in English was worthwhile even though it took time away from speaking the target language.	78.4	10.8	10.8
32. My friends and I all perform at the Advanced level.	11.8	11.8	76.5

Open ended questions. Please use the back of your Scantron form to answer the following questions.

33. Imagine that a new student came to your foreign language class last week as you were preparing for your final performance assessment. What would you tell him / her is the best thing about performance assessment in your foreign language class?

34. If there were one thing you could change about about the performance assessment, what would it be?

35. What outside experience have you had in the foreign language you are studying? (be specific)

36. What is your expected grade in this class?

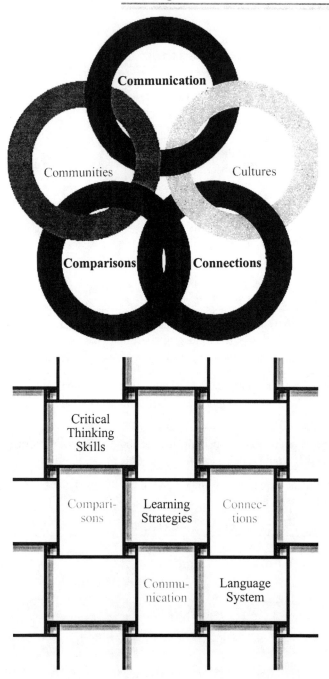

Critical Thinking and Reflective Learning in the Latin Classroom

John Muccigrosso

Drew University

Deborah Pennell Ross

University of Michigan

This chapter looks at specific ways in which critical thinking skills can be fostered and refined in the language classroom, and how the foreign language student can be encouraged to become a more self-reliant and reflective learner. We propose a set of attitudes and behaviors on the part of students which we have observed to be characteristic of strong language students, and we balance these with a set of suggested teacher attitudes and behaviors designed to encourage those outlined for students. Although the examples in this chapter pertain to the Latin classroom, the concepts and techniques we present here are also applicable to the learning and teaching of all languages and even of non-language topics.

The aspects of language learning we address here correspond in the Standards for Classical Language Learning (1997) to Goal 1, Communication, both in and of itself and as it weaves through Goal 3, Connections, and Goal 4, Comparisons. With reference to the National Standards for Foreign Language Learning (1996), our work highlights the "weave elements" of language system, critical thinking, and learning strategies.

This chapter will not concentrate on language-learning theory but will present the practical knowledge we have gained in helping beginning and intermediate Latin students develop critical-thinking skills and self-directed learning strategies. Thus, we report on knowledge derived from "knowing in action" (Schön, 1987). The student voices heard in the chapter were collected from our students via self-reflective, written analyses of test errors, and the teacher voices are those of our colleagues, graduate student instructors, and participants in Latin pedagogy workshops. The voice echoing throughout this chapter is that of our late colleague, Glenn M. Knudsvig, whose creative thinking and passion for teaching and learning we have endeavored to represent here.

What Is Critical Thinking?

Critical thinking has been defined in various ways. Chaffee (1991, p. 35) characterizes it as "an active, purposeful organized process we use to make sense of our world by carefully examining our thinking and the thinking of others, in order to clarify and improve our understanding." In this chapter, we focus on the organized examination of one's own thinking, and use "critical thinking" to mean the reflective integration of lower-level thinking skills into higher-level decisions and analysis. It is essentially a hierarchical construct, one which incorporates categories and subcategories of information as well as a "top-down/bottom-up" processing model. In particular, we will refer to a model of critical thinking developed by Smith et al. (1998) which organizes information under the rubrics of **topic/class/description/relevance**, hereafter TCDR. Here is an example of a very simple TCDR analysis (Smith et al., 1998, p. 4):

A hammer is a tool, consisting of a handle with a heavy "head" placed on one end, used for pounding.

a hammer	the **topic** of the material
a tool	the **class**, the higher level, the main heading
a handle with a heavy head on one end used for pounding	the **description**, the characteristics the **relevance** or use

Here is an example of the same analysis applied to Latin:

The ablative is a case, marked in nouns by the endings -*ā*, -*ō*, -*e*, -*ī*, -*ū*, and -*ē* in the singular and -*īs*, -*ibus*, and -*bus* in the plural, and in adjectives by

-*ā, -ō, -ī,* and -*e* in the singular and -*īs* and -*ibus* in the plural. It expresses various types of adverbial information, including instrument, agent, manner, cause, time, place, accompaniment, and comparison.

the ablative	the **topic**
a case	the **class**
marked by the	the **description**
endings -ā, -ō, etc.	
expresses various types of	the **relevance**
adverbial information	

(To distinguish between generic and technical uses of "topic," we will refer to the TCDR headings in bold face: **topic, class,** etc.)

We refer above to "top-down/bottom-up" processing in reading. This is a vertical model representing both the more general "top-down" knowledge a reader brings, or is expected to bring, to a text, and the linguistic facts which must be brought to bear hierarchically from the "bottom-up" in order to comprehend the text. Processing from both directions is necessary to read effectively and with understanding (Crowder & Wagner, 1992; Smith, 1988; Swaffar et al., 1991). For a discussion of top-down/bottom-up in Latin, see Gruber-Miller (1998).

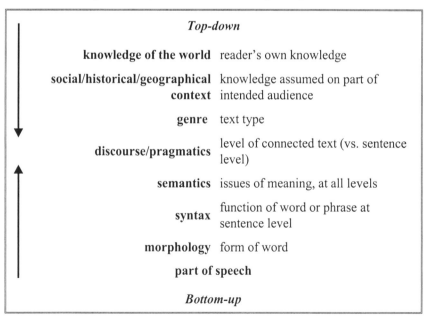

	Top-down
knowledge of the world	reader's own knowledge
social/historical/geographical context	knowledge assumed on part of intended audience
genre	text type
discourse/pragmatics	level of connected text (vs. sentence level)
semantics	issues of meaning, at all levels
syntax	function of word or phrase at sentence level
morphology	form of word
part of speech	
	Bottom-up

In language learning, we can apply the TCDR model not only to the acquisition of information, i.e., the learning of language facts, but also to the process of reading and interpreting the target language, i.e., as a strategy for reading.

What Is Reflective Learning?

We propose that reflective learning has three main aspects. First, reflective learning of new information involves relating the new to the old in the context of TCDR, asking the questions "am I adding a totally new category or class? what previously established category or class am I expanding? am I learning new factual information or new procedural information?" Reflective learners use reflective strategies when processing, i.e., they are aware of themselves as learners involved in the process of learning. They are able to step back from the process and consider their role in it. This calls for questions such as "where am I? how does what I see shape my expectation of what I am going to encounter next?" Third, reflective learning is a component in self-evaluation: "what am I monitoring in my work? am I still making the same errors? am I getting better? faster? reading with more comprehension? am I reading or working with a higher degree of mastery of fundamentals?" (See Barnett, Tulou & Pettigrew, and Wenden, this volume.)

Reflective readers are also aware of their "top-down/bottom-up" processing and are able, when running into difficulty, to isolate the level at which the problem lies. As they struggle with comprehension of the text, they check for specific errors from the bottom-up, asking: "do I have the right part of speech for this word? did I misidentify a form? is there another possible syntactic function for this word?" But they are also conscious of the top-down levels: "am I missing some crucial cultural information that would clarify this? do I understand the referent of this pronoun?"

What Do Critical Thinking and Reflective Learning Look Like in the Latin Classroom?

In the Latin classroom, the critical thinking model of TCDR can be used by the teacher to present new information or topics, by the student to demonstrate comprehension of information or topics, and by both teacher and student for evaluative purposes to determine if the student understands a given topic and the various classes to which it belongs. On a meta-level, the teacher can use it to evaluate the descriptive adequacy of the textbook and other materials in use, in order to assess what needs to be added to provide students with comprehensive information. Any topic in the Latin language, be it case use, verb conjugation, adjectival modification, subordination, inflection, noun equivalence, etc., can be placed in a TCDR paradigm, to ensure that students can discriminate the **topic** from its higher **class**, or its **description** (how do I know one when I see one?) from its **relevance** (what good does it do me to know about this? where will it make a difference in my comprehension? my translation? my analysis?). Fuzzy thinking with respect to TCDR information is common in the classroom. For example, students will often confuse the **class** "part of speech" with various features of the **topics** in that **class**. When asked to give the gender of the noun *virum* [man], the student will respond instead with "noun."

Reflective learning requires a self-aware, active learner who questions both teacher and self for the "why" and "how" as well as the "what." This can be promoted at even a very rudimentary level in the Latin classroom. When responding to a question such as "what is the subject of the sentence *Canem videt vir* [The man sees the dog]?" students can be encouraged to first ask themselves "how is the subject of a sentence marked in Latin?" and as a follow-up, "what thinking did I use to arrive at my decision?"

Learner and Teacher Attitudes in this Model

A fundamental attitude for both learner and teacher in the critical thinking/reflective learning model is a commitment to the learner's establishing ownership of the material. The learner needs to approach the acquisition of such "facts" of the language as part of speech, morphology, and basic rules of syntax with the attitude that these form a necessary basis without which higher-level processing, such as reading, is not possible. To support the learner, teachers in turn must take that same attitude and convey their belief to the learner. Teachers must also acknowledge the importance of the student's internal motivation for the learning process.

Critical Thinking for the Learner

Attitudes of the Strong Learner to Be Encouraged by the Teacher

There are a number of attitudes that characterize the strong language learner and the effective reader. Students may come to the study of Latin with some of these already in place, and others may need to be fostered by the teacher. In our experience, the most significant of these are:

Expects the Language to Make Sense

Critical-thinking students expect the Latin language to make sense. They are not content with an interpretation or a translation which is non-sensical, whether the confusion lies at the syntactic, semantic, or discourse level. Such students will continually look for ways to "make sense" of what they are reading. With the proper coaching, they can learn useful strategies to resolve their difficulties, but if left to their own devices, they may fall back on their native language intuitions rather than the rules of Latin and compound their original errors.

Trusts Own Abilities

In addition to the belief that the Latin text expresses something intelligible, the strong student also trusts his own abilities in working with the language, and expects to be able to "make sense" of what is being read, given that the bottom-up information is correct.

Willing to Work toward Mastery

As mentioned above, a key attitude for reflective learners is the willingness to work toward mastery of basic knowledge and skills. Underlying this attitude toward mastery, however, is the realization that such a layer of basic knowledge and skills exists, and the acceptance that control of it is a pre-requisite for reading and comprehending Latin texts. The most obvious example of this in Latin is control of morphology. Learners are likely to be more willing to master material which is clearly useful and relevant; the ability to discriminate between the accusative and ablative forms of nouns or between finite and non-finite verbs is meaningful only if there is a consequent reward, such as increased ease of processing.

Willing to Take Ownership

When students are willing to assume ownership of their learning—both the process and the result—they are more active and engaged learners (see Barnett and Lavine, this volume). Latin is no different from any other subject matter in this respect. The attitude of "taking ownership" carries with it a sense of control of one's own destiny, and a vested interest in finding out about techniques and strategies that can improve performance.

Willing to Tolerate Uncertainty and Ambiguity

Another important attitude of the critically thinking learner is a willingness to tolerate the uncertainties and ambiguities of human language, especially those presented by Latin for the native speaker of English. Students who can "wait for/expect the verb" instead of finding it necessary to "find the verb," who can "hold that thought" instead of needing to "complete that thought," who approach Latin without assuming a one-to-one correspondence with English are much more likely to read with ease and confidence and less inclined to throw up their hands in frustration when encountering bumpy places in the road. Students who read a sentence beginning *canem vir* [dog (accusative,direct object) man (nominative, subject)] can tell themselves that the man is doing something to the dog and that when they encounter the verb they will know what he is doing have more effective reading strategies than students who cannot make sense out of these two words without a verb. Likewise, in reading the sentence *Consilium gladiator qui vivere vult in harena capit* [The gladiator who wishes to live forms a plan in the arena], the syntactic ambiguity of *consilium* (formally ambiguous as to subject or direct-object function) is resolved immediately upon seeing the unambiguously nominative *gladiator*, and it is unnecessary and time-consuming to hunt for *capit* to determine that *consilium* must be the direct object.

Trusts Own Knowledge

Hand in hand with the students' tolerance of the limits of their own knowledge at any given point, strong learners have sufficient confidence that their knowledge is valuable and useful and can be a resource for solving problems. When making decisions about which adjectives go with which nouns, for instance, a strong Latin student will rely on the knowledge that adjectives agree in case, number, and gender with the nouns they modify, and make fewer errors in this area. A weaker student, while perhaps able to rattle off the rule, will not use it as the primary guideline in making such decisions and may instead fall back on compatible word meanings or word proximity.

Josh, a second-semester student at the University of Michigan, made the following comment after assigning the adjective *brevi* to the wrong noun in the sentence beginning *Brevi tempore Pelias sciens patrem Jasonis...* [Within a short time Pelias, knowing that Jason's father...]:

> I *knew brevi* wasn't nominative, but I thought it meant "brave," and "time" can't be "brave," so I put it with the king *Pelias*. I realize now I should have trusted the rule that adjectives agree with the nouns they modify.

Behaviors of the Strong Learner to Be Encouraged by the Teacher

The attitudes described above can translate into specific student behaviors which are able to be modeled and observed.

Uses Critical Thinking in Both Learning
New Material and Problem Solving

The use of the TCDR model in learning and incorporating new information requires first a conscious assessment of the relationship between the new information and that previously known. In our experience, when learners encounter unfamiliar circumstances, they will attempt to analyze them in terms of previous knowledge and experience. If such a link between the known and the unknown is not explicit, a connection will still be made with whatever seems logical, regardless of its validity. For students, the deliberate integration of new with known information is a habit of thinking that needs to be overtly described, carefully modeled, and continuously encouraged by the teacher. For example, a student who understands the syntactic relationship of adjectives to the nouns they modify will more readily be able to handle relative clauses if he or she can classify them both as two **topics** of the same **class**, i.e., adjectival modifiers.

The TCDR critical-thinking model is valuable not only for learning new material, but also for making decisions in reading. The key to its successful application lies first in recognizing that in any given instance there may be a number of possible TCDR perspectives, and second, in determining which are most productive in a given context. Consider the Latin infinitive *facere* in the sentence *Caesar milites pontem facere dixit* ("Caesar said that the soldiers were building a bridge"). A less-proficient reader may know that an infinitive (**topic**) is a non-finite verb form (**class**), and that the English equivalent for this form is "to ____ ," but may not know (or be able to use the knowledge) that in different environments infinitives may have different syntactic roles, not all of which are expressed in English in the same way. This weaker reader's **description** of an infinitive in a given sentence would probably be limited to the morphological details of the infinitive itself (i.e., that it ends in *-re*) and the **relevance** in this analysis might be that such a form (usually) does not function as a main verb and is translated "to ____ ." A typical translation of this sentence by a student using this thinking would be "Caesar said the soldiers to build a bridge." This ill-formed English sentence renders the infinitive with the "to-" form in English, but shows that the student has not considered the meaning of the semantic relationship between the infinitive clause and the main clause, nor the meaning of the sentence as a whole. This is precisely the situation which gives rise to the plaint, "I translated all the words, but I don't understand what it means," particularly when the ideas expressed are more abstract than those in the sample sentence.

For a stronger reader, able to access a number of TCDR profiles, this sentence presents a **description** of "accusative + infinitive + verb of the head," which in turn will trigger the **topic** "indirect statement," and its **relevance**, namely that it expresses the substance of a speech act or thought, and that this is expressed by a finite clause in English, resulting not only in comprehension for the reader, but also in a well-formed translation such as "Caesar said that the soldiers were building a bridge."

Links Separate Categories of Knowledge and Information

The learner who actively engages in critical thinking can link separate categories of information, seeing the hierarchical relationships of **topic** and **class** clarified by the TCDR format as well as those present between the various levels in top-down/bottom-up processing. This ability to link information allows students to form more accurate expectations as they read and thus increases comprehension. For example, when reading a sentence beginning with the word *postquam*, a student who activates only lexical information will assign the English equivalent "after" to the word but will not be able to form clear syntactic and semantic expectations, since in English "after" could be a preposition, an adverb, or a subordinating conjunction. Time spent processing will be longer, and the potential for error higher. But the student who links two categories for *postquam*, that of meaning and that of part of speech, can form clear expectations about the remainder of the sentence: since *postquam* is a subordinating conjunction meaning "after," the sentence will contain a minimum of two finite clauses, the first of them a dependent clause expressing temporal information, and the second the main clause.

Assesses Recursively When Working through Text

The proficient reader uses prediction and recursive assessment to maintain comprehension while working through text (see Smith, 1988, pp. 30ff, on the role of prediction in reading). This involves reading in a linear, left-to-right fashion with an awareness of both the linear sequence of information as well as the non-linear, rhetorical structure of the text. Efficient reading combines linear processing with self-awareness, with students asking themselves questions such as "am I in a main or dependent clause? How (and when) do I know?" These readers use previous context to inform their subsequent decisions, both at sentence and text levels. Michael, a student at the University of Michigan who placed into a third-semester course, remarked:

> My approach to Latin was pretty much just look up the meanings of words and then find the verb. I was all over the sentence trying to figure it out. Now I see how reading left to right in chunks really makes sense. No one reads by jumping all around—certainly the Romans didn't do it that way.

Uses a Strategic Rather than a Random Approach to a Text

Strong readers approach a text with a conscious set of strategies. They work top-down by gaining as much information as possible about the background relevant to the text, they consider features of the genre of the text, and they are prepared to track discourse markers such as pronouns, implied or "understood" subjects, and sentence connectors such as *itaque* [therefore] and *enim* [for]. Working from the bottom up, they use information about parts of speech to streamline morphological decisions and consider syntactic possibilities on the basis of morphology. If readers lack a clear protocol to follow when faced with a text, their approach is often random and based heavily on the English meanings of Latin words. A resulting translation or interpretation is then based on whatever coherent meaning the student has been able to create on the basis of those English meanings rather than on the structure of the Latin.

Behaviors of the Reflective Learner

In addition to the behaviors described above for the student engaged in critical thinking, there are several types of self-aware, reflective behaviors which strengthen the learner.

Sets and Reviews Goals Periodically

The establishment of goals is important for all learning; if the student does not have a goal to work toward, tasks become meaningless and progress difficult to measure. Goals can be simple, such as "expand vocabulary by three new words per day" or "master the paradigm of third declension adjectives," or they can be more complex, such as "read in linear chunks" or "increase speed in resolving ambiguous forms and structures." A reflective learner not only sets goals, but periodically reviews them and sets new ones. This habit of goal setting is a hallmark of a student who is assuming ownership of the learning process.

Assesses Strengths and Weaknesses

A reflective approach to language study translates into real learning only when change results from it. The student who acknowledges errors, and even corrects them ad hoc, but commits them repeatedly is not actively working toward improvement. A student engaged in more reflective learning will assess his or her own strengths and weaknesses and target those areas most in need of work. Such a student, in preparing for a test, might review errors on previous exams in order to make certain that the mistakes are not repeated, and that previously unclear material is now understood. The results of this self-assessment of strong and weak areas would then be used to guide the preparation for the up-coming test. As Sarah, a first-semester student at the University of Michigan, reflected:

I just looked back at my other tests, and I can't *believe* I'm making this mistake over and over. I can't seem to get it through my head that the present participle is 3rd declension. This time I'm really going to *learn* this rule, so I don't have to do this correction again!

Conscious of the Relative Magnitude of Errors

The strong Latin student can discriminate between the major errors which can utterly confound meaning and comprehension, such as interpreting a Latin verb as a noun or an ablative noun as the subject of a sentence, and relatively minor infractions, such as translating a singular verb as plural, or using the wrong preposition to express a noun in the ablative case. Major errors are usually those that assign words or phrases to an inappropriate high-level category—the parts of speech or the major syntactic divisions of the sentence (the kernel or core elements of subject, verb, direct object, modification, connection). Confusion between **topics** in the same **class** are often less likely to seriously impede comprehension. A student may be unable to determine whether the information conveyed by a dependent adverbial clause is temporal or comparative, but he or she will still recognize the clausal structure of the sentence. Mistaking a subordinating conjunction for a preposition, however, is a high-level error which obscures the syntactic relationships.

Teacher Attitudes and Behaviors that Encourage the Critical-Thinking Learner

Necessary Teacher Attitudes

How students feel about their learning and how they go about it are to a great extent affected by the attitude of their teachers. Therefore, we present here a set of teacher attitudes that promote the critical-thinking, reflective learner.

Critical Thinking Can Be Taught

The primary attitude necessary for the teacher is that critical thinking skills can be taught. Just as students must expect that they can achieve mastery, the teacher needs to expect that students are able to learn how to think in critical ways and that he or she is able to convey those ways to them. Critical thinking is not an unconscious skill that students can "just pick up" but a set of techniques we can teach explicitly and students can apply deliberately.

Reading Strategies for Latin Can Be Taught

Following this attitude about teaching critical thinking is the attitude that, in particular, reading strategies for Latin can be taught. Since many expert readers of Latin (including teachers) were not taught such strategies and so at their advanced stage do not consciously use them, they can underplay and devalue the use of deliberate strategies. The teacher who accepts that such strategies are useful and can be learned even by the beginning student will convey them to learners more successfully.

Students Have Various Learning Styles

The teacher can be more effective by recognizing that students learn in different ways and have strengths in different areas. This means that the teacher will not evaluate a student on the basis of one task or one kind of task, but rather will provide different and varying approaches to a topic and attempt to have the student think critically about a topic in different ways.

Modeling Is Necessary to Ensure Desired Student Performance

It is important that the teacher recognize that modeling is a crucial element in successful teaching. Specifically, the teacher must model for students how to perform exercises, that is, the student must be shown the correct way of doing tasks before being expected to do them. Modeling for the Latin student is not limited to exercises and drills, however. It can cover reading strategies and the appropriate questions to consider as the reader thinks through a text. Without good modeling, one might very well test the student's ability to catch on quickly or even the teacher's ability to give clear and accurate instruction.

A Hierarchical Presentation Is Important for Critical Thinking

Finally, the teacher must be conscious of the hierarchical nature of critical thinking. Students will find it difficult to think in terms of **topic** and **class** if such relationships are not made explicit, and the textbook may not present all the **classes** of information the teacher feels are important. Teachers should be prepared to explain to students the distinction between **topic** and **class**, and to provide a comprehensive list of those **topics** and **classes** with which the students should be familiar.

Teacher Behaviors Necessary for Improved Student Performance

As with those of the student, the attitudes of the teacher can be expected to result in certain kinds of behavior, either in the classroom or by extension in assignments and testing.

Presents the Various Systems of the Latin
Language in a Hierarchical Format

When the teacher presents information about the various systems of the Latin language (e.g., morphology, syntax, and semantics) in a hierarchical format, the student can incorporate any new information in the appropriate cognitive place. This teacher behavior also includes explicitly linking like material so that the student perceives not only the vertical relationships and patterns but also the horizontal ones. An example of this linking is teaching the noun paradigm vertically as the representation of all cases in a single pattern,

	nominative	rex
	genitive	regis
singular	dative	regi
	accusative	regem
	ablative	rege
	nominative	reges
	genitive	regum
plural	dative	regibus
	accusative	reges
	ablative	regibus

but also teaching horizontally across the declensions, looking at all endings (-ā, -ō, -e, -ī, -ū -ē), or allomorphs, of the ablative singular, so that the student sees all the possible endings which mark that case, e.g.,

1st declension	*2nd declension*	*3rd declension*
hōrā	animō	rege

4th declension	*5th declension*
manū	rē

In TCDR terms, this involves specifying the various **classes** to which **topics** belong, but also providing examples, where possible and relevant, of other **topics** within a given **class**. One way to implement this is to specify a **topic**, such as "noun relative clause," and ask students to name the **class** and other parallel **topics** in the same **class**. A given **topic** can be a member of a variety of **classes**, e.g., relative clauses, dependent clauses, finite clauses, noun equivalents. Each **class** will have its own list of parallel **topics**, and students can see that a single structure may be part of several patterns. As Cynthia, a Latin teacher participating in a pedagogy workshop, noted:

> I've always called the various indeclinable words in Latin (e.g., adverbs, conjunction, particles) "junk" words. But it's clear to me now that these words are important for reading comprehension, especially their part of speech. I'm going to start calling them "key" words.

Models Desired Student Behavior

Student performance improves when teachers model desired student behaviors and demonstrate their consequences. This is particularly important in teaching reading strategies, where students working with texts often have developed deeply rooted personal strategies that interfere with efficient reading, such as relying on word meaning for syntactic information. This is especially true in highly inflected languages, like Latin, that rely much less on word order than English does for syntactic information. To change such behavior, it is necessary to replace the inefficient strategies with more effective ones so that students can actively turn their attention to something concrete and to demonstrate that the new approach is do-able and productive. In modeling a strategy like the one given here, the teacher can create and demonstrate the consequences of student decisions. This basic reading strategy has readers employ recursively the following three questions, the answer to each dependent on the one preceding:

quid video? ("what do I see?")	elicits part of speech and morphological information, which provides the context for answering
ergo, quid habeo? ("therefore, what do I have")	elicits the syntactic role of the word or phrase and provides the context for answering
ergo, quid exspecto? ("therefore, what do I expect?")	asks the reader to think about the syntactic (and possibly semantic) expectations raised by the word in question and to consider what might be yet to come in the sentence.

The *ergo* component of this strategy is extremely important, as it reminds the reader to link each piece of information with the decision at the next level. A very simple example of this type of processing is found in the word *virum* ("man"). Assuming it to be the first word in a sentence, the question *quid video?* elicits "noun, accusative singular masculine"; *ergo, quid habeo?* "direct object"; *ergo, quid exspecto?* "a nominative noun acting as subject and a transitive verb in the active voice." As each word or group of words is encountered, the questions are used recursively to keep the reader on track.

The Teacher as Learner: Working toward Reflective Practice

Since reflective learning is at the heart of the TCDR model of critical thinking, it is not limited to the learner but is applicable also to the teacher. In this case we broaden our terminology to speak of the "reflective practitioner." (This term is taken from Schön, 1987.) There are a number of pedagogical areas we feel benefit from reflective practices.

Cycles in the Curriculum

Evaluation of the curriculum is an area in which reflective practices are especially useful. The teacher should ask on a larger scale the student's question of "where am I?" At the curricular level, this translates into the recognition that a hierarchically structured curriculum is cyclical, rather than linear in nature. This means that the full complement of major categories, such as basic sentence elements (or kernel), modification, and connection, are introduced in the first cycle, and additional members are added in subsequent cycles. For an example of a Latin textbook that establishes major, high-level categories in the initial lessons and builds on them by adding individual **topics**, see Knudvig and Seligson (1986). One result of this curriculum design is a concern that the lower levels of the curriculum do indeed correspond to the higher levels. The goal for the teacher would be to have a clear notion of the categories or **classes** which he or she wishes to establish at the highest level, and to be sure to introduce them as soon as possible, so that they are available for building upon. Even if the desired categories are not explicitly named and described in the textbook in use, they can still be introduced, and the information contained in the lessons classified accordingly. Useful questions for the teacher to ask in this regard include "are the initial cycles of my curriculum designed with the later cycles clearly in mind? does my teaching emphasize those hierarchies and categories I wish to establish in my students' minds?"

Priorities for Students

At the same time as the teacher is building a cyclical curriculum, there is a need to set priorities for students, to ensure that the most time is spent on the most important concepts. This is especially relevant in these days of one-or two-year language requirements, when we can no longer expect to have students in the Latin classroom year after year. Therefore information should be introduced when it is important and relevant and not before. Learners remember concepts and information better when they have a context for them and when they use them. One guideline for using the TCDR model is to introduce **topics** only when students need to use them. For example, it is counter-productive for students to worry about all six noun cases when they will be using only the nominative and accusative for the following month. As the students meet more syntactic elements of the language, they can be introduced to more morphological elements (namely, the further **topics** of the other noun cases). Another aspect of this approach is waiting to introduce a **class** until the students meet more than one **topic** belonging to it. For example, the **class** of verbal mood needs to be introduced only when students meet something which contrasts with the indicative (which in most instances they will use exclusively for the first portion of the course). The introduction of material only when necessary and useful complements and strengthens the reflective learner's goal of relating new material to previous knowledge.

Set Goals and Review Them

Another "where am I?" imperative for the teacher is to set goals for student progress. Where should the student be in two days, two weeks, two months, or two years? The answers will help determine what material is presented and emphasized.

This reflective monitoring mirrors the student's self-monitoring and leads to the teacher's goal-setting at all levels: the course, unit, week, day, even task. No class ever goes entirely as planned, as both learners and teachers surpass and fall short of expectations, so continued review of these goals is necessary both during and after the completion of tasks.

Consider Assumptions about Students

Even teachers' assumptions about learners can benefit from scrutiny. Are they valid? In particular, the teacher should be concerned with evaluating the various student learning styles. Correspondingly, the teacher needs to find out how much of the material being taught the learners actually understand. This can be done by various types of diagnostic tasks. One specific kind of approach is to use writing tasks frequently during and outside class. In this system, students are asked to answer a question, provide an explanation, or perform an analysis of some Latin text. In our classes, students often do this first on paper individually before answering orally. In this way each student must attempt an answer even though only one or a few will actually answer out loud. All students, though, can get feedback on their own answer and, if the practice is added to their individual learning habits, have a powerful new tool for learning. Written analytical test corrections that ask the student to explain the thinking that led to their original error and provide a rationale for the right answer can bring to light some amazing misconceptions and fuzzy thinking and produce clarification. These writing tasks provide valuable information for the teacher about the effectiveness of both teaching and learning, and can be used by the reflective teacher to improve approaches to both teaching and evaluating students. Ann, a graduate student instructor in Latin at the University of Michigan, observed:

> I was experiencing great difficulties with my beginning Latin class. I spent several class periods explaining perfective aspect, but they still did poorly on the quizzes. Finally I stopped lecturing so much and had them do the explaining in writing tasks; they did much better. I guess I thought that if I wasn't working hard (i.e., talking), I wasn't really teaching, but that's clearly not the case.

Conclusion

In our experience, students respond well to an approach to language learning that incorporates critical thinking and reflection. We have seen strong students acquire a effective set of reading strategies that have served them well in more advanced coursework in Latin. Even less-proficient students are able to approach a text with more confidence and success. Many students who have extensive but undifferentiated knowledge of the Latin language and who have, by their own account, been ineffective readers in the past have found that a critical-thinking approach based on the TCDR method enables them to organize this knowledge and become proficient and successful readers.

References

American Classical League. (1997). *Standards for classical language learning.* Oxford, OH: Author.

Chaffee, J. (1991). *Thinking critically* (3rd ed.). Boston: Houghton Mifflin.

Crowder, R. G., & Wagner, R. K. (1992). *The psychology of reading.* New York: Oxford University Press.

Gruber-Miller, J. (1998). Toward fluency and accuracy: A reading approach to college Latin. In LaFleur (Ed.), *Latin for the 21st century.* Glenview, IL: Scott Foresman-Addison Wesley.

Knudsvig, G. M., & Seligson, G. A. (1986). *Latin for reading: A beginner's textbook with exercises.* (Rev. ed.). Ann Arbor: University of Michigan Press.

National Standards for Foreign Language Learning Project. (1996). *Standards for foreign language learning: Preparing for the 21st century.* Yonkers, NY: Author.

Schön, D.A. (1987). *Educating the reflective practitioner.* San Francisco: Jossey-Bass.

Smith, D.E.P., Knudsvig, G.M., & Walter, T.L. (1998). *Critical thinking: Building the basics.* Belmont, CA: Wadsworth.

Smith, F. (1988). *Understanding reading.* Hillsdale, NJ: Lawrence Erlbaum.

Swaffar, J.K., Arens, K.M., & Byrnes, H. (1991). *Reading for meaning.* Englewood Cliffs, NJ: Prentice Hall.

Oxford and Carpenter address …

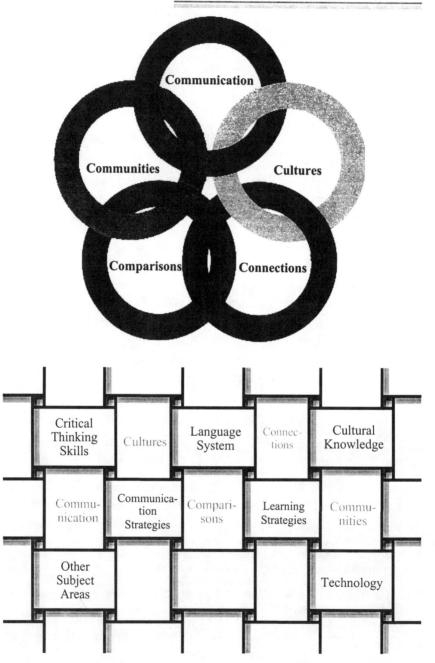

Learner Autonomy, National Standards, and Language Learners of Tomorrow

Rebecca Oxford

University of Alabama

Angela Carpenter

Wellesley College

H ow can tomorrow's language learners move toward language proficiency with greater effectiveness and more commitment, and how can teachers help this happen? This question has special meaning as U.S. foreign language learners and teachers, armed with the new National Standards for Foreign Language Learning (1996; see also Lafayette, 1996; Phillips, 1999) enter the next millennium. To answer the question, the authors in this book describe an innovative vanguard composed of today's learners, who are just beginning to be guided by the National Standards and by the notion of learner autonomy that appears to infuse these standards. Our chapter explains how learner autonomy and the National Standards relate to learners (and teachers) mentioned in the previous chapters, encapsulates the main points of the chapters, and offers implications for future research.

In the National Standards' spirit of "weaving," this chapter weaves together our two viewpoints as co-authors. We differ in geographic location, age, experience, and ethnicity, although our gender and nationality are the same. I, Rebecca, have taught languages at the secondary and university levels and am now a researcher, author, international speaker, associate dean, and teacher of language teachers. Angela Carpenter is a senior at Wellesley College majoring in Language Studies. Her interest in languages and cultures caused her to return to school to complete her undergraduate degree after a 20-year absence. Although Angela may not be a typical learner (is there any such creature?), nevertheless her strong presence in this chapter helps break down artificial boundaries that often separate "researchers," "teachers," and "learners." I was invited to provide objective comments, while Angela was asked to offer personal reactions. Our chapter is an ongoing dialog, as shown by the use of regular type (Rebecca) interspersed with large blocks of italics (Angela).

Overview

Rebecca: It is important to review a few concepts. *Learner autonomy* might be defined as the learner's willingness to take responsibility for learning and the behaviors or processes by which the learner makes this self-responsibility a reality.[1] Intertwined with the National Standards are "weave elements," two of which are among the most crucial processes or behaviors for learner autonomy: learning strategies and critical thinking skills. *Learning strategies* are specific steps, techniques, or actions (which might or might not be observable by the teacher or researcher) taken by learners to enhance their own learning. One of these steps is self-assessment, assessing one's own learning progress, and is often viewed as a metacognitive (from Greek meaning "beyond the cognitive") learning strategy. *Critical thinking skills* are higher-order mental abilities such as analyzing, synthesizing, and evaluating. Critical thinking also involves making informed judgments about when to deploy various types of thinking to fit the current task or need; even lower-level forms such as recognition have their place. Virtually all the chapters in this book touch on learning strategies and critical thinking skills, no matter what kind of wording the chapter authors use.

Additional "weave elements" are found in this book. These include language as a system (see especially the chapter by John Muccigrosso and Deborah Pennell Ross), cultural knowledge (chapters by Roberta Lavine, Lina Lee, and Vicki Galloway), communication strategies (chapter by

Ghislaine Tulou and Frances Pettigrew), technology (chapter by Lina Lee), and relationships with other subject areas and fields (chapters by Anna Chamot, Marva Barnett, and Roberta Lavine). Before discussing any of the chapters in detail, let us consider learner autonomy and the National Standards a little further.

Angela: A dominant theme woven throughout the chapters of this volume is the learner-centered classroom that fosters autonomous language learning. In that classroom, language learners exercise a significant amount of control over their own learning, help select instructional themes and tasks, engage in self-assessment, and provide feedback to the teacher about their individual learning processes. This development is heartening for learners everywhere, but particularly in the foreign language (we might call it the "world language") classroom. This development reflects a paradigm shift. In various ways, the authors in this volume provide recommendations that break up the old paradigm and give students more of a role in their own learning—all the while allowing teachers to do what they do best.

Rebecca: In this paradigm shift, the autonomous learner takes ultimate responsibility for his or her own language learning. This shift demands changes in attitudes and beliefs, with significant implications for classroom roles. Compared to old-fashioned language instruction, learner-centered instruction focused on autonomy requires a more active, more central, and more crucial role for language students. No longer does the teacher have roles such as (on the more positive side) director, fount of all wisdom, or orchestra leader nor (on the more negative side) zookeeper, hanging judge, or baby sitter. When the autonomous learner becomes a focal point, teachers necessarily take on new roles—guide, facilitator, catalyst, counselor, opportunity-provider, and co-creator of knowledge—that emphasize ways in which they can empower the learner. Such role changes embody a fundamental shift in classroom power relationships.

Learner autonomy does not just "happen." It requires a transformation in the hearts and minds of language learners and teachers. The National Standards, with their "weave elements" related to learner autonomy (learning strategies and critical thinking skills), encourage such a transformation. Here is a summary of the standards:

Goal 1: *Communicate in languages other than English* in a variety of ways, for different purposes, and in different settings.
Goal 2: *Gain knowledge and understanding of other cultures,* through exploring those cultures' perspectives, practices, and products.

Goal 3: *Connect with other disciplines and acquire information* by using the foreign language
   and by recognizing distinctive viewpoints that the language and culture reveal.
Goal 4: Through *comparing one's home language and culture with other languages and
   cultures,* demonstrate understanding of the nature of language and the concept of culture.
Goal 5: *Participate in multicultural communities at home and abroad* by using the language
   in multiple settings and by becoming lifelong learners of the language.

Keep in mind the National Standards and the concept of learner autonomy as we discuss the contributions made by each of the chapter authors.
The standards and the notion of autonomy are woven into every chapter.

Specific Contributions by the Authors

The sequence of our discussion moves from a chapter on principles of
learner autonomy (Wenden) to various manifestations of learner autonomy promoted by different instructional techniques or program types
(Chamot, Barnett, Lavine, Lee, Galloway, Tulou and Pettigrew, and Muccigrosso and Ross). All chapters except two (Wenden, Chamot) concern
foreign language learners in secondary schools or universities. With the
exception of Muccigrosso and Ross, who discuss strategies for learning
Latin, the authors focus on modern languages.

Wenden Explores Learner Autonomy

Rebecca: Anita Wenden addresses the development of learner autonomy through a case study of a Japanese business manager who has lived
in Germany and the United States. According to Wenden, learner autonomy depends on learning strategies, task knowledge, and person knowledge. The ultimate goal of language learning is to develop competence in
using the language in socially appropriate ways in a variety of settings
and for various purposes.

An especially valuable part of the chapter is the discussion of causes
of resistance to learner autonomy: cultural values, beliefs about the
teacher's role, and beliefs about language learning. Wenden emphasizes
that learners must see the relevance of becoming more autonomous and
must, with the teacher's help, discard negative attitudes and beliefs that
work against taking greater personal responsibility for learning. She emphasizes the national standards of Communication, Connections, and
Communities, all required for learner autonomy, and highlights the stand-

ards of Cultures and Comparisons, in which cultural belief systems play a major role.

Angela: Wenden's chapter demonstrates the level of responsibility students have to assume in order to take charge of their own learning. To be autonomous, learners have to become metacognitively aware of their own learning processes. They also need to feel positive about their ability to influence the teacher's instructional style. It is important for learners to develop realistic assessments of their own progress, not simply measuring their foreign language ability against their ability in the native language. They need to have clear expectations of where they are and should be.

As Wenden notes, teachers have a large role to play in transitioning students to their new role. However awkward this might be at the start, the potential rewards are tremendous. The authors of the other chapters in this book show ways by which they as teachers have created learner-centered classrooms in their educational settings and demonstrate the excellent results and rewards that are possible.

Chamot Uncovers Learning Strategies of Young Students

Rebecca: Anna Uhl Chamot examines the learning strategies of young (kindergarten through sixth-grade) students in two full immersion programs, one in French and the other in Spanish, and a Japanese partial immersion program. In immersion programs, students learn some or all of their academic subjects through the target language. Chamot's research methodology included "think-alouds," in which the young children in this study talked about their learning strategies as they did language tasks. Learners' comments were audiotaped and later transcribed.

As reported by Chamot, the children used a variety of learning strategies and talked about them articulately, a remarkable finding given the ages involved. Less-able and younger students in this K–6 study exhibited greater use of phonetic coding (sounding out syllables), while more-effective and older students employed more sophisticated strategies, such as predicting and elaborating. The investigation also found that children in immersion programs developed foreign language reading and writing skills in ways similar to children in non-immersion, native language programs.

Chamot offers instructional applications of this research, focusing on a metacognitive model for strategic learning (planning, monitoring, problem-solving, and evaluating) and a framework for learning-strategies instruction drawn from the Cognitive Academic Language Learning Approach she developed earlier with J. Michael O'Malley. Of all the National Standards, the one most clearly reflected in this chapter is Connections. Immersion programs are uniquely situated to allow learners to learn other subjects via the foreign language, so connections with other disciplines are rapidly and thoroughly made. Though this was not highlighted as much, the fact is that students fortunate enough to be in a strategy-enriched immersion program would also be privileged in regard to the Communication standard.

Angela: As noted above, a surprising finding in Chamot's chapter is that children as young as kindergarten-age are aware of the learning strategies they use and can describe these strategies while going through them. These children, because of their immersion setting, are also able to describe their metacognitive awareness in the target language. Such awareness on the part of young learners offers educators additional avenues to help students facilitate their own learning. Students who are conscious of how they learn can become better learners, especially in areas that give them difficulty. Additionally, as Chamot points out, learning strategies identified in a foreign language immersion setting are transferable to all areas of learning.

The students in Chamot's study who were specifically taught strategies stated they considered these strategies to be useful. This finding reinforces my personal experience that, especially when faced with a new subject, it really helps to have the teacher outline good strategies for learning. Unfortunately, I did not come to this realization until I was in college. Chamot demonstrates that young learners who are encouraged to be metacognitively aware of how they learn (and how to learn) from a tender age gain a wonderful, lifelong advantage. This empowers them to meet the challenges they will continue to face inside the language classroom, in other classrooms, and at home, both now and well into the future.

Barnett Co-Creates a Language
Course with Her Students

Rebecca: Employing the idea of greater autonomy with learners of French, Marva Barnett shows how language learners can create a language course hand in hand with their teachers. Shifting the focus to the learner involves defining expectations rather than hiding them, engaging students directly, evaluating the course frequently, offering challenges and supports to students, giving clear feedback, and using a variety of instructional techniques (e.g., cooperative learning, technology). Teachers who share their power experience benefits not otherwise possible, such as freedom, student responsiveness, interpersonal connections, and new ideas.

Learners in such a situation demonstrate greater confidence, are more engaged in language learning, have a conscious sense of responsibility and a feeling of community, use thinking skills more effectively, and deploy an array of useful metacognitive and cognitive strategies. According to Barnett, they necessarily deal with standards such as Communication, Connections, Communities, and Cultures. This chapter is enhanced by the use of abundant, highly practical appendices that offer specific ideas about how to conduct a co-created language course.

Angela: Barnett describes very positive results of having students work with the teacher to create the course. I love this idea. As she states, it is very easy for students to fall into traditional roles where they simply show up for class, read the syllabus, and spit out what is expected of them on tests and quizzes. In trying to learn a foreign language, it is easy to learn grammatical forms without really learning how to use the language. To foster greater learner self-direction, the teacher needs to help students create new expectations for the course; a co-created course does not operate just like other courses do. Barnett's type of course incorporates general learning strategies that would be useful in many other subject fields.

A co-created course also calls for greater student input. In Barnett's example, I was struck by the teacher's actually changing the final exam on the basis of suggestions from students. Now that reveals a major acceptance of student input. With such acceptance throughout the course, it is no wonder that the students became invested. If I were in that situation, I wouldn't want to miss class. I would prepare better, making this class a priority. I would be irritated if other students were lax and failed to contribute to the group effort.

Lavine Gives Student Management Teams Creative Responsibility

Rebecca: Another proponent of learner autonomy, Roberta Lavine demonstrates that business-related principles drawn from the Total Quality Management (TQM) model can change language classroom dynamics.

From TQM Lavine has selected the technique of implementing "management teams" (similar to "quality circles") that allow workers to provide constant input into decisions related to their work, their satisfaction level, and the progress of the corporation. In courses on Business Spanish and Cross-cultural Communications, Lavine has created Student Management Teams and uses them to obtain students' feedback and ideas about group processes, content, assignments, and other aspects of teaching and learning. According to Lavine, Student Management Teams relate to at least three of the national standards: Communication, Connections, and the lifelong-learning aspect of Communities.

Lavine explains the theory from which Student Management Teams are derived. She also offers very specific suggestions about ways to use this cooperative instructional mode, and her own rich descriptions make these suggestions concrete. For example, the story about the fantasy "dolareso" illustrates a reality some language teachers have yet to encounter —the fact that when students are asked to provide creative ideas and are given a systematic way to do so, significant improvement can occur in instruction and student motivation, interest, and involvement.

Angela: The Student Management Team empowers students. The professor and the team work together to create a learning environment in which student input is sought out and students' needs are heard in order to facilitate learning. Lavine found that her Student Management Teams took their responsibilities seriously and avoided making capricious demands.

Like the other approaches in this book, the Student Management Team puts more responsibility on students than the traditional quiescent student role dictates. We all respond well when we perceive that we are being treated with respect. When students sense the genuine respect and inclusiveness that is driving the teacher's desire to give them more of a say in their learning experience, students will step up to the plate to accept more responsibility. However, students need to understand fully what is being attempted in this endeavor. Lavine's model includes a thorough explanation of what the team is, how it fits into the class structure, and what is expected of the students.

Technology-Aided Language
Learning Is Lee's Contribution

Rebecca: Lina Lee suggests a language teaching-and-learning model involving Internet technology: using online Spanish-language newspapers and two online Spanish-language chat rooms. Reading online newspapers in the target language, according to Lee, helps students achieve the 5 C's: Communication, Cultures, Comparisons, Connections, and Communities. However, the chapter focuses more on the students' perceptions of their learning than on the teacher's.

Learner autonomy is implicit in the online activities Lee describes. In fact, some of the key perceptions of students included a greater sense of control, heightened engagement, and increased use of learning strategies, all of which contribute to or reflect autonomy. Online reading of newspapers in the foreign language allows students to explore freely and independently the language and culture, without the teacher hovering over them. Online chats allow students to be as autonomous as they care to be. Lee observes that some students, seeking the security of the familiar, preferred to talk with their same-language peers rather than with Spanish speakers during the online chats, but many students were enthusiastic about online conversations with native speakers. Lee notes occasional problems with access to computers and printers, but this did not significantly dampen the spirits of the learners.

Angela: Having read Lee's chapter and the overall positive comments from her students, I just had to experience a Spanish chat room for myself. I have used Spanish online newspapers and found that they instantly drew me into the pulse of the particular city; however, I had never tried online chatting in Spanish. My search on the Internet pointed me to several chat rooms, two of which I joined. After quietly observing the interchanges for a while, I was greeted by several other chatters and jumped into the conversation. What fun! There were chatters from all over the Spanish-speaking world sending greetings, talking about themselves and their cities, and, in general, making friends. Being a non-academic chat room, the conversation was informal, but I discovered that I could keep up (the responses scroll up the screen at a fairly rapid pace) and even add a little to the conversation. No wonder Lee's students were so enthusiastic!

It is widely acknowledged that the World Wide Web provides access to a vast amount of information; but, as Lee points out, online technology also offers opportunities for cross-cultural interaction. My limited expo-

sure to chat rooms demonstrated some immediate benefits. First, partici-pating in online conversation imparts a feeling of inclusiveness with na-tive speakers. The anonymity of an online chat reduced my anxiety, and soon I felt on an equal footing with other chatters, free to express myself. Another benefit is the exposure to idiomatic expressions from different countries. In the chat room, I had time to notice such expressions and to try to figure them out without the pressures of real-time, face-to-face con-versation. In some cases, I had to ask what something meant and received immediate answers, thereby allowing me to negotiate meaning and stay engaged in the conversation. Most importantly, I truly felt a part of the Spanish-speaking world, welcome to return.

Galloway Writes an Ode to Cultural Differences

Many of Vicki Galloway's passages read like prose-poems. The sen-sory, evocative style of this chapter breathes life into the Cultures and Communication goals. In Galloway's view, language teachers are actu-ally teachers of culture at heart. Using a host of authentic examples start-ing on the very first page, Galloway demonstrates that bridges (or simi-larities) across cultures are not as profoundly important as boundaries (or dissimilarities) between cultures. Understanding the perspectives of other cultures requires entering the mindspace of those cultures and refusing the temptation to view other cultures through one's own cultural lens.

How does this chapter relate to learner autonomy? The chapter shows how students can learn to think independently about cultures. Developing deep cultural understanding—that is, "growing the cross-cultural mind" —requires the learner to strengthen the ability to observe and interpret cultures objectively. This means moving away from the herd mentality of long-held cultural stereotypes. Such an inner movement could be consid-ered a special, culturally relevant form of autonomous learning. If teach-ers give more attention to this type of learning, students will be more likely to become culturally aware and adept.

Angela: In this chapter, Galloway really gets under the skin of culture. She goes beyond just learning about the products of the culture, the out-ward manifestations, to the real differences that exist between cultures. Galloway views these differences as boundaries between "separate reali-ties." Acknowledging boundaries instead of blurring them allows students to negotiate their way in the new culture from the perspective of that culture and not their own. This level of introspection and confrontation cannot be easy, and, I daresay, could make for some tense and upsetting moments in the classroom. However, as Galloway documents, this effort results in students' beginning to understand that language is only the medium and that culture is the real message.

Galloway's approach is far different from the pre-packaged cultural snapshots often presented in the classroom. I am reminded of the slide presentations of Spanish culture I watched in high school. They were little more than tourist guides showing beautiful architecture, colorful costumes, and exotic flamenco dancing. The pictures were pretty but left me with no feeling or connection whatsoever to the people or the place. I particularly like Galloway's insistence on presenting authentic images to her students, allowing them to see the lens through which they interpret the images and then guiding them to an understanding of how the images are viewed and interpreted by the people of the target culture. In the process, students learn about themselves and about the collective assumptions and stereotypes in their own culture.

Galloway's examples involve college students. However, getting beyond the surface of a culture is possible for language students of all ages. For example, students can be stimulated to write about their own customs that might seem strange to another culture. Galloway cites a discussion in which students talked about times in their lives when they were the "different" one and how that made them feel. These explorations are appropriate for students of any age.

Tulou and Pettigrew Help Students Assess Their Performance

Rebecca: As we have already seen, self-assessment is one of the key components of learning strategies and autonomous learning. Ghislaine Tulou and Frances Pettigrew offer an integrated assessment system known as Performance Assessment for Language Students (PALS). This system highlights student involvement in assessment and leads to greater student engagement in language learning. Performance assessment, including learner self-assessment of performance, uses lifelike language and culture tasks. These tasks are so realistic that they enhance students' development vis-à-vis most of the National Standards, in my opinion, with special emphasis on the goal areas of Communication, Comparisons, and Cultures, and with lifelong spinoffs into the Communities standard. Once learners have experience in creating assessments and assessing themselves, they take that experience with them wherever they go.

Performance assessment demands clear expectations for learning and teaching from the outset. In performance assessment, the emphasis on authentic, socioculturally appropriate language tasks and on collaborative assessments obviates the fierce, student-versus-student competition that is so often found in non-performance-based classes. In the version of performance assessment described by Tulou and Pettigrew, students have a real role in using the assessment tools, assessing their own progress, and viewing themselves as cooperative rather than competitive.

Angela: PALS dares to ask the question, "Do we actually assess progress and mastery by the end of the year?" (emphasis added). The beauty of the PALS approach lies in the way it involves the student. By having very clear guidelines as to how each performance task will be assessed, students can enjoy a sense of control over how well they do in the class. There is no mystery about how their grade is determined. Furthermore, the clear feedback students get shows them the areas in which they need to improve. An important first step is involving students in using the scoring rubrics so they become personally invested in the assessment process.

Performance tasks, all based on real-world situations, immediately bring home to students the relevance of the language. I especially like the idea of having more than one "right answer." As a student, this gives me the freedom to be creative within the language, to remove the language from the realm of the typical academic subject where I give back to teachers just what they want to hear or will accept as correct. I especially responded to the Performance Improvement Plan, or PIP, because of its demonstration that students can look at their individual learning process critically, with a view to improvement. I was also interested in the fact that students responded favorably to measuring themselves against the ACTFL standards, which were built into PALS. This would especially appeal to students who want to know where they fit into the larger, national picture of language proficiency.

Muccigrosso and Ross Encourage
Critical Thinking and Reflective Learning

Rebecca: In this chapter, which is devoted to the learning of Latin, John Muccigrosso and Deborah Pennell Ross emphasize critical thinking, which they define as the integration of lower-level thinking skills into higher-level thinking skills. A different way of saying this is that the learner draws upon *all* levels of thinking. Muccigrosso and Ross's system involves learning strategies that use hierarchical, logical analysis. These strategies help students identify four important factors: Topic, Class, Description, and Relevance (TCDR). These strategies inherently require reflective learning, defined by these authors as the learners' relating of new information to what they already know.

To use the system, learners must be willing to work toward mastery, take ownership of learning, accept ambiguity, trust their own knowledge, and expect that the language will make sense. Learners must be self-directed as they link categories, assess and review recursively, and use a strategic rather than random approach. The teacher can help by modeling the attitudes and strategies that learners should use; after all, say the authors, the teacher is a learner, too.

Angela: Often a student can be so involved in the minutiae of translating that he or she misses the sense of the passage, thereby losing what is being communicated. This is a common problem for many of us as we progress from the intermediate levels of a language to reading authentic texts that are more advanced. Suddenly we feel thrown into unknown territory, and the relative mastery we felt we had developed seems to evaporate overnight. At this point critical thinking can be of real benefit. As the authors very reasonably state, critically thinking students should expect Latin—or any language—to make sense. The confusion we feel when something is not making sense should be the signal to slip into critical-thinking gear, where we pull out the reading strategies that we have learned since our early reading days in our own language. Many of the reading strategies we learned then can be transferred from our native language to the language we are acquiring. In order to do this, we need to trust what we know.

In the midst of what feels like a language breakdown, when our knowledge seems to be falling apart, it might seem counterintuitive to trust what we know, but that is precisely what Muccigrosso and Ross encourage us to do. It is at that time that we must call on the knowledge we do *have with the confidence that what we know can give us access to what we don't know. The pitfall to avoid is doubting what we have already learned or second-guessing what we already know. While this chapter speaks specifically about Latin, the principles of critical thinking and reflective learning apply in all learning situations. The more I understand the over-*

riding principles of being in charge of my own learning, the better learner I become.

Pulling the Strands Together

Rebecca: As we have discovered, the National Standards and the concept of autonomous learning permeate the chapters in this book. These themes emerge in varied ways and with contrasting emphases, just as the multiple sides of a prism sparkle with different lights. All the chapters ultimately point to an image of a (potentially) more-conscious, more-aware, more-autonomous learner who actively seeks to use the language for multiple purposes. For such a learner, the language serves as a means of communication, a window into the target culture and (by comparison) the home culture, a link with other disciplines, and a lifelong means of participating in multilingual communities. Perhaps the learner described here at the end of the second millennium foreshadows a more frequently found and more powerful third-millennium language learner.

Angela: However, it is wise to insert a note of caution. In our enthusiasm to promote learner-centered classrooms and autonomous language learning, we need to realize that the scope of the work goes beyond *the foreign (or world) language classroom. A learner-centered way of teaching should pervade instruction in all fields and subjects, not just language instruction. As Wenden points out, the changes students need to make to become more autonomous learners could cause them to be "resistant, unwilling, and uncooperative." This negative energy could very well turn toward the target language and the language teacher.*

Autonomous learning, as practiced in the learner-centered classroom, should be part of the entire educational curriculum in all areas. Ideally, education administrators should be the driving force behind this institution-wide approach, giving individual departments and teachers latitude in how to help learners implement autonomous learning in their area of specialty. This broad-based approach would reinforce the principles of autonomous learning at every level and through all subjects. Perhaps it will take the efforts of foreign (world) language teachers in documenting the improved quality of the learning experience to convince other educators to join them in developing learner-centered classrooms. The point is that learner-centered classrooms should not be the sole province of the language teacher.

Rebecca: If it "takes a village" to bring up a child, then it does indeed make sense that it should take the efforts of many teachers—not just the language teacher—to help every student develop into an autonomous learner. Autonomous learning, which is by nature active and self-propelled, could be a key goal of all teachers and could certainly make their instruction far more effective. Optimally fostering learner autonomy would require good communication among language teachers, among teachers in multiple subject areas, and among different educational levels.

Similarly, the truest and most widespread fulfillment of the National Standards for Foreign Language Learning could occur if many teachers outside the language field, as well as within the language area, take an active interest in building interdisciplinary connections and cross-cultural understanding. History, geography, political science, sociology, psychology, and literature are obvious examples of areas where such interdisciplinary and cross-cultural prospects are good. Business is increasingly taught at the undergraduate and graduate level with an emphasis on cultural awareness, in many instances combined with instruction in languages.

Even mathematics and the so-called hard sciences could be taught in ways that encourage students to seek knowledge across disciplines and understand the contributions of multiple cultures. My university asked me, as a "dyed-in-the-wool" language person with an interest in innovative teaching, to conduct seminars for engineering, mathematics, and science professors on cooperative, interdisciplinary, learner-centered instructional techniques. Disciplinary barriers *can* come down.

How does all this occur? As mentioned earlier, it begins with changes in attitude and behavior on the part of learners and teachers. We have to start with ourselves. We can also look outside the language domain to find allies in other fields. Team-teaching courses with someone from a different field, establishing a pilot immersion program that allows learning of multiple subjects via the target language, talking about learner-centered instruction at interdepartmental faculty meetings, holding seminars on learner autonomy, and setting up a task force to make the curriculum more interdisciplinary and more supportive of learner autonomy — all these are within the realm of practical possibility for many of us, either now or in the near future. Such efforts take time, but consider where they might take language teachers and learners.

Even if we work toward the National Standards and learner autonomy strictly within the language field, language teachers can communicate with and support each other (and their students) far more than we have done to date. Inside individual language classrooms, it is possible to implement the kinds of creativity supported by the National Standards and by the learner autonomy movement, as long as the needed seeds have been sown.

Future Research Directions

Rebecca: We need attitudinal and behavioral change if we want learner autonomy to flourish in the foreign or world language field. By the same token, the National Standards demand alterations in attitudes and behaviors on the part of learners as well as teachers. Qualitative research is valuable because it can provide rich detail about variables that inhibit attitudinal and behavioral change, and it can bring forth suggestions about what to do about those variables. Quantitative research can offer more structured information about each learner's attitudes and behaviors (especially learning strategies), information that for some purposes can be combined across learners to give a group picture.

Upcoming investigations, building on studies reported in this book and those published in professional journals, could evaluate in greater depth the success of attempts to implement the National Standards and parallel efforts to encourage learner autonomy in various contexts. To use the weaving metaphor once more, the authors in this book have shown us many ways to use the loom, thread, and spindles. Which ways are most effective in which contexts? Do we have to invent still other ways that fit better with particular students in certain settings? Language learning, like any other type of learning, always occurs within a social and institutional context. Ignoring that context is at best misleading, and at worst it could imperil even the best-intentioned efforts. That is why research on effects of instructional innovation in various learning environments is so important.

As we expect of our students, we, too, must adopt a stance of sensitive, active, critical awareness so that we can understand what works, what does not work, and why. Such reflectiveness, along with expanded communication and cooperation among teachers and learners, could lead to increased insight into the meaning of the National Standards, more autonomous language learning, and more effective language teaching.

Note

[1]The language learning autonomy movement began during the early 1970s in Europe and then spread elsewhere. However, learner autonomy was also discussed in adult education circles in various parts of the world the 1960s.

References

Lafayette, R. C. (Ed.). (1996). *National standards: A catalyst for reform.* ACTFL Foreign Language Education Series. Lincolnwood, IL: National Textbook Company.

National Standards in Foreign Language Education Project. (1996). *Standards for foreign language learning: Preparing for the 21st century.* Yonkers, NY: Author.

Phillips, J. K., & Terry, R. M. (Eds.). (1999) *Foreign language standards: Linking research, theories, and practices.* ACTFL Foreign Language Education Series. Lincolnwood, IL: National Textbook Company.

About the Authors

Martha G. Abbott is the Foreign Language Coordinator in Fairfax County Public Schools in Fairfax, Va., where she supervises a K–12 foreign language program. She taught Spanish and Latin at the elementary and secondary school levels for 14 years and currently teaches as an adjunct instructor for George Mason University. She served on the Task Force that developed National Standards in Foreign Language Education and subsequently the committee that developed standards for Classical Languages. She is also the chair of the 1999 Northeast Conference on the Teaching of Foreign Languages.

Marva A. Barnett is the Director of the Teaching Resource Center and holds the rank of professor at the University of Virginia, where she teaches in the Department of French. Her current research project is a cross-cultural analysis of thinking skills and expectations in the U.S. and France; other research interests include the second-language reading process, with an emphasis on reader strategies, foreign-language methodology, and teacher training. The author of the reading strategies text *Lire avec plaisir* and the theoretical *More than meets the eye: Foreign language reading, theory and practice*, she publishes in such journals as the *Modern Language Journal*, *Foreign Language Annals*, and the *ADFL Bulletin*.

Angela Carpenter is currently a senior at Wellesley College, majoring in Language Studies. As a recipient of the Mellon Minority Undergraduate Fellowship, she has recently completed her honors thesis, "Factors that Affect Second Language Proficiency." At Wellesley College, she serves as a writing tutor with a focus on non-native speakers of English. She has studied Spanish and Italian, spending the past two summers in Costa Rica and Italy, respectively. Angela returned to college to complete her bachelor's degree after a 21-year break to raise her family and now plans to study linguistics in graduate school.

Anna Chamot is Associate Professor in the area of ESL teacher preparation in the Graduate School of Education and Human Development at The George Washington University. She serves as Associate Director of the Georgetown University/George Washington University/Center for Applied Linguistics National Capital Language Resource Center, and conducts research, training, and materials development in areas such as language learning strategies, immersion, portfolio assessment, and literacy development. Dr. Chamot's publications include several books, *Learning strategies in second language acquisition*, *The CALLA handbook: How to implement the Cognitive Academic Language Learning approach*, and *The language learning strategies handbook*, articles in *TESOL Quarterly*, *Language Learning*, *NABE Journal*, and *Bilingual Research Journal*, and instructional materials in EFL and ESL.

Vicki Galloway is currently Professor of Spanish at Georgia Institute of Technology where she teaches language, literature, and culture at all levels and shares responsibility for direction of an intensive program in Spanish for Business and Technology. She is the author of several foreign language textbooks for college, secondary, and middle-school levels and has published actively in various books and journals, including *The Modern Language Journal*, *Northeast Conference Reports*, *ACTFL Language Education Series*, and a volume of the American Educational Research Association.

Margaret Ann Kassen is Associate Professor and Language Program Coordinator in the Department of Modern Languages at The Catholic University of America in Washington, DC. She works closely with graduate teaching assistants and undergraduate teacher candidates and teaches courses in pedagogy, phonetics, and language acquisition. Her research interests include FL writing, portfolio assessment, FL technology, and teacher development. She is the author of *Motifs: An Introduction to French* and other publications.

Roberta Z. Lavine is Associate Professor and Associate Chair of the Department of Spanish and Portuguese at the University of Maryland. She is also Director of Undergraduate Studies for that department and specializes in methodology and pedagogy. Her other areas of expertise include Business Spanish and instructional technology. Her research and publishing interests include language learning styles and strategies, learning disabilities and language learning, and language for specific purposes.

Lina Lee is Assistant Professor of Spanish at the University of New Hampshire where she coordinates the Basic Language Program, trains teaching assistants, teaches foreign language teaching methods, and supervises foreign language interns. Her research in the areas of portfolio assessment and Internet technology for teaching foreign language and culture have been published in *Hispania*, *Foreign Language Annals*, *CALICO* and the *Northeast Conference Newsletter*. She is the author of websites for two Spanish textbooks: *Mosaicos* and *Puentes*.

John Muccigrosso received his PhD in 1998 from the Department of Classical Studies at the University of Michigan. He is currently Assistant Professor of Classics at Drew University. His research interests include Latin pedagogy, Roman history, and Italian archaeology. Most recently, he has been finishing work on excavations at Paestum, Italy.

Rebecca Oxford is Associate Dean of the College of Education at the University of Alabama. She has authored or coauthored three books, *Language learning strategies: What every teacher should know, Patterns of cultural identity*, and *The tapestry approach: The Individual in the communicative classroom*; has edited two books, *Language learning strategies around the world: Cross-cultural perspectives* and *Language learning motivation: Pathways to the new century*; and has coedited the *Tapestry program*, a collection of over 30 textbooks for college-age ESL students. In her many publications and presentations, she has contributed to a greater understanding of learner characteristics that influence the language learning process.

Frances Pettigrew is a Spanish teacher and chairman of the foreign language department at McLean High School, McLean, Va. She is also a resource teacher in the Office of Foreign Language Instruction in Fairfax County, Va. She has been on the PALS curriculum development task force since its beginning in the summer of 1995 and has taught seminars and classes on performance assessment to Fairfax County foreign language teachers. She has also made presentations at the local, state and national level on performance assessment. She is currently working with Fairfax County's Assessment Review Committee and with ACTFL's pilot of Performance Assessment Units.

Deborah Pennell Ross is Adjunct Assistant Professor in the Department of Classical Studies at the University of Michigan and is currently serving as Director of the Elementary Latin Program there. She has teaching experience in Latin at the high-school as well as at the college level, and is particularly concerned with teaching Latin for reading and other aspects of Latin pedagogy. A linguist by training, her research is in the areas of Indo-European studies, functional grammar, and discourse analysis, and she has published on word order and discourse issues in Latin, as well as on Latin pedagogy.

Ghislaine Tulou is a French teacher and staff development coordinator at McLean High School in McLean, Va. She has been on the PALS curriculum development task force since its beginning in the summer of 1995 and is currently the chair. She has taught seminars and classes on performance assessment to Fairfax County foreign language teachers and has also made presentations on this topic at local, state, and national conferences. She is currently working with Fairfax County's Assessment Review Committee and with ACTFL's pilot of Performance Assessment Units.

Anita Wenden is professor of ESL at York College (City University of New York). Her professional interests are in metacognition, specifically adult L2 learners' beliefs, and in the development of methods and materials for promoting learner autonomy in language learning. Her books on these topics include *Learner strategies in language learning* (co-edited with Joan Rubin in 1987) and *Learner strategies for learner autonomy* (1991).

Northeast Conference Reports 1954–1998

Foreign Language Teachers and Tests. *Hunter Kellenberger, Editor. Committee on the Qualifications of Foreign Language Teachers*, Stephen A. Freeman, Chairman; Theodore Andersson, Finis E. Engleman, E. Duncan Grizzell, John Holden, Kathryn L. O'Brien, T. M. Stinnett: *Committee on Foreign Language Instruction in Elementary Schools*, Arthur M. Selvi, Chairman; Lillian S. Adams, Nelson Brooks, Dorothy Chamberlain, Vincenzo Cioffari, Ann Foberg, Howard Garey, Manuel H. Guerra, Victoria Lyles, Mary P. Thompson, Olga Scherer Virski: *Committee on Tests*, Nelson Brooks, Chairman; Frederick B. Agard, Anne-Marie de Commaille, Howard Garey, Archibald T. MacAllister, Kathryn L. O'Brien, Henry B. Richardson, Edith A. Runge, Stanley M. Sapon, Paula Thibault: *Committee on the Teaching of Literature*, Norman L. Torrey, Chairman; Esther M. Eaton, Archibald T. MacAllister, Olga Scherer Virski, Donald D. Walsh: *Committee on the Role of Foreign Languages in American Life*, Theodore Andersson, Chairman; Leon Dostert, Herbert G. Espy, Stephen A. Freeman, Henri Peyre, Henry Lee Smith, Wilmarth H. Starr: *Committee on Linguistic Aids*, Richard H. Walker, Chairman; F. B. Agard, William N. Locke, Edmond A. Meras, Robert Politzer, Fred H. Tone, W. Freeman Twaddell: and *The Foreign Language Program*, speech given by W. R. Parker. 1954

Culture, Literature and Articulation. *Germaine Brée, Editor. Committee on the Role of Literature in Language Teaching*, Archibald T. MacAllister, Chairman; Mrs. Germaine Cressey, Edwin M. Faust, Joseph Genna, Joseph Stookins, Olga Scherer Virski: *Committee on the Place of Culture and Civilization*, Laurence Wylie, Chairman; Joseph B. Casagrande, A. Irving Hallowell, John B. Hughes, Otto Klineberg, Mrs. Dolores Andújar de MacDonald, David C. McClelland, Albert H. Marckwardt, Eric Rosenbaum, William C. Sayres, Mrs. Rose Scheider, Elbridge Sibley, Theodore C. Wright: *Committee on Foreign Language Instruction in Elementary Schools*, Mary P. Thompson, Chairman; Sandra Adler, Julius Arnold, Joseph Astman, Marion Digisi, Marguerite Eriksson, James Grew, Lucrecia Lopez, Susan Scott, Sylvia Smith, Alex Szogyi, Olga Scherer Virski: *Committee on Foreign Languages in Secondary Schools*, Robert G. Mead, Jr., Chairman; Louis González, Audrey Havican, Joseph LoBue, Louise Theurer: *Classical and Modern Foreign Languages: Common Areas and Problems*, Barbara P. McCarthy, Chairman; Josephine P. Bree, Helen E. Bridey, Austin M. Lashbrook, Alice Nesta Lloyd Thomas, C. Arthur Lynch, Edmond A. Meras: *Committee on Tests*, Nelson Brooks, Chairman; Ramona Beeken, Anne-Marie de Commaille, Durand Echeverria, Sarah W. Lorge, Kathryn L. O'Brien, Edith Runge, Stanley Sapon, James Stephens, Paula Thibault: *Committee on the Preparation of Foreign Language Teachers*, Alonzo G. Grace, Chairman; Stephen Freeman, Henry Herge, John R. Matthew, Arthur Selvi: *Committee on Teaching Aids and Techniques*, Jeanne Varney Pleasants, Chairman; Douglas W. Alden, Armand Bégué, Jean Benoît-Levy, Pierre Crénesse, Renée Jeanne Fulton, Daniel Girard, Pierre Guédenet, Robert M. Hankin, Sylvia N. Levy, Sister Margaret Thérèse, Richard H. Walker, Ruth Hirsch Weinstein, Edward Williamson: *Committee on the Role of Foreign Languages in Ameri-*

can Life, Wilmarth Starr, Chairman; Theodore Andersson, Lilian Avila, Yaroslav Chyz, Leonard Covello, Rachel DuBois, Joseph Monserrat, Alfred Pellegrino, Nora Wittman. 1955

Foreign Language Tests and Techniques. *Margaret Gilman, Editor. Committee on Teaching Aids and Techniques,* Frederick D. Eddy, Chairman; John B. Archer, Grace A. Crawford, Kathryn Fellows, Daniel P. Girard, Karl Kellermann, E. Wesley O'Neill, Hubert S. Packard, Fred B. Painter, Tilla Thomas, Mrs. Ruth Hirsch Weinstein, Mrs. Margaret V. Wojnowski, Mrs. Jeanne Varney Pleasants: *Committee on Tests*, Stanley M. Sapon, Chairman; Simon Belasco, Nelson Brooks, Charles Choquette, Paula Thibault: *Committee on Foreign Language Instruction in Elementary Schools*, Mary P. Thompson, Chairman; Joyce Greene, Paul F. Poehler, Mrs. Ina C. Sartorius, Katherine Scrivener, Sylvia Smith: *Committee on Foreign Language Instruction in Secondary Schools*, Mrs. Ruth P. Kroeger, Chairman; Joseph LoBue, Alexander D. Gibson, Blanche A. Price, Frank M. Soda, Elizabeth White, Alfred J. Wright: *Committee on the Teaching of Classical and Modern Foreign Languages, Common Areas and Problems*, Josephine P. Bree, Chairman; Allan Hoey, Sister Marie Louise, Barbara P. McCarthy, Kenneth Meinke, Esther Tabor, Ralph Ward: *Committee on the Role of Literature in Language Teaching*, Robert J. Clements, Chairman; Annette Emgarth, Laurent LeSage, Grace Myer, Charlotte Pekary, Sanford Shepart, Adeline Strouse, Floyd Zulli: *Committee on the Place of Culture and Civilization in Foreign Language Teaching*, John B. Carroll, Chairman; William C. Sayres, Otto Klineberg, William G. Moulton, Mrs. Rose M. Scheider, Gerald E. Wade, Theodore C. Wright: *Committee on the Role of Foreign Languages in American*

Life, Wilmarth Starr, Chairman; Yaroslav Chyz, Leonard Covello, Rachel DuBois, Joseph Monserrat, Alfred Pellegrino, Nora Wittman. 1956

The Language Classroom. *William F. Bottiglia, Editor. Committee on Materials and Methods for Teaching Literature in Secondary School in Preparation for Admission to College with Advanced Standing,* Blanche A. Price, Chairman; Morton W. Briggs, Georgette Galland, DeVaux de Lancey, Marthe Lavallée, Edward P. Morris, Rose Presel, Olga S. Virski: *Committee on Tests*, Nelson Brooks, Chairman; Stanley M. Sapon, Simon Belasco, Charles Choquette, Fernand Marty, Paula Thibault: *Committee on the Place of Grammar and the Use of English in the Teaching of Foreign Languages at Various Levels*, James Grew, Chairman; Nelson Brooks, Elliott Grant, Paul Gropp, Paul S. Hennessey, Emilie Margaret White: *Committee on the Drop-Out of Students in High School Language Classes*, Renée J. Fulton, Chairman; Thomas V. Banks, Josephine R. Bruno, A. Louise Carlson, Emilio Guerra, Alice F. Linnehan, Nita Willits Savage, Mary M. Stavrinos: *Committee on the Philosophy of the Language Laboratory*, John B. Archer, Chairman; Frederick D. Eddy, Mrs. Lois S. Gaudin, Joyce E. Greene, Sister Julie, S.N.D., Rudolph V. Oblum, Geneviève Wantiez, Mrs. Margaret V. Wojnowski: *Committee on Teaching Aids and Techniques*, Jeanne Varney Pleasants, Chairman; Pierre Capretz, Kathryn F. Fellows, Manuel H. Guerra, Paul King, Theodore Mueller, William Nemser, Marcella Ottolenghi, Pierre Oustinoff, S. E. Schmidt, Richard H. Walker, Elizabeth Young. 1957

The Language Teacher. *Harry L. Levy, Editor. Committee on the Teaching of Writing*, Jeannette Atkins, Chairman; Jean-

Pierre Cossnard, Elliott M. Grant, Mrs. Glenda G. Richards: *Committee on Single Versus Multiple Languages in Secondary Schools*, James H. Grew, Chairman; Thelma B. DeGraff, Arthur Howe, Jr., William N. Locke, Paul H. Phaneuf, A. Marguerite Zouck: *Committee on the Foreign Language Program, Grades 3–12*, Margaret E. Eaton, Chairman; Dorothy Chamberlain, Janet Jones, Filomena C. Peloro, Elizabeth H. Ratte, Mrs. Anne Slack, Emily L. Snow: *Committee on Patterns as Grammar*, Mrs. Dorothy Brodin, Chairman; Sidney D. Braun, J. Donald Bowen, Nelson Brooks, Catherine Davidovitch, Naomi Goldstein, Frederick Kempner: *Committee on "The Ghosts in the Language Classroom*," Donald D. Walsh, Chairman; Nelson Brooks, Margaret Gilman, S. A. Kendrick, Oliver A. Melchior, Archibald K. Shields: *Committee on Means of Meeting the Shortage of Teachers*, Carolyn E. Bock, Chairman; Mrs. Genevieve S. Blew, William Brunt, Grace A Crawford, Otis N. Jason, William J. Nelligan, Carl A. Tyre, Mrs. Eleanor Young. 1958

The Language Learner. *Frederick D. Eddy, Editor. Modern Foreign Language Learning: Assumptions and Implications,* Wilmarth H. Starr, Chairman; Alfred G. Pellegrino, Frederick H. Dedmond, James H. Grew, Elizabeth H. Ratte, Clyde Russell; *A Provisional Program to Implement the Report of Committee I: A Six-Year Sequence from Grade Nine through the Second Year of College,* Gordon R. Silber, Chairman; Jeannette Atkins, Paul M. Glaude, Richard R. Miller, Jouquina Navarro, W. Napoleon Rivers, Nita W. Savage: *Elementary and Junior High School Curricula,* Filomena C. Peloro, Chairman; Alexander S. Hughes, J. Donald Bowen, Doris Dunn, Mary Lou Washburn, Ismael Silva-Fuenzalida: *Definition of Language Competences through*

Testing, Nelson Brooks, Chairman; James M. Ferrigno, Charles A. Choquette, Esther M. Eaton, Mary E. Hayes, Maxim Newmark, Perry Sturges: *Committee on Resolutions,* Harry L. Levy, Chairman; Archibald T. MacAllister, Mary P. Thompson. 1959

Culture in Language Learning. *G. Reginald Bishop, Jr., Editor. Working Committee I: An Anthropological Concept of Culture,* Ernestine Friedl, Chairman; Edward M. Bruner, Regina Flannery Herzfeld: *Working Committee II: Language as Culture,* William E. Welmers, Chairman; Alexander Hull, Eva Douglas, Dan Desberg: *Working Committee III: Teaching of Western European Cultures,* Ira Wade, Chairman; Joseph M. Franckenstein, Daniel Girard, Maria Sora, Fernand Vial: *Working Committee IV: Teaching of Classical Cultures,* Doris E. Kibbe, Chairman; Moses Hadas, Ralph Marcellino, Irene E. Stanislawczyk, John Rowe Workman: *Working Committee V: Teaching of Slavic Cultures,* Leon I. Twarog, Chairman; Edward J. Brown, William E. Harkins, Alfred E. Senn, Johannes Van Straalen, Wiktor Weintraub. 1960

Modern Language Teaching in School and College. *Seymour L. Flaxman, Editor. Working Committee I: The Preparation of Secondary School Teachers,* Genevieve S. Blew, Chairman; Wesley Childers, Alice A. Arana, Philip E. Arsenault, Anna Balakian: *Working Committee II: The Preparation of College and University Teachers,* Jack M. Stein, Chairman; Helen M. Mustard, Patricia O'Connor, Francis Rogers, Wilmarth Starr: *Working Committee III: The Transition to the Classroom,* Evangeline Galas, Chairman; Remunda Cadoux, Sister Margaret Pauline, Robert Serafino, Herbert Schueler: *Working Committee IV: Coordination between Classroom and Laboratory,*

Guillermo del Olmo, Chairman; Jeannette Atkins, Dora S. Bashour, Pierre Capretz, Clark A. Vaughan. 1961

Current Issues in Language Teaching. *William F. Bottiglia, Editor. Working Committee on Linguistics and Language Teaching,* Robert A. Hall, Jr., Chairman; Raleigh Morgan, Jr., Josephine R. Bruno, Paul M. Glaude, William D. Ilgen, James P. Soffietti, Seymour O. Simches: *Working Committee on Programmed Learning,* Alfred S. Hayes, Chairman; Harlan L. Lane, Theodore Mueller, Waldo E. Sweet, Wilmarth H. Starr: *Panel on FLES Practices,* Mary A. Brophy, Chairman; Nancy V. Alkonis, Alice Arana, Randall Marshall, Andre Paquette, Laurence G. Paquin, Beverly Sherp, Mary P. Thompson: *Panel on Televised Teaching,* M. Jeannette Atkins, Chairman; Dorothy Brodin, Robert W. Cannaday, Jr., Benito L. Lueras, Robert Serafino. 1962

Language Learning: The Intermediate Phase. *William F. Bottiglia, Editor. Working Committee on the Continuum: Listening and Speaking,* Simon Belasco, Chairman; Eleanor Bingham, Dan Desberg, Stanley M. Sapon, Albert Valdman, Filomena Peloro Del Olmo: *Working Committee on Reading for Meaning,* George A. C. Scherer, Chairman; Delvin Covey, Sharon Entwistle, Wallace E. Lambert, Dean H. Obrecht, Betty Robertson, Alfred S. Hayes: *Working Committee on Writing as Expression,* Marina Prochoroff, Chairman; Richard Burgi, Jacques Ehrmann, George Krivobok, Mary P. Thompson. 1963

Foreign Language Teaching: Ideals and Practices. *George Fenwick Jones, Editor. Working Committee I: Foreign Languages in the Elementary School,* Conrad J. Schmitt, Chairman; Marjorie P. Bowen, Janice S. Calkin, Gladys Lipton, Protase E.

Woodford, Seymour O. Simches: *Working Committee II: Foreign Languages in the Secondary School,* Milton R. Hahn, Chairman; Colette Garimaldi, Jack B. Krail, James F. McArthur, Arnold Tauber, Joseph Tursi, Russell Webster, M. Jeannette Atkins: *Working Committee III: Foreign Languages in Colleges and Universities,* Roger L. Hadlich, Chairman; Harlan P. Hanson, James H. Harris, Robert J. Nelson, Arthur M. Selvi, Ralph L. Ward, Delvin L. Covey. 1964

Foreign Language Teaching: Challenges to the Profession. *G. Reginald Bishop, Jr., Editor. A Discussion Panel—The Case for Latin,* William R. Parker, Chairman; Clara West Ashley, Margaret Gill, John F. Latimer, Edward A. Robinson, Edward D. Sullivan: *Working Committee I: Study Abroad,* Stephen A. Freeman, Chairman; Donald Bigelow, Leonard Brisley, George E. Diller, John A. Garraty, Francis Rogers: *Working Committee II: The Challenge of Bilingualism,* A. Bruce Gaarder, Chairman; Joshua A. Fishman, Wallace E. Lambert, Elizabeth Anisfeld, Gerard J. Brault, Pauline M. Rojas, Louis L. Curcio, Norman D. Kurland: *Working Committee III: From School to College: The Problem of Continuity,* Micheline Dufau, Chairman; Miriam M. Bryan, John W. Kurtz, Theodore Nuzzi, Josephine Bruno Pane. 1965

Language Teaching: Broader Contexts. *Robert G. Mead, Jr., Editor. Discussion Panel: Research and Language Learning,* Edward D. Sullivan, Chairman; John B. Carroll, Noam Chomsky, Charles A. Furguson, with comments by Harlan L. Lane, W. Freeman Twaddell, Douglas C. Sheppard; *Working Committee I: Content and Crossroads: Wider Uses for Foreign Languages,* Brownlee Sands Corrin, Chairman;

William F. Bottiglia, Cleophas W. Boudreau, James H. Grew, W. Roy Phelps, Helen P. Warriner: *Working Committee II: Coordination of Foreign Language Teaching: A Contemporary View of Professional Leadership,* Genevieve S. Blew, Chairman; John W. Gartner, Sister Charlotte Marie, Frank M. Soda, June U. Stillwell, Marilyn E. Wolf. 1966

Foreign Languages: Reading Literature Requirements. *Thomas E. Bird, Editor. Working Committee I: The Teaching of Reading,* William G. Moulton, Chairman; Hugh Campbell, Doris E. Kibbe, Albert M. Reh, Dorothy S. Rivers, Kimberly Sparks: *Working Committee II: The Times and Places for Literature,* F. Andre Paquette, Chairman; Anna Benjamin, Hugh M. Davidson, Gladys Lipton, Chris N. Nacci, Filomena Del Olmo, Robert H. Spaethling, James P. Ward: *Working Committee III: Trends in FL Requirements and Placement,* John F. Gummere, Chairman; Robert L. Hinshalwood, Mrs. Herbert F. McCollom, Gordon R. Silber. 1967

Foreign Language Learning: Research and Development. *Thomas E. Bird, Editor. Working Committee I: Innovative FL Programs,* Oliver Andrews, Jr., Chairman; Carolyn E. Bock, Grace A. Crawford, A. Bruce Gaarder, Elton Hocking, Paul C. McRill, Mabel W. Richardson, George E. Smith: *Working Committee II: The Classroom Revisited,* Seymour O. Simches, Chairman; Josephine Bruno Pane, Richard M. Penta, James R. Powers, Dorothy S. Rivers, Marigwen Schumacher, Symond Yavener: *Working Committee III: Liberated Expression,* Mills F. Edgerton, Jr., Chairman; Dwight Bolinger, Thomas W. Kelly, Gail E. Montgomery, Donald G. Reiff. 1968

Sight and Sound: The Sensible and Sensitive Use of Audio-Visual Aids. *Mills F. Edgerton, Jr., Editor. Non-Projected Visuals* by Brenda Frazier: *Sound Recordings* by Jermaine Arendt (Using Taped Material in Studying Goethe's *Faust* in High School: A Slide-Tape Demonstration - by Margaret Shryer): *Slides and Filmstrips* by Rev. Hilary Hayden, O.S.B. (*Combray:* A Multi-Media Introduction to the World of Marcel Proust by Pierre Capretz): *The Overhead Projector* by James J. Wrenn, *Motion Pictures* by Allan W. Grundstrom (Motion-Picture Film: A Demonstration - by Mills F. Edgerton, Jr.): *Television* by Joseph H. Sheehan (Demonstration of the Use of Television in the Training of Foreign-Language Teachers - by Joseph Sheehan and Robert Willis): *Let us Build Bridges* by Stephen A. Freeman. 1969

Foreign Languages and the "New" Student. *Joseph A. Tursi, Editor. A Relevant Curriculum: An Instrument for Polling Student Opinion,* Robert P. Serafino, Chairman; Joan L. Feindler, F. André Paquette, John J. Reilly and consultant Leon A. Jakobovits: *Motivation in Foreign-Language Learning,* Robert J. Nelson, Chairman; Leon A. Jakobovits, Filomena Peloro Del Olmo, Rev. Daniel R. Kent, Wallace E. Lambert, Elaine C. Libit, Jane W. Torrey, G. Richard Tucker: *Foreign Languages For All Students?* Eleanor L. Sandstrom, Chairman; Paul Pimsleur, Michael E. Hernick, Gertrude Moskowitz, Frank Otto, Frederick J. Press, Mary L. Robb, Pearl M. Warner: *The Rung and the Ladder* by Nelson Brooks. 1970

Leadership for Continuing Development. *James W. Dodge, Editor. Professional Responsibilities,* James R. Powers, Chairman; Nelson Brooks, A. Bruce Gaarder, Stowell C. Goding, John F. Latimer, John P. Nionakis, Rebecca Valette, and consultants Frank Di Giammarino, Frederick D. Eddy, Ronald Fitzgerald: *Inservice Involvement in the Process of Change,* Jerome G. Mirsky, Chairman; Edward H. Bourque, Jerald R. Green, Norma Enea Klayman, Gladys C. Lipton, Harriet Norton: *Innovative Trends in Foreign-Language Teaching,* François Hugot, Chairman; Genelle Caldwell, Nancyanne Fitzgibbons, Judith Le Bovit, Frank Otto, Ferdinand Ruplin, Brother Dean Warthen, C.F.X.: *Literature for Advanced Foreign-Language Students* by Harry L. Levy. 1971

Other Words, Other Worlds: Language-in-Culture. *James W. Dodge, Editor. On Teaching Another Language as Part of Another Culture* by Joey L. Dillard, Mary R. Miller and William A. Stewart: *Sociocultural Aspects of Foreign-Language Study* by G. Richard Tucker and Wallace E. Lambert: *Ancient Greek and Roman Culture* by Samuel Lieberman: *France* by Gerard J. Brault: *Some Suggestions for Implementing the Report on France* by Joan L. Feindler: *Quebec: French Canada* by Marine Leland: *An Approach to Courses in German Culture* by Harry F. Young: *Italy and the Italians* by Joseph Tursi: *Japan: Spirit and Essence* by Walter J. Odronic: *The Soviet Union* by Irina Kirk: *Spain* by John W. Kronik: *Spanish America: A Study in Diversity* by Frank N. Dauster: *Some Suggestions for Implementing the Report on Spanish America* by Jerome G. Mirsky: *Teaching Foreign Languages: A Brief Retrospect and Prospect* by Robert G. Mead, Jr.: *Individualizing Instruction through Team Teaching* by Frank Otto: *La Révolte des jeunes or An Experiment in Relevancy* by Michael Agatstein. 1972

Sensitivity in the Foreign-Language Classroom. *James W. Dodge, Editor. Interaction in the Foreign-Language Class,* Gertrude Moskowitz, Chairman; Jacqueline Benevento, Norma Furst: *Teaching Spanish to the Native Spanish Speaker,* Herman LaFontaine, Chairman; Evelyn Colón, Marco Hernández, Awilda Orta, Muriel Pagan, Carmen Pérez, Nathan Quiñones, Sonia Rivera: *Individualization of Instruction,* Ronald L. Gougher, Chairman; Howard B. Altman, John F. Bockman, Aline C. Desbonnet, Philip D. Smith, Lorraine A. Strasheim and consultants Tora T. Ladu and Alfred D. Roberts: *Meditations on Being a Foreign-Language Teacher* by Freeman Twaddell: *The Audio-Motor Unit: A Listening Comprehension Strategy that Works* by Theodore B. Kalivoda, Genelle Morain, and Robert J. Elkins. 1973

Toward Student-Centered Foreign-Language Programs. *Warren C. Born, Editor. Training for Student-Centered Language Programs,* Annette S. Baslaw, Co-Chairwoman, Joan S. Freilich, Co-Chairwoman; William E. De Lorenzo, Thomas H. Geno, Charles R. Hancock, Robert R. Sherburne and consultants Howard B. Altman, Leo Benardo and Barbara E. Elling: *Implementing Student-Centered Foreign-Language Programs,* Anthony Papalia, Chairman; Peter Boyd-Bowman, Dale V. Lally, Jr., Helene Loew, Stefano Morel, Roland Obstfeld, Anne Slack, Harry Tuttle and consultant Toby S. Tamarkin: *Careers, Community, and Public Awareness,* René L. Lavergneau, Chairman; Marguerite D. Bomse, Beverly Butler Lavergneau, Diane F. Menditto, Richard W. Newman, Toby S. Tamarkin, Blanca G. Wright and consultant Doris Marks: *Curriculum Perspectives: The Need for Diversified Services* by Emma Birkmaier: *Penetrating the Mass Media: A Unit to Develop Skill in Reading Spanish Newspaper Headlines* by H. Ned Seelye and J. Laurence Day. 1974

Goals Clarification: Curriculum Teaching Evaluation. *Warren C. Born, Editor. Committee on Curriculum,* Stephen L. Levy, Chairman; Muriel H. Goldstein, Mark Levine, June K. Phillips, Pearl M. Warner, and consultants Gladys C. Lipton, Helen Z. Loew, Rose Marie Roccio: *Committee on Teaching,* Ann A. Beusch, Chairman; Jane M. Bourque, Roberta Cohen, William E. De Lorenzo, and consultant Philip Arsenault: *Committee on Evaluation,* John L. D. Clark, Chairman; Virginia S. Ballard, John P. Nionakis, Richard C. ten Eyck, and consultant Brenda Frazier Clemons: *Gladly Teche ... and Gladly Lerne* by Donald D. Walsh: *Fusion of the Four Skills: A Technique for Facilitating Communicative Exchange* by Robert J. Elkins, Theodore B. Kalivoda, and Genelle Morain. 1975

Language and Culture: Heritage and Horizons. *Warren C. Born, Editor. Committee on the Classics,* Grace Crawford, Chairperson; Marigwen Schumaker, William Ziobro, and consultants Marie Cleary, John Latimer, Meyer Reinhold: *Committee on the French-Speaking,* Normand C. Dube, Chairperson; Gerard J. Brault, Guy F. Dubay and consultants Madeleine D. Giguere, Roger Grindle, Roger Paradis: *Committee on the German-Speaking,* Helene Z. Loew, Chairperson; Barbara Elling, LaVern J. Rippley, William I. Schreiber: *Committee on the Spanish-Speaking,* John M. Darcey, Chairperson; Milagros Carrero, Rosemary Weinstein Dann, John Leach, Toby Tamarkin, Penny A. Zirkel and consultants, Janet Baird, Janie L. Duncan, Dora Kennedy: *Retrospect and Prospect* by Nelson Brooks: *Changing Goals for Foreign Language Education* by Ted T. Grenda: *The Imaginative Use of Projected Visuals* by Thomas P. Carter. 1976

Language: Acquisition, Application, Appreciation. *Warren C. Born, Editor. Working Committee on Acquisition,* Pierre F. Cintas, Chairperson; Nelson Brooks, Yvonne Escola, Robert C. Gardner, John S. Rohsenow, Ernest A. Scatton and consultant Seok Choong Song: *Working Committee on Application,* Kenneth Lester, Chairperson; Merriam Moore, Flora O'Neill, Symond Yavener and consultant Philip Arsenault: *Working Committee on Appreciation,* Germaine Brée, Chairperson; Claude Chauvigne, Micheline Dufau, Enrique H. Miyares: *The Link between Language and Ethnicity: Its Importance for the Language Teacher* by Joshua A. Fishman: *Affective Learning Activities* by Clay Benjamin Christensen. 1977

New Contents, New Teachers, New Publics. *Warren C. Born, Editor. Working Committee on New Contents,* Rebecca M. Valette, Chairman; Pietro Frassica, Gesa Kandeler, Gene S. Kupferschmid, Cathy Linder, Helene B. Mensh, Elaine V. Uzan, Freidrich Winterscheidt and consultant Peter A. Eddy: *Working Committee on New Teachers,* William E. De Lorenzo, Chairman; Ann A. Beusch, Yvonne Escola, Charles R. Hancock, Anthony Mistretta, Sara Schyfter and consultants Peter A. Eddy, James S. Greenberg and Dora Kennedy: *Working Committee on New Publics,* Joseph A. Tursi, Chairman; Ruth L. Bennett, Alain Blanchet, Richard I. Brod, Helene Z. Loew, Anita Monsees and consultant Peter A. Eddy: *Interaction Activities in the Foreign Language Classroom, or How to Grow a Tulip-Rose* by Christina Bratt Paulston. 1978

The Foreign Language Learner in Today's Classroom Environment. *Warren C. Born, Editor. The View on the Way Up: A Wider Perspective* by Wilga M. Rivers: *Educational Goals: The Foreign Language*

Teacher's Response by Wilga M. Rivers: *Cindy: A Learner in Today's Foreign Language Classroom* by Carol Hosenfeld: *The Second Language Teacher: Reconciling the Vision with the Reality* by Gilbert A. Jarvis: *The Combining Arrangement: Some Techniques* by I.S.P. Nation, New Zealand. 1979

Our Profession/Present Status & Future Directions. *Thomas H. Geno, Editor. Present Status of Foreign Language Teaching: A Northeast Conference Survey* by Peter A. Eddy: *Toward an Articulated Curriculum* by Robert C. Lafayette: *Competence in a Foreign Language: A Valuable Adjunct Skill in the Eighties* by Mills F. Edgerton, Jr.: *Educational Technology* by James W. Dodge: *New Approaches to Assessment of Language Learning* by Helen L. Jorstad: *The American Language Association: Toward New Strength, Visibility, an Effectiveness as a Profession* by David P. Benseler: *Diagnosing and Responding to Individual Learner Needs* by Diane W. Birckbichler and Alice C. Omaggio. 1980

New Cases for Foreign Language Study. [A special publication project.] *Compiled by June K. Phillips. Language and Global Awareness* by George W. Bonham: *Escalating the Campaign Against Provincialism* by S. Frederick Starr: *Why Study Foreign Languages?* by F. Andre Paquette: *We Think We Are "Evening in Paris," But We're Really "Chanel"* by Gilbert A. Jarvis: *Educational Goals: The Foreign Language Teacher's Response* by Wilga M. Rivers: *Developing Foreign Language Curriculum in the Total School Setting: The Macro-Picture* by Robert S. Zais: *Defending the FL Requirement in the Liberal Arts Curriculum* by Thomas J. Bugos: *Views on the Foreign Language Requirement in Higher Education* by Norma Enea Klayman: *The Resurgence of Foreign Language Study* by John

K. Primeau: *Special Curricula for Special Needs* by Barbara Elling: *Rationales for Foreign Language Study: What Are Our Goals?* by Gerd K. Schneider: *Views of Secondary School Superintendents on Foreign Language Study: A Support-Constraint Analysis* by Dominick DeFilippis: *Students' Beliefs on the Importance of Foreign Languages in the School Curriculum* by Anthony Papalia: *Why Study Foreign Languages? A Junior Orientalist's Perspective* by John Buscaglia. 1981

Foreign Language and International Studies—Toward Cooperation and Integration. *Thomas H. Geno, Editor. A Chronicle: Political, Professional, and Public Activities surrounding the President's Commission on Foreign Language and International Studies* by Thomas H. Geno: *Global Responsibility: The Role of the Foreign Language Teacher;* Donald H. Bragaw, Helene Z. Loew, Judith S. Wooster: *Exchanges and Travel Abroad in Secondary Schools* by Claudia S. Travers: *Toward an International Dimension in Higher Education* by Richard C. Williamson: *International Training* by Lucia Pierce. 1981

The Foreign Language Teacher: The Lifelong Learner. *Robert G. Mead, Jr., Editor. Less Frequently Taught Languages: Basic Information and Instruction: American Sign Language* by Marilyn Conwell and April Nelson; *Chinese* by David N. Gidman; *Japanese* by Jean-Pierre Berwald and Toshiko Phipps; *Latin* by Marie Cleary; *Portuguese* by Rosemarie Pedro Carvalho; *Russian* by Robert L. Baker; *Comtemporary Cultures: Issues and Answers: La France Comtemporaine* by Pierre Maubrey; *Die Bundesrepublik Deutschland heute-zeitgemäße Betrachtungen* by Barbara Elling and Karl Elling; *L'Italia Contemporanea* by Romo J. Trivelli; *La España de Hoy* by John

M. Darcey; *La Cultura Contemporánea de Hispanoamérica* by Frank Dauster: *Methodology and Evaluation: Merging Methods and Texts: A Pragmatic Approach* by Elizabeth G. Joiner and June K. Phillips: *Proficiency Testing in Second Language Classrooms* by Judith E. Liskin-Gasparro and Protase E. Woodford: *Technology and the Foreign Language Classroom: Audiovisual Materials and Techniques for Teaching Foreign Languages* by Carolyn Parks: *Applications of Computer Technology in Foreign Language Teaching and Learning* by John S. Harrison. 1982

Foreign Languages: Key Links in the Chain of Learning. *Robert G. Mead, Jr., Editor. Elementary School Foreign Language: Key Link in the Chain of Learning,* Myriam Met, Chair; Helena Anderson, Evelyn Brega, Nancy Rhodes: *Foreign Language in the Secondary School: Reconciling the Dream with the Reality,* Alice C. Omaggio, Chair; Anthony J. DeNapoli, Paul T. Griffith, Dora F. Kennedy, Stephen L. Levy, Gladys Lipton, Helene Z. Loew: *"Nuturing the Ties that Bind": Links Between Foreign Language Departments and the Rest of the Post-secondary Educational Enterprise,* Claire Gaudiani, Chair; Patricia Cummins, Humphrey Tonkin: *Foreign Language and the "Other" Student* by Vicki Galloway: *Toward a Multidimensional Foreign Language Curriculum* by H. H. Stern: *Thirty Years of the Northeast Conference: A Personal Perspective* by Jane McFarland Bourque. 1983

The Challenge for Excellence in Foreign Language Education. *Gilbert A. Jarvis, Editor. For Teachers: A Challenge for Competence* by Barbara H. Wing: *The Challenge of Proficiency: Student Characteristics* by Diane W. Birckbichler: *Testing in a Communicative Approach* by Michael Canale: *Of Computers and Other Technologies* by Glyn Hol-

mes: *The Challenge for Excellence in Curriculum and Materials Development* by Christine L. Brown. 1984

Proficiency, Curriculum, Articulation: The Ties that Bind. *Alice C. Omaggio, Editor. Designing the Proficiency-Based Curriculum* by Frank W. Medley, Jr.: *The Development of Oral Proficiency* by Jeannette D. Bragger: *Teaching toward Proficiency: The Receptive Skills* by Heidi Byrnes: *Teaching and Testing Proficiency in Writing: Skills to Transcend the Second-Language Classroom* by Sally Sieloff Magnan: *Toward Cultural Proficiency* by Wendy W. Allen: *A Continuing Chronicle of Professional, Policy, and Public Activities in Foreign Languages and International Studies* by J. David Edwards and Melinda E. Hanisch. 1985

Listening, Reading, and Writing: Analysis and Application. *Barbara H. Wing, Editor. Listening in the Native Language* by Carolyn Gwynn Coakley and Andrew D. Wolvin: *Listening in the Foreign Language* by Elizabeth G. Joiner: *Reading in the Native Language* by Michael L. Kamil: *Reading in the Foreign Language* by Elizabeth B. Bernhardt: *Writing in the Native Language* by Kathryn K. Osterholm: *Writing in the Foreign Language* by Trisha Dvorak. 1986

The Language Teacher: Commitment and Collaboration. *John M. Darcey, Editor. The Importance of Collaboration* by Claire L. Gaudiani: *Grassroots and Treetops: Collaboration in Post-secondary Language Programs* by Humphrey Tonkin: *Incorporating an International Dimension in Education Reform: Strategies for Success* by Gordon M. Ambach: *Baltimore's Foreign Language Mandate: An Experiment that Works* by Alice G. Pinderhughes: *Commitment to Excellence: Community Col-*

laboration in Pittsburgh by Richard C. Wallace, Jr., Mary Ellen Kirby and Thekla F. Fall: *Parents: The Child's Most Important Teachers* by Madeline Ehrlich: *Canadian Parents for French: Parent Action and Second Official Language Learning in Canada* by Carolyn E. Hodych: *The Role of the Foreign Language Teacher in American Corporate Education* by Badi G. Foster. 1987

Toward a New Integration of Language and Culture. *Alan J. Singerman, Editor. Language and Culture at the Crossroads* by Peter Patrikis: *Semiotic and Sociolinguistic Paths to Understanding Culture* by Angela Moórjani and Thomas T. Field: *Integrating the Teaching of Culture into the Foreign Language Classroom* by Robert C. Lafayette: *The Cultural Discourse of Foreign Language Textbooks* by Claire J. Kramsch: *Mass Media and Authentic Documents: Language in Cultural Context* by Jean-Pierre Berwald: *Integrating Language and Culture through Video: A Case Study from the Teaching of Japanese* by Seiichi Makino: *Linguistic and Cultural Immersion: Study Abroad for the Younger Student* by Aleidine J. Moeller: *Linguistic and Cultural Immersion: Study Abroad for the College Student* by Norman Stokle: *Learning Culture through Local Resources: A Hispanic Model* by Barbara Lotito and Mireya Pérez-Erdélyi. 1988

Shaping the Future: Challenges and Opportunities. *Helen S. Lepke, Editor. Teacher Education: Target of Reform* by June K. Phillips: *Elementary School Foreign Languages: Obstacles and Opportunities* by Carol Ann Pesola and Helena Anderson Curtain: *The Secondary Program, 9–12* by Helen P. Warriner-Burke: *Re-shaping the "College-level" Curriculum: Problems and Possibilities* by Dorothy James: *The Less Commonly Taught Languages in the*

Context of American Pedagogy by Galal Walker: *Beyond the Traditional Classroom* by Emily L. Spinelli. 1989

Shifting the Instructional Focus to the Learner. *Sally Sieloff Magnan, Editor. Attending to the Affective Domain in the Foreign Language Classroom* by Elaine K. Horwitz: *Language Learning Strategies and Beyond: A Look at Strategies in the Context of Styles* by Rebecca L. Oxford: *Child Development and Academic Skills in the Elementary School Foreign Language Classroom* by Nancy Rhodes, Helena Curtain and Mari Haas: *The Exploratory Years: Foreign Languages in the Middle-Level Curriculum* by Anne G. Nerenz: *Learning Foreign Language in High School and College: Should It Really Be Different?* by Thomas Cooper, Theodore B. Kalivoda and Genelle Morain: *Foreign Language Proficiency and the Adult Learner* by Katherine M. Kulick. 1990

Building Bridges and Making Connections. *June K. Phillips, Editor. Adapting an Elementary Immersion Approach to Secondary and Postsecondary Language Teaching: The Methodological Connection* by Eileen W. Glisan and Thekla F. Fall: *ESL and FL: Forging Connections* by Diane Larsen-Freeman: *Higher-Level Language Abilities: The Skills Connection* by Karen E. Breiner-Sanders: *Building Multiple Proficiencies in New Curricular Contexts* by Barbara Schnuttgen Jurasek and Richard T. Jurasek: *Linking the Foreign Language Classroom to the World* by Juliette Avots: *Connecting Testing and Learning in the Classroom and on the Program Level* by Elana Shohamy. 1991

Languages for a Multicultural World in Transition. *Heidi Byrnes, Editor. Societal Multilingualism in a Multicultural World in Transition* by Ofelia García: *The Role of the*

Foreign Language Teaching Profession in Maintaining Non-English Languages in the United States by Guadalupe Valdés: *Area Studies for a Multicultural World in Transition* by Claire Gaudiani: *Toward a Cultural Reading of Authentic Texts* by Vicki Galloway: *The Changing Goals of Language Instruction* by John M. Grandin, Kandace Einbeck and Walter von Reinhart: *Technology at the Cutting Edge: Implications for Second Language Learning* by Clara Yu. 1992

Reflecting on Proficiency From the Classroom Perspective. *June K. Phillips, Editor. Proficiency-Oriented Language Learning: Origins, Perspectives, and Prospects* by Alice Omaggio Hadley: *Proficiency as a Change Element in Curricula for World Languages in Elementary and Secondary Schools* by Robert LaBouve: *Using Foreign Languages to Learn: Rethinking the College Foreign Language Curriculum* by Janet Swaffar: *Proficiency as an Inclusive Orientation: Meeting the Challenge of Diversity* by Marie Sheppard: *Perspectives on Proficiency: Teachers, Students, and the Materials that They Use* by Diane W. Birckbichler and Kathryn A. Corl: *On Becoming a Teacher: Teacher Education for the 21st Century* by Anne Nerenz: *Forty Years of the Northeast Conference: A Personal Perspective* by Stephen L. Levy. 1993

Teaching, Testing, and Assessment: Making the Connection. *Charles R. Hancock, Editor. Teaching, Testing, and Assessment: Conceptualizing the Relationship* by Rebecca M. Valette: *Developments in Foreign Language Testing and Instruction: A National Perspective* by Charles W. Stansfield: *Toward More Authentic Assessment of Language Performances* by Grant Wiggins: *Assessing the Speaking Skill in the Classroom: New Solutions to an Ongoing Problem* by Peggy Boyles: *Listening Skills: Acquisition and Assessment* by

Donna Reseigh Long and Janice Lynn Macián: *Authentic Assessment: Reading and Writing* by James J. Davis: *The Portfolio and Testing Culture* by Zena T. Moore: *Affective Considerations in Developing Language Tests for Secondary Students* by Pat Barr-Harrison and Elaine K. Horwitz: *Assessment in Foreign Language Teacher Education* by Leslie L. Schrier and JoAnn Hammadou: *Glossary of Selected Terms* by Charles R. Hancock: *Annotated Bibliography* by Graduate Students at Ohio State University. 1994

Voices From the Field: Experiences and Beliefs of Our Constituents. *Trisha Dvorak, Editor. Voices from the Field: An Introduction* by Rebecca R. Kline: *Voices from the Traditional Classroom: Learner Reflections* by Joan Kelly Hall and Jackie Davis: *Voices from Beyond the Classroom: Foreign Language Learners in Non-Traditional Environments* by Gwendolyn Barnes-Karol: *Native Speakers as Language Learners* by María Teresa Garretón: *Voices from Down the Hall: The Reflections of Non-Foreign Language Teachers* by Frank B. Brooks: *Voices Outside Academia: The View from the Center* by Susan Terrio and Mark Knowles: *Venerable Voices* by Dolly Jesúsita Young and Mary M. Kimball: *Voices from the Field: Conclusion* by Trisha Dvorak. 1995

Foreign Languages for All: Challenges and Choices. *Barbara H. Wing, Editor. Foreign Languages for All: Challenges and Choices—An Introduction* by Barbara H. Wing: *The Case for Multilingual Citizens in the 21st Century* by Jeffrey J. Munks: *Starting Early: Foreign Languages in the Elementary and Middle Schools* by Barbara H. Wing: *Meeting the Challenges of the Diverse Secondary School Population* by Emily Spinelli: *Choices in Postsecondary Foreign Language Programs* by Susan M. Bacon: *National Standards and the Chal-*

lenge of Articulation by Claire W. Jackson: *Technological Choices to Meet the Challenges* by Sue K. Otto and James P. Pusack: *R(T)eaching All Students: Necessary Changes in Teacher Education* by Diane J. Tedick and Constance L. Walker: *State Foreign Language Standards Projects—A Sampling* by S. Paul Sandrock. 1996

Collaborations: Meeting New Goals, New Realities. *June K. Phillips, Editor. Collaborations: Meeting New Goals, New Realities* by June K. Phillips. *Professional Collaboration: A Perspective from the Mathematics Standards* by Mary Montgomery Lindquist and Linda P. Rosen. *The Teacher's Voice: A View from a National Standards Site* by Kathleen M. Riordan and Rita A. Oleksak. *Communication Goal: Meaning Making through a Whole Language Approach* by Bonnie Adair-Hauck and Philomena Cumo-Johanssen. *Connections: A K–8/University Collaboration to Promote Interdisciplinary Teaching* by Eileen B. Lorenz and Pierre Verdaguer. *Linguistic and Cultural Comparisons: Middle School African American Students Learning Arabic* by Zena Moore and Mark Anthony English. *Reflections on the Collaborative Projects: Two Perspectives, Two Professionals* by Dale L. Lange and Joseph A. Wieczorek. *Video Guide to* Collaborations: Meeting New Goals, New Realities. 1997

Stories Teachers Tell: Reflecting on Professional Practice. *Douglas K. Hartman, Editor. The Sea of Stories* by Douglas K. Hartman. *Reading the Stories Teachers Tell* by Colleen M. Fairbanks. *I Am Quite Sure of It* by Courtney Stewart. *Outsiders Becoming Insiders* by Bonnie Rorrer. *Gold Is Where You Find It* by Kristine Olin Finnegan. *Learning to Think in French (Cartesian Elixir)* by Mary Gegerias. *Turning Two Ways at Once* by Shannon M. Gallagher. *Every Day and in Every Way I Get Better and Better* by Brooke Walters. *A West Side Story* by John Figueroa. *Vignettes in a Latin Key* by Christine Sleeper. *Be a Good Sport, Sensei!* By Yoko Morimoto. *Room to Grow* by Ruth Supko. *The Year* by Laura Condron Flores. *The Past in Present Tense* by Mark Demkee. *Just One Little Boy* by Regla Armengol. *In the Beginning There Was a Word* by Joseph Ferdinand. *Moving toward the Middle* by Diane Sturgis. *"Mami"* by Melvy E. Jensen. *Montrer Patte Blanche (To Show a White Paw)* by Gloria Pollard. *Traduttori Traditori (Translators Are Traitors)* by Elaine Cerul Eisenhauer. *Memoirs of a Former Spanish Teacher* by Milton R. Hahn. *Same Time Next Year: Same Year Next Time?* by Tom Markham. *Reflections on the Stories Teachers Tell* by G. Richard Tucker. 1998

Northeast Conference Reports
Editors and Authors 1954–1998

Adair-Hauck, Bonnie 1997
Adams, Lillian S. 1954
Adler, Sandra 1955
Agard, Frederick B. 1954
Agatstein, Michael 1972
Alden, Douglas W. 1955
Alkonis, Nancy V. 1962
Allen, Wendy W. 1985
Altman, Howard B. 1973, 1974
Ambach, Gordon M. 1987
Anderson, Helena. See Curtain.
Andersson, Theodore 1954, 1955
Andrews, Oliver, Jr. 1968
Anisfeld, Elizabeth 1965
Arana, Alice A. 1961, 1962
Archer, John B. 1956, 1957
Arendt, Jermaine 1969
Armengol, Regla 1998
Arnold, Julius 1955
Arsenault, Philip E. 1961, 1975, 1977
Ashley, Clara West 1965
Astman, Joseph 1955
Atkins, Jeannette M. 1958, 1959, 1961, 1962, 1964
Avila, Lilian 1955
Avots, Juliette 1991
Bacon, Susan M. 1996
Baird, Janet 1976
Baker, Robert L. 1982
Balakian, Anna 1961
Ballard, Virginia S. 1975
Banks, Thomas V. 1957
Barnes-Karol, Gwendolyn 1995
Barr-Harrison, Pat 1994
Bashour, Dora S. 1961

Baslaw, Annette S. 1974
Beeken, Ramona 1955
Bégué, Armand 1955
Belasco, Simon 1956, 1957, 1963
Benardo, Leo 1974
Benevento, Jacqueline 1973
Benjamin, Anna 1967
Bennett, Ruth L. 1978
Benoît-Levy, Jean 1955
Benseler, David P. 1980
Bernhardt, Elizabeth B. 1986
Berwald, Jean-Pierre 1982, 1988
Beusch, Ann A. 1975, 1978
Bigelow, Donald 1965
Bingham, Eleanor 1963
Birckbichler, Diane W. 1980, 1984, 1993
Bird, Thomas E. Ed. 1967, Ed. 1968
Birkmaier, Emma 1974
Bishop, G. Reginald, Jr. Ed. 1960, Ed. 1965
Blanchet, Alain 1978
Blew, Genevieve S. 1958, 1961, 1966
Bock, Carolyn E. 1958, 1968
Bockman, John F. 1973
Bolinger, Dwight 1968
Bomse, Marguerite D. 1974
Bonham, George W. 1981
Born, Warren C. Ed. 1974, Ed. 1975, Ed. 1976, Ed. 1977, Ed. 1978, Ed. 1979
Bottiglia, William F. 1957, Ed. 1962, Ed. 1963, 1966
Boudreau, Cleophas W. 1966
Bourque, Edward H. 1971
Bourque, Jane McFarland 1975, 1983

Davis, Jackie 1995
Davis, James J. 1994
Day, J. Laurence 1974
de Commaille, Anne-Marie 1954, 1955
de Lancey, DeVaux 1957
de MacDonald, Dolores Andújar 1955
Dedmond, Frederick H. 1959
DeFilippis, Dominick 1981
DeGraff, Thelma B. 1958
del Olmo, Filomena Peloro 1963, 1967, 1970
del Olmo, Guillermo 1961
De Lorenzo, William E. 1974, 1975, 1978
Demkee, Mark 1998
DeNapoli, Anthony J. 1983
Desberg, Dan 1960, 1963
Desbonnet, Aline C. 1973
Di Giammarino, Frank 1971
Digisi, Marion 1955
Dillard, Joey L. 1972
Diller, George E. 1965
Dodge, James W. Ed. 1971, Ed. 1972, Ed. 1973, 1980
Dostert, Leon 1954
Douglas, Eva 1960
Dubay, Guy F. 1976
Dube, Normand C. 1976
DuBois, Rachel 1955, 1956
Dufau, Micheline 1965, 1977
Duncan, Janie L. 1976
Dunn, Doris 1959
Dvorak, Trisha 1986, Ed. 1995
Eaton, Esther M. 1954, 1959
Eaton, Margaret E. 1958
Echeverria, Durand 1955
Eddy, Frederick D. 1956, 1957, Ed. 1959, 1971
Eddy, Peter A. 1978, 1980
Edgerton, Mills F. 1968, Ed. 1969, 1980
Edwards, J. David 1985

Ehrlich, Madeline 1987
Ehrmann, Jacques 1963
Einbeck, Kandace 1992
Eisenhauer, Elaine Cerul 1998
Elkins, Robert J. 1973, 1975
Elling, Barbara E. 1974, 1976, 1981, 1982,
Elling, Karl 1982
Emgarth, Annette 1956
Engleman, Finis E. 1954
English, Mark Anthony 1997
Entwistle, Sharon 1963
Eriksson, Marguerite 1955
Escola, Yvonne 1977, 1978
Espy, Herbert G. 1954
Eyck, Richard C. ten 1975
Fairbanks, Colleen M. 1998
Fall, Thekla F. 1987, 1991
Faust, Edwin M. 1955
Feindler, Joan L. 1970, 1972
Fellows, Kathryn F. 1956, 1957
Ferdinand, Joseph 1998
Ferrigno, James M. 1959
Field, Thomas T. 1988
Fishman, Joshua A. 1965, 1977
Figueroa, John 1998
Finnegan, Kristine Olin 1998
Fitzgerald, Ronald 1971
Fitzgibbons, Nancyanne 1971
Flaxman, Seymour L. Ed. 1961
Foberg, Ann 1954
Foster, Badi G. 1987
Franckenstein, Joseph M. 1960
Frassica, Pietro 1978
Freeman, Stephen A. 1954, 1955, 1965, 1969
Freilich, Joan S. 1974
Friedl, Ernestine 1960
Fulton, Renée Jeanne 1955, 1957
Ferguson, Charles A. 1966
Furst, Norma 1973

Gaarder, A. Bruce 1965, 1968, 1971

Galas, Evangeline 1961

Gallagher, Shannon M. 1998

Galland, Georgette 1957

Galloway, Vicki 1983, 1992

García, Ofelia 1992

Gardner, Robert 1977

Garey, Howard 1954

Garimaldi, Colette 1964

Garraty, John A. 1965

Garretón, María Teresa 1995

Gartner, John W. 1966

Gaudiani, Claire 1983, 1987, 1992

Gaudin, Mrs. Lois S. 1957

Gegerias, Mary 1998

Genna, Joseph 1955

Geno, Thomas H. 1974, Ed. 1980, Ed. 1981

Gibson, Alexander D. 1956

Gidman, David N. 1982

Giguere, Madeleine D. 1976

Gill, Margaret 1965

Gilman, Margaret Ed. 1956, 1958

Girard, Daniel 1955, 1956, 1960

Glaude, Paul M. 1959, 1962

Glisan, Eileen W. 1991

Goding, Stowell C. 1971

Goldstein, Muriel H. 1975

Goldstein, Naomi 1958

González, Louis 1955

Gougher, Ronald L. 1973

Grace, Alonzo G. 1955

Grandin, John M. 1992

Grant, Elliott, M. 1957, 1958

Green, Gerald R. 1971

Greenberg, James S. 1978

Greene, Joyce E. 1956, 1957

Grenda, Ted T. 1976

Grew, James H. 1955, 1957, 1958, 1959, 1966

Griffith, Paul T. 1983

Grindle, Roger 1976

Grizzell, E. Duncan 1954

Gropp, Paul 1957

Grundstrom, Allan W. 1969

Guédenet, Pierre 1955

Guerra, Emilio 1957

Guerra, Manuel H. 1954, 1957

Gummere, John F. 1967

Haas, Mari 1990, 1997

Hadas, Moses 1960

Hadlich, Ralph L. 1964

Hahn, Milton R. 1964, 1998

Hall, Joan Kelly 1995

Hall, Robert A., Jr. 1962

Hallowell, A. Irving 1955

Hammadou, JoAnn 1994

Hancock, Charles R. 1974, 1978, Ed. 1994

Hanisch, Melinda E. 1985

Hankin, Robert M. 1955

Hanson, Harlan P. 1964

Harkins, William E. 1960

Harris, James H. 1964

Harrison, John S. 1982

Hartman, Douglas K. 1998, Ed. 1998

Havican, Audrey 1955

Hayden, Hilary 1969

Hayes, Alfred S. 1962, 1963

Hayes, Mary E. 1959

Hennessey, Paul S. 1957

Herge, Henry 1955

Hernández, Marco 1973

Hernick, Michael E. 1970

Herzfeld, Regina Flannery 1960

Hinshalwood, Robert L. 1967

Hocking, Elton 1968

Hodych, Carolyn E. 1987

Hoey, Allan 1956

Holden, John 1954

Holmes, Glyn 1984

Horwitz, Elaine K. 1990, 1994

Hosenfeld, Carol 1979
Howe, Arthur, Jr. 1958
Hughes, Alexander S. 1959
Hughes, John B. 1955
Hugot, François 1971
Hull, Alexander 1960
Ilgen, William D. 1962
Jackson, Claire W. 1996
Jakobovits, Leon A. 1970
James, Dorothy 1989
Jarvis, Gilbert A. 1979, 1981, Ed. 1984
Jason, Otis N. 1958
Jensen, Melvy E. 1998
Joiner, Elizabeth G. 1982, 1986
Jones, George Fenwick Ed. 1964
Jones, Janet 1958
Jorstad, Helen L. 1980
Jurasek, Barbara Schnuttgen 1991
Jurasek, Richard T. 1991
Kalivoda, Theodore B. 1973, 1975, 1990
Kamil, Michael L. 1986
Kandeler, Gesa 1978
Kavanaugh, Mark S. 1997
Kellenberger, Hunter Ed. 1954
Kellermann, Karl 1956
Kelly, Thomas W. 1968
Kempner, Frederick 1958
Ken, Rev. Daniel R. 1970
Kendrick, S. A. 1958
Kennedy, Dora 1976, 1978, 1983
Kibbe, Doris E. 1960, 1967
Kimball, Mary M. 1995
King, Paul 1957
Kirby, Mary Ellen 1987
Kirk, Irina 1972
Klayman, Norma Enea 1971, 1981
Kline, Rebecca R. 1995
Klineberg, Otto 1955, 1956
Knowles, Mark 1995
Krail, Jack B. 1964

Kramsch, Claire J. 1988
Krivobok, George 1963
Kroeger, Ruth P. 1956
Kronik, John W. 1972
Kulick, Katherine M. 1990
Kupferschmid, Gene S. 1978
Kurland, Norman D. 1965
Kurtz, John W. 1965
LaBouve, Robert 1993
Ladu, Tora T. 1973
Lafayette, Robert C. 1980, 1988
LaFontaine, Herman 1973
Lally, Dale V., Jr. 1974
Lambert, Wallace E. 1963, 1965, 1970, 1972
Lane, Harlan L. 1962, 1966
Lange, Dale L. 1997
Larsen-Freeman, Diane 1991
Lashbrook, Austin M. 1955
Latimer, John F. 1965, 1971, 1976
Lavallée, Martha 1957
Lavergneau, Beverly Butler 1974
Lavergneau, René L. 1974
Le Bovit, Judith 1971
Leach, John 1976
Leland, Marine 1972
Lepke, Helen S. Ed. 1989
LeSage, Laurent 1956
Lester, Kenneth 1977
Levine, Mark 1975
Levy, Harry L. Ed. 1958, 1959, 1971
Levy, Stephen L. 1975, 1983, 1993
Levy, Sylvia N. 1955
Libit, Elaine C. 1970
Lieberman, Samuel 1972
Linder, Cathy 1978
Lindquist, Mary Montgomery 1997
Linnehan, Alice F. 1957
Lipton, Gladys C. 1964, 1967, 1971, 1975, 1983
Liskin-Gasparro, Judith E. 1982

LoBue, Joseph 1955, 1956
Locke, William N. 1954, 1958
Loew, Helene Z. See Zimmer-Loew.
Long, Donna Reseigh 1994
Lopez, Lucrecia 1955
Lorenz, Eileen B. 1997
Lorge, Sarah W. 1955
Lotito, Barbara 1988
Lueras, Benito L. 1962
Lyles, Victoria 1954
Lynch, C. Arthur 1955
MacAllister, Archibald T. 1954, 1955, 1959
Macián, Janice Lynn 1994
Magnan, Sally Sieloff 1985, Ed. 1990
Makino, Seiichi 1988
Marcellino, Ralph 1960
Marckwardt, Albert H. 1955
Markham, Tom 1998
Marks, Doris 1974
Marshall, Randall 1962
Marty, Fernand 1957
Matthew, John R. 1955
Maubrey, Pierre 1982
McArthur, James F. 1964
McCarthy, Barbara P. 1955, 1956
McClelland, David C. 1955
McCollom, Mrs. Herbert F. 1967
McRill, Paul C. 1968
Mead, Robert G., Jr. 1955, Ed. 1966, 1972, Ed. 1982, Ed. 1983
Medley, Frank W., Jr. 1985
Meinke, Kenneth 1956
Melchior, Oliver A. 1958
Menditto, Diane F. 1974
Mensh, Helene B. 1978
Meras, Edmond A. 1954, 1955
Met, Myriam 1983
Miller, Mary R. 1972
Miller, Richard R. 1959
Mirsky, Jerome G. 1971, 1972

Mistretta, Anthony 1978
Miyares, Enrique H. 1977
Moeller, Aleidine 1988
Monsees, Anita 1978
Monserrat, Joseph 1955, 1956
Montgomery, Gail E. 1968
Moore, Merriam 1977
Moore, Zena T. 1994, 1997
Moorjani, Angela 1988
Morain, Genelle 1973, 1975, 1990
Morel, Stefano 1974
Morgan, Raleigh 1962
Morimoto, Yoko 1998
Morris, Edward P. 1957
Moskowitz, Gertrude 1970, 1973
Moulton, William G. 1956, 1967
Mueller, Theodore 1957, 1962
Munks, Jeffrey J. 1996
Mustard, Helen M. 1961
Myer, Grace 1956
Nacci, Chris N. 1967
Navarro, Jouquina 1959
Nelligan, William J. 1958
Nelson, April 1982
Nelson, Robert J. 1964, 1970
Nemser, William 1957
Nerenz, Anne G. 1990, 1993
Newman, Richard W. 1974
Newmark, Maxim 1959
Nionakis, John P. 1971, 1975
Norton, Harriet 1971
Nuzzi, Theodore 1965
O'Brien, Kathryn L. 1954
O'Connor, Patricia 1961
O'Neill, E. Wesley 1956
O'Neill, Flora 1977
Oblum, Rudolph V. 1957
Obrecht, Dean H. 1963
Obstfeld, Roland 1974
Odronic, Walter J. 1972
Oleksak, Rita A. 1997

Sandstrom, Eleanor L. 1970

Sapon, Stanley M. 1954, 1955, 1956, 1957, 1963

Sartorius, Ina C. 1956

Savage, Nita Willits 1957, 1959

Sayres, William C. 1955, 1956

Scatton, Earnest A. 1977

Scheider, Rose 1955, 1956

Scherer, George A. C. 1963

Schmidt, S. E. 1957

Schmitt, Conrad J. 1964

Schneider, Gerd K. 1981

Schreiber, William I. 1976

Schrier, Leslie L. 1994

Schueler, Herbert 1961

Schumacher, Marigwen 1968, 1976

Schwartz, Ana María 1997

Schyfter, Sara 1978

Scott, Susan 1955

Scrivener, Katherine 1956

Seelye, H. Ned 1974

Selvi, Arthur M. 1954, 1955, 1964

Senn, Alfred E. 1960

Serafino, Robert P. 1961, 1962, 1970

Sheehan, Joseph H. 1969

Shepart, Sanford 1956

Sheppard, Douglas C. 1966

Sheppard, Marie 1993

Sherburne, Robert R. 1974

Sherp, Beverly 1962

Shields, Archibald K. 1958

Shohamy, Elana 1991

Shryer, Margaret 1969

Sibley, Elbridge 1955

Silber, Gordon R. 1959, 1967

Silva-Fuenzalida, Ismael 1959

Simches, Seymour O. 1962, 1964, 1968

Singerman, Alan J. Ed. 1988

Sister Charlotte Marie 1966

Sister Julie, S.N.D. 1957

Sister Margaret Pauline 1961

Sister Margaret Thérèse 1955

Sister Marie Louise 1956

Slack, Anne 1958, 1974

Sleeper, Christine 1998

Smith, George E. 1968

Smith, Henry Lee 1954

Smith, Philip D. 1973

Smith, Sylvia 1955, 1956

Snow, Emily L. 1958

Soda, Frank M. 1956, 1966

Soffietti, James P. 1962

Song, Seok Choong 1977

Sora, Maria 1960

Spaethling, Robert H. 1967

Sparks, Kimberly 1967

Spinelli, Emily L. 1989, 1996

Stanislawczyk, Irene E. 1960

Stansfield, Charles W. 1994

Starr, S. Frederick 1981

Starr, Wilmarth H. 1954, 1955, 1956, 1959, 1961, 1962

Stavrinos, Mary M. 1957

Stein, Jack M. 1961

Stephens, James 1955

Stern, H. H. 1983

Stewart, Courtney 1998

Stewart, William A. 1972

Stillwell, June U. 1966

Stinnett, T.M. 1954

Stokle, Norman 1988

Stookins, Joseph 1955

Strasheim, Lorraine A. 1973

Strouse, Adeline 1956

Sturges, Perry 1959

Sturgis, Diane 1998

Sullivan, Edward D. 1965, 1966

Supko, Ruth 1998

Swaffar, Janet 1993

Sweet, Waldo E. 1962

Szogyi, Alex 1955

Tabor, Esther 1956

Tamarkin, Toby S. 1974, 1976
Tauber, Arnold 1964
Tedick, Diane J. 1996
Terrio, Susan 1995
Theurer, Louise 1955
Thibault, Paula 1954, 1955, 1956, 1957
Thomas, Alice Nesta Lloyd 1955
Thomas, Tilla 1956
Thompson, Mary P. 1954, 1955, 1956, 1959, 1962, 1963
Tone, Fred H. 1954
Tonkin, Humphrey 1983, 1987
Torrey, Jane W. 1970
Torrey, Norman L. 1954
Travers, Claudia S. 1981
Trivelli, Romo J. 1982
Tucker, G. Richard 1970, 1972, 1998
Tursi, Joseph A. 1964, Ed. 1970, 1972, 1978
Tuttle, Harry 1974
Twaddell, W. Freeman 1954, 1966, 1973
Twarog, Leon I 1960
Tyre, Carl A. 1958
Uzan, Elaine V. 1978
Valdés, Guadalupe 1992
Valdman, Albert 1963
Valette, Rebecca M. 1971, 1978, 1994
Van Straalen, Johannes 1960
Vaughan, Clark A. 1961
Verdaguer, Pierre 1997
Vial, Fernand 1960
Virski, Olga Scherer 1954, 1955, 1957
von Reinhart, Walter 1992
Wade, Gerald E. 1956
Wade, Ira 1960
Walker, Constance L. 1996
Walker, Galal 1989
Walker, Richard H. 1954, 1955, 1957
Wallace, Richard C., Jr. 1987
Walsh, Donald D. 1954, 1958, 1975

Walters, Brooke 1998
Wantiez, Geneviève 1957
Ward, James P. 1967
Ward, Ralph 1956, 1964
Warner, Pearl M. 1970, 1975
Warriner-Burke, Helen P. 1966, 1989
Warthen, Dean 1971
Washburn, Mary Lou 1959
Webster, Russell 1964
Weinstein, Ruth Hirsch 1955, 1956
Weintraub, Wiktor 1960
Welmers, William E. 1960
White, Elizabeth 1956
White, Emilie Margaret 1957
Wieczorek, Joseph A. 1997
Wiggins, Grant 1994
Williamson, Edward 1955
Williamson, Richard C. 1981
Willis, Robert 1969
Wing, Barbara H. 1984, Ed. 1986, Ed. 1996
Winterscheidt, Friedrich 1978
Wittman, Nora 1955, 1956
Wojnowski, Margaret V. 1956, 1957
Wolf, Marilyn E. 1966
Wolvin, Andrew D. 1986
Woodford, Protase E. 1964, 1982
Wooster, Judith S. 1981
Workman, John Rowe 1960
Wrenn, James J. 1969
Wright, Alfred J. 1956
Wright, Blanca G. 1974
Wright, Theodore C. 1955, 1956
Wylie, Laurence 1955
Yavener, Symond 1968, 1977
Young, Dolly Jesúsita 1995
Young, Eleanor 1958
Young, Elizabeth 1957
Young, Harry F. 1972
Yu, Clara 1992
Zais, Robert S. 1981

Zimmer-Loew, Helene 1974, 1975, 1976, 1978, 1981, 1983
Ziobro, William 1976

Zirkel, Penny A. 1976
Zouck, A. Marguerite 1958
Zulli, Floyd 1956

Abbott, Martha G., Fairfax County (VA) Public Schools, Director 1994-97.

Alexander, Elizabeth, Burlington (VT) HS, Director 1997-2000.

Anderson, Nancy E., ETS, Director 1990-93, ACTFL Representative 1994, Consultant to the Chair 1996.

Andersson, Theodore†, [Yale U]* U of Texas, Director 1954-56.

Andrews, Oliver, Jr., U of Connecticut, Director 1971-74.

Arndt, Richard, Columbia U, Director 1961.

Arsenault, Philip E., Montgomery County (MD) Public S, Local Chair 1967, 1970; Director 1971, 1973-74; Vice Chair 1975; Conference Chair 1976.

Atkins, Jeannette, Staples (Westport, CT) HS, Director 1962-65.

Baird, Janet, U of Maryland, Local Chair 1974.

Baker, Robert M.†, Middlebury C, Director 1987-90.

Bashour, Dora, [Hunter C], Secretary 1963-64; Recording Secretary 1965-68.

Baslaw, Annette S., [Teachers C], Hunter C, Local Chair 1973.

Bayerschmidt, Carl F., [Columbia U], Conference Chair 1961.

Bennett, Ruth, Queens C, Local Chair 1975-76.

Bertin, Gerald A., Rutgers U, Local Chair 1960.

Berwald, Jean-Pierre, U of Massachusetts-Amherst, Director 1980-83.

Bird, Thomas E., Queens C, Editor 1967-68; Director 1969.

Bishop, G. Reginald, Jr., Rutgers U, Editor 1960, 1965; Director 1961-62, 1965, 1968; Vice Chair 1966; Conference Chair 1967.

Bishop, Thomas W., New York U, Local Chair 1965.

Born, Warren C., [ACTFL], Editor 1974-79.

Bostroem, Kyra, Westover S, Director 1961.

Bottiglia, William F., MIT, Editor 1957, 1962-63; Director 1964.

Bourque, Jane M., [Stratford (CT) Public S], Mt. Vernon (NY) Public S, Director 1974-75; Vice Chair 1976; Conference Chair 1977.

Brée, Germaine, [New York U, U of Wisconsin], Wake Forest U, Conference Chair 1955; Editor 1955.

Brennan, Judith, Virginia Beach Public S, Director 1995-98

Bressler, Julia T., Nashua (NH) Public S, Director 1991-94; Vice Chair 1995, Conference Chair 1996.

Brod, Richard I., MLA, Consultant to the Chair, 1983; Director 1985-88.

Brooks, Nelson†, [Yale U], Director 1954-57, 1960-61; Vice Chair 1959.

Brooks-Brown, Sylvia R., [Baltimore (MD) City S], Baltimore County (MD) Public S, Director 1988-92; Vice Chair 1993, Conference Chair 1994.

Brown, Christine L., [West Hartford (CT) Public S], Glastonbury (CT) Public S, Director 1982-85; Vice Chair 1986; Conference Chair 1987.

Byrnes, Heidi, Georgetown U, Director 1985-88; Vice Chair 1989; Conference Chair 1990; Editor 1992.

Cadoux, Remunda†, [Hunter C], Vice Chair 1969; Conference Chair 1970.

Campbell, Hugh, [Roxbury Latin S], Rocky Hill Country Day S, Director 1966-67.

Cannon, Adrienne G., Prince George's Co (MD) Public S, Director 1993-96.

Carr, Celestine G., Howard County (MD) Public S, Director 1993-96.

Churchill, J. Frederick, Hofstra U, Director 1966-67; Local Chair 1971-72.

Ciotti, Marianne C., [Vermont State Department of Education, Boston U], Barre (VT) Public S, Director 1967.

Cincinnato, Paul D., Farmingdale (NY) Public S, Director 1974-77; Vice Chair 1978; Conference Chair 1979.

Cintas, Pierre F., [Dalhousie U], Pennsylvania State U-Ogontz, Director 1976-79.

Cipriani, Anita A., Hunter C Elem S, Director 1986-89.

Clark, John L.D., [CAL], DLI, Director 1976-78; Vice Chair 1979; Conference Chair 1980.

Clark, Richard P., Newton (MA) HS, Director 1967.

Clemens, Brenda Frazier, [Rutgers U, U of Connecticut], Howard U, Director 1972-75.

Cobb, Martha, Howard U, Director 1976-77; Recording Secretary 1978.

Covey, Delvin L., [Montclair State C], Spring Arbor C, Director 1964-65.

Crapotta, James, Barnard C, Director 1992-95.

Crawford, Dorothy B., Philadelphia HS for Girls, Conference Chair 1956.

Dahme, Lena F., Hunter C, Local Chair 1958; Director 1959.

Darcey, John M., West Hartford (CT) Public S, Director 1978-81; Vice Chair 1982; Conference Chair 1983; Editor 1987.

Dates, Elaine, Burlington (VT) HS, Recording Secretary 1991.

Del Olmo, Filomena Peloro, [Hackensack (NJ) Public S], Fairleigh Dickinson U, Director 1960-63.

De Napoli, Anthony J., Wantagh (NY) Public S, Local Chair 1980-82, 1987; Director 1982-85.

Di Donato, Robert, MIT, Consultant to the Chair 1986.

Díaz, José M., Hunter C HS, Director 1988-91; Vice Chair 1992; Conference Chair 1993; Consultant to the Chair 1995 and 1997.

Didsbury, Robert, Weston (CT) JHS, Director 1966-69.

Dodge, James W.†, [Middlebury C], Editor 1971-73; Secretary-Treasurer 1973-89.

Dodge, Ursula Seuss, Northeast Conference Secretariat, Interim Secretary-Treasurer 1990.

Donato, Richard, U of Pittsburgh, Director 1993-96, Vice Chair 1997.

Dostert, Leon E., [Georgetown U], Occidental C, Conference Chair 1959.

Duclos, Marie, Nashua (NH) Public S, Newsletter Editor 1996.

Dufau, Micheline†, U of Massachusetts, Director 1976-79.

Dvorak, Trisha, U of Michigan, Editor 1995.

Dye, Joan C., Hunter C, Local Chair 1978.

Eaton, Annette, Howard U, Director 1967-70.

Eddy, Frederick D.†, [U of Colorado], Editor 1959; Director 1960.

Eddy, Peter A., [CAL/ERIC], CIA Language S, Director 1977-78.

Edgerton, Mills F., Jr., Bucknell U, Editor 1969; Director 1970; Vice Chair 1971; Conference Chair 1972.

Elkins, Robert, West Virginia U, Director 1991-94.

Elling, Barbara E., SUNY-Stony Brook, Director 1980-83.

Feindler, Joan L., East Williston (NY) Public S, Director 1969-71; Vice Chair 1972; Conference Chair 1973.

Flaxman, Seymour, [New York U], City C of New York, Editor 1961; Director 1962.

Freeman, Stephen A., [Middlebury C], Director 1957-60.

Fulton, Renee J., New York City Board of Education Director 1955.

Gaarder, A. Bruce, [USOE], Director 1971-74.

Galloway, Vicki B., [ACTFL], Georgia Technological U, Consultant to the Chair 1985.

Geary, Edward J., [Harvard U], Bowdoin C, Conference Chair 1962.

Geno, Thomas H., U of Vermont, Director 1975-76; Vice Chair 1977; Conference Chair 1978; Recording Secretary 1979; Editor 1980-81.

Gilman, Margaret†, Bryn Mawr C, Editor 1956.

Glaude, Paul M., New York State Dept of Education, Director 1963-66.

Glisan, Eileen W. Indiana U of Pennsylvania, Director 1992-95, Vice Chair 1996, Conference Chair 1997.

Golden, Herbert H., Boston U, Director 1962.

Goldfield, Joel, Fairfield U, Director 1995-98.

Grandin, John M., U of Rhode Island, Director 1999-2002.

Grew, James H., [Phillips Acad], Director 1966-69.

Gutiérrez, John R., Pennsylvania State U, Director 1988-91.

Hancock, Charles R., The Ohio State University, Editor 1994

Hartie, Robert W., Queens C, Local Chair 1966.

Harrison, John S., Baltimore County (MD) Public S, Local Chair 1979, 1983; Director 1983-86; Recording Secretary 1988-89.

Harris-Schenz, Beverly, [U of Pittsburgh], U of Massachusetts-Amherst, Director 1988-91.

Hayden, Hilary, OSB, St. Anselm's Abbey S, Vice Chair 1970; Conference Chair 1971.

Hayes, Alfred S.†, CAL, Vice Chair 1963; Conference Chair 1964.

Henderson, John S., Dickinson C (emeritus), *Review* Editor 1998-.

Hernandez, Juana A., Hood C, Director 1978-81.

Holekamp, Elizabeth L., Executive Director 1990-95.

Holzmann, Albert W.†, Rutgers U, Director 1960.

Hurtgen, André, St. Paul's School (NH), Director 1992-95.

Claire Jackson, Brookline (MA) Public S, Director 1996-99.

Jalbert, Emile H., [Thayer Acad], Berkshire Comm C, Local Chair 1962.

Jarvis, Gilbert A., Ohio State U, Editor 1984.

Jebe, Suzanne, [Guilford (CT) HS], Minnesota Dept of Education, Director 1975-76; Recording Secretary 1977.

Johnston, Marjorie C., [USOE], Local Chair 1964.

Jones, George W., Jr.†, Norfolk (VA) Public S, Director 1977-80.

Kahn, Timothy M., S Burlington (VT) HS, Director 1979-82.

Kassen, Margaret Ann. Catholic U of America, Director 1997-2000, *Reports* Editor 1999.

Keesee, Elizabeth, [USOE], Director 1966-70.

Kellenberger, Hunter†, [Brown U], Conference Chair 1954, Editor 1954.

Kennedy, Dora F., Prince George's County (MD) Public S, Director 1985-88; Recording Secretary 1990; Consultant to the Chair 1991.

Kesler, Robert, Phillips Exeter Acad, Director 1957.

Kibbe, Doris E., Montclair State C, Director 1968-69.

Kline, Rebecca, [Dickinson C], Pennsylvania State U, Director 1990-93, Vice-Chair 1994, Conference Chair 1995, Executive Director 1995-.

Koenig, George, State U of New York-Oswego, Recording Secretary, 1993.

Kramsch, Claire J., [MIT], Cornell, Director 1984-87.

La Follette, James E., Georgetown U, Local Chair 1959.

La Fountaine, Hernan, New York City Board of Education, Director 1972.

Lenz, Harold, Queens C, Local Chair 1961.

Lepke, Helen S., [Kent State U], Clarion U of Pennsylvania, Director 1981-84;

Vice Chair 1985; Conference Chair 1986; Editor 1989.

Lester, Kenneth A., Connecticut State Dept of Education, Recording Secretary 1982.

Levy, Harry†, [Hunter C], Fordham U, Editor 1958; Director 1959-61; Conference Chair 1963.

Levy, Stephen L., [New York City Board of Education], Roslyn (NY) Public S, Local Chair 1978, 1980-82, 1984-85, 1987-present; Director 1980-83; Vice Chair 1984; Conference Chair 1985; Consultant to the Chair 1994.

Lieberman, Samuel, Queens C, Director 1966-69.

Lipton, Gladys C., [New York City Board of Education, Anne Arundel County (MD) Public S], U of Maryland-Baltimore County, Director 1973-76; *Newsletter* Editor 1993-95.

Liskin-Gasparro, Judith E., [ETS], Middlebury C, Recording Secretary 1984; Director 1986-89; Vice Chair 1990; Conference Chair 1991.

Lloyd, Paul M., U of Pennsylvania, Local Chair 1963.

Locke, William N.†, MIT, Conference Chair 1957; Director 1958-59.

MacAllister, Archibald T.†, [Princeton U], Director 1955-57, 1959-61.

Magnan, Sally Sieloff, University of Wisconsin-Madison, Editor 1990.

Masciantonio, Rudolph, School District of Philadelphia, Director 1969- 71.

Mead, Robert G., Jr.†, U of Connecticut, Director 1955; Editor 1966; Vice Chair 1967; Conference Chair 1968; Editor 1982-83.

Medley, Frank W. Jr., West Virginia U, Director 1996-99; Vice Chair 1999.

Mesnard, Andre, Barnard C, Director 1954-55.

Micozzi, Arthur L., [Baltimore County (MD) Public S], Local Chair 1977, 1979, 1983, 1986; Director 1970-82.

Mirsky, Jerome G.†, [Jericho (NY) SHS], Shoreham-Wading River (NY) HS, Director 1970-73; Vice Chair 1974; Conference Chair 1975.

Mulhern, Frank, Wallingford-Swarthmore (PA) Public S, Director 1999-2002.

Nelson, Robert J., [U of Pennsylvania], U of Illinois, Director 1965-68.

Neumaier, Bert J., Timothy Edwards (S Windsor, CT) MS, Director 1988-92.

Neuse, Werner†, [Middlebury C], Director 1954-56.

Nionakis, John P., Hingham (MA) Public S, Director 1984-87; Vice Chair 1988; Conference Chair 1989.

Obstfeld, Roland, Northport (NY) HS, Recording Secretary 1976.

Omaggio, Alice C., U of Illinois, Editor 1985.

Owens, Doris Barry, West Hartford (CT) Public S, Recording Secretary 1983.

Pane, Remigio U., Rutgers U, Conference Chair 1960.

Paquette, Andre, [Middlebury C], Laconia (NH) Public S, Director 1963- 66; Vice Chair 1968; Conference Chair 1969.

Parks, Carolyn, [U of Maryland], French International S, Recording Secretary 1981.

Peel, Emily S., Wethersfield (CT) Public S, Director 1991-94.

Perkins, Jean, Swarthmore C, Treasurer 1963-64; Conference Chair 1966.

Petrosino, Vince J., Baltimore (MD) City S, Local Chair 1986.

Phillips, June K., [Indiana U of Pennsylvania, Tennessee Foreign Language Institute, US Air Force Acad], Weber State U, Director 1979-82; Vice Chair 1983; Conference Chair 1984; Consultant to the Chair 1986, 1989, 1990, 1992; Editor 1991, 1993, 1997.

Prochoroff, Marina, [MLA Materials Center], Director 1974.

Ramos, Alicia, Indiana U of Pennsylvania, *Newsletter* Editor 1995-97.

Reilly, John H., Queens C, Local Chair 1968-69; Director 1970.

Remillard, Vincent., St. Francis C (PA), Recording Secretary 1997.

Renjilian-Burgy, Joy, Wellesley C, Director 1987-90; Vice Chair 1991; Chair 1992.

Reutershan, Donald H., Jr., Maine Dept. of Ed., Director 1997-2000.

Riley, Kerry, U of Maryland, Consultant to the Chair 1986.

Riordan, Kathleen M., Springfield (MA) Public S, Director 1988-91; Recording Secretary 1992.

Rochefort, Frances A., Cranston (RI) Public S, Director 1986-89.

Rosser, Harry L., Boston College, Director 1994-97.

Russo, Gloria M., [U of Virginia], Director 1983-86.

Sandstrom, Eleanor L., [School District of Philadelphia], Director 1975-78.

Selvi, Arthur M., Central Connecticut State C, Director 1954.

Senn, Alfred, U of Pennsylvania, Director 1956.

Serafino, Robert, New Haven (CT) Public S, Director 1969-73.

Sheppard, Douglas C., [SUNY-Buffalo], Arizona State U, Director 1968-71.

Shilaeff, Ariadne, Wheaton C, Director 1978-80.

Shrum, Judith, Virginia Tech U, Director 1996-99.

Shuster, George N.†, [U of Notre Dame], Conference Chair 1958.

Simches, Seymour O., Tufts U, Director 1962-65; Vice Chair 1965.

Sims, Edna N., U of the District of Columbia, Director 1981-84.

Singerman, Alan J., Davidson C, Editor 1988.

Sister Margaret Pauline, [Emmanuel C], Director 1957, 1965-68; Recording Secretary 1969-75.

Sister Margaret Therese, Trinity C, Director 1959-60.

Sister Mary Pierre, Georgian Court C, Director 1961-64.

Sousa-Welch, Helen Candi, West Hartford (CT) Public S, Director 1987-90.

Sparks, Kimberly, Middlebury C, Director 1969-72.

Starr, Wilmarth H., [U of Maine], New York U, Director 1960-63, 1966; Vice Chair 1964, Conference Chair 1965.

Steer, Alfred G., Jr., Columbia U, Director 1961.

Stein, Jack M.†, [Harvard U], Director 1962.

Stracener, Rebecca J., Edison (NJ) Public S, Director 1984-87.

Sturgis, Diane, Oxford Hills (South Paris, ME) HS, Director 1999-2002.

Tamarkin, Toby, Manchester (CT) Comm C, Director 1977-80; Vice Chair 1981; Conference Chair 1982; Recording Secretary 1987.

Thompson, Mary P., [Glastonbury (CT) Public S], Director 1957-62.

Trivelli, Remo J., U of Rhode Island, Director 1981-84.

Tursi, Joseph, [SUNY-Stony Brook], Editor 1970; Director 1971-72; Vice Chair 1973; Conference Chair 1974.

Valette, Rebecca, Boston C, Director 1972-75.

Vasquez-Amaral, Jose, Rutgers U, Director 1960.

Walker, Richard H., Bronxville (NY) HS, Director 1954.

Walsh, Donald D.†, [MLA], Director 1954; Secretary-Treasurer 1965-73.

Walton, A. Ronald†, U of Maryland, Director 1990-93.

Warner, Pearl M., New York City Public S, Recording Secretary 1985.

Webb, John, Hunter College HS, Consultant to the Chair 1993; Director 1995-98.

White, Arlene, Salisbury State U, Recording Secretary 1994.

White, Emile Margaret, [District of Columbia Public S], Director 1955- 58.

Williamson, Richard C., Bates C, Director 1983-86; Vice Chair 1987; Conference Chair 1988.

Wing, Barbara H., U of New Hampshire, Editor 1986; *Newsletter* Editor 1987-93; Recording Secretary 1995; Editor 1996.

Woodford, Protase E., ETS, Director 1982-85.

Yakobson, Helen B., George Washington U, Director 1959-60.

Yu, Clara, Middlebury College, Director 1994-97.

Zimmer-Loew, Helene, [NY State Education Dept], AATG, Director 1977-79; Vice Chair 1980; Conference Chair 1981.

NORTHEAST CONFERENCE ON THE
TEACHING OF FOREIGN LANGUAGES

Language Learners of
TOMORROW
Process and Promise

Margaret Ann Kassen, **Editor**

Martha G. Abbott, **Chair 1999**

National Textbook Company
a division of NTC/CONTEMPORARY PUBLISHING GROUP
Lincolnwood, Illinois USA

1999 Board of Directors

Martha G. Abbott, *Chair,*
Fairfax County (VA) Public Schools

Frank W. Medley, Jr., *Vice Chair,*
West Virginia University

Acknowledgments

Permission to use the "rings and weave" pattern granted on behalf of the National Standards Collaborative Board.

Questionnaire on page 57, "Questionnaire to Evaluate Use of Learning Strategies." From: Chamot, A. U., Barnhardt, S., El-Dinary, P. B., & Robbins, J. (2000). *The learning strategies handbook* (pp. 137–138). White Plains, NY: Addison Wesley Longman, Inc. Permission granted by Addison Wesley Longman, Inc.

Poetry pages 167, 170 from Tino Villanueva "Convocación de palabras." In A. Labarca & R. Halty Pfaff. (1991). *Convocación de palabras.* Boston: Heinle& Heinle. Permission granted by Heinle & Heinle.

Figure, page 173, "The Kluckhohn Model of Value Orientations and Ranges of Variation." In Kluckhohn, F. R., & Strodtbeck, F. L. (1976). *Variations in value orientations.* Westport, CT: Greenwood Publishing Group, Inc.

ISBN:0-8442-2855-9

Published by National Textbook Company,
A division of NTC/Contemporary Publishing Group, Inc.,
4255 West Touhy Avenue,
Lincolnwood (Chicago), Illinois 60646-1975 U.S.A.
© 1999 NTC/Contemporary Publishing Group, Inc.